MONEY
FROM
THIN
AIR

THE STORY OF CRAIG McCAW, THE VISIONARY

WHO INVENTED THE CELL PHONE INDUSTRY,

AND HIS NEXT BILLION-DOLLAR IDEA

O. CASEY CORR

CROWN
BUSINESS
NEW YORK

Published by Crown Publishers, New York, New York. Member of the
Crown Publishing Group.

Random House, Inc. New York, Toronto, London, Sydney, Auckland
www.randomhouse.com

CROWN is a trademark and the Crown colophon is a registered
trademark of Random House, Inc.

Design by Robert Bull Design

Library of Congress Cataloging-in-Publication Data
Corr, O. Casey
Money from thin air : the story of Craig McCaw, the visionary
who invented the cell phone industry, and his next
billion-dollar idea / O. Casey Corr.— 1st ed.
p.   cm.
ISBN 0-8129-2697-8
1. McCaw, Craig.   2. Cellular telephone systems—United States.
3. Cellular telephones—United States.   I. Title.
HE8815 .C67 2000
384.5'3'092—dc21
[B] 99-089068

10   9   8   7   6   5   4   3   2   1

First Edition

To Sally Tonkin
Virtus in Arduis

Contents

Preface

More than any other individual alive, Craig McCaw embodies the incredible transformation and likely future of the telecommunications industry. He is one of the most fascinating executives in business today, an acknowledged visionary in communications, the billionaire whom even other billionaires find interesting.

This book's title refers to McCaw's long-term business focus: invisible airwaves that carry high-profit voice and data services. But it also suggests a deeper theme—the managerial magic he brings to business. McCaw is astonishingly good at finding value where others see obstacles, doom, or just plain nothing. He seems to make money from thin air.

Describing himself as the master of the obvious, McCaw has redefined the idea of the executive. This is one guy rarely found in a suit, in the office, at a desk. More likely, he's kayaking, waterskiing, or piloting his jet high above the islands of British Columbia. When he talks about the freedom that wireless communications brings to the mobile worker, he knows it because he lives it. Contacting subordinates by voice mail, he is the virtual executive, more felt than seen. He makes money the new-fashioned way.

For the first eighty years of the twentieth century, people like McCaw had no place in telecommunications. The industry revolved around men in blue suits, white shirts, and sensible shoes who spent their lives inside a single gigantic company, AT&T, which resisted ideas that threatened its monopoly. Creative thinkers and quirky personalities worked elsewhere. Bill McGowan's MCI provided the notable exception, but the universe remained Ma Bell's until AT&T was broken up in 1984.

Today the telecom world is in turmoil. Giant companies are vulnerable because of their entrenchment in old technology and high cost. So they merge: Bigger must be better. At a different level, start-ups tap new pools of capital and maneuver to exploit opportunities created by stumbling giants and collapsing regulation. Everyone wants a share of the profit created by huge demand from businesses and consumers tapping the Internet. Increasingly, it's a game for the nimble and the daring. The telecommunications world has come around to Craig McCaw's way of business.

McCaw made one fortune in cable TV and another in cellular telephones. Now he's building a telecommunications empire of staggering potential through a collection of companies he controls: Teledesic, a satellite partnership with Microsoft's Bill Gates that is building a global "Internet in the Sky"; NEXTLINK, a company positioning itself to rival the Baby Bells with its own vast network of fiber-optic cable, wireless transmission services, and switching systems; CablePlus, a company that provides voice service, Internet access, and TV signals through coaxial cable; and Nextel, an international wireless telephone company with an expanding role in data services.

Each company is breathtaking in its ambition, hunger for capital, and risk-taking management style. Together, they provide a glimpse of McCaw's possible goal: one company capable of providing high-speed access to any point in the world, be it a cabin in the Cascade Mountains or a remote village in Asia. On the ground, a Teledesic community could also be served by a wireless network. For the Third World, that's the telecommunications equivalent of jumping from the nineteenth century to the twenty-first century. The idea has enormous social implications, and the potential for equally enormous profits.

Though this book focuses on McCaw, his story represents how the entrepreneur has moved from the fringes of the telecommunications business to the forefront. People such as McCaw, not the executives of major companies, have emerged as the visionaries who can adapt to a rapidly changing competitive landscape. They are the hunters, not the hunted. The management style and values they used to reach this point will be crucial in the future as the Internet fuels huge demand for sophisticated data services.

This book shows how McCaw's unique management style evolved by instinct and from periods of intense personal reflection and self-scrutiny. His emergence as a remarkable presence in global communications began with a crucial event in his youth.

MONEY FROM THIN AIR

CHAPTER

1

"That Man Behind the Curtain"

A Family Fortune Is Lost

On a cool, cloudy morning in August 1969, a young man was walking through the halls of his family's mansion. It sat on forested acreage near a bluff north of Seattle, overlooking Puget Sound and the snowy Olympic Mountains, part of a guarded enclave originally founded by timber barons and now housing some of the Northwest's wealthiest families. The community name was as much a statement of status as its elevation over the waters: The Highlands.

The young man, a nineteen-year-old sophomore at Stanford University, was Craig McCaw. He still had the look of an undeveloped youngster: His mouth and head seemed disproportionately large, his arms hung awkwardly from narrow shoulders, and his feet pointed inward as he walked. At a time when most American teens let their hair tumble over their eyes and ears, McCaw kept his dark, almost black, hair neatly trimmed. He avoided large groups, spoke in a murmur, treated others with almost excessive politeness, preferred chess to football, and kept private his struggles with dyslexia.

McCaw was a prankster—a dead aim with a squirt gun—but at times his long, introspective silences made people nervous. Those who made the effort to know him discovered a keen intelligence and a veiled competitiveness. Perhaps his eyes told the tale—dark almost to blackness, revealing nothing, but fiercely alert.

On this August morning, McCaw could not anticipate the crisis that was about to batter his family and help define the rest of his life. The summer of '69 was one of America's most turbulent, marked by violent protests over race and the Vietnam War, the countercultural watershed of Woodstock, and the ultimate technological triumph of the Apollo moon landing. But Craig McCaw and his three brothers lived a sheltered life.

Craig, Bruce, John, and Keith relished comforts unimaginable to most American teens. The McCaws' 20,000-square-foot mansion— built in 1915 by the Boeings, founders of the aircraft company—was a veritable fortress, with stucco walls eighteen inches thick. The lifestyle it housed was equally unusual. Beyond the ski lessons, orthodontia, European vacations, and other common badges of the ascendant class, from their early teens the McCaw boys enjoyed access to cars, airplanes, a yacht, and even a Learjet, as well as the services of a phalanx of employees who cooked, cleaned, gardened, and kept track of the family's expanding wealth.

Their mother, Marion Oliver McCaw, was a poised, elegant woman of charm and intelligence. She had grown up in Washington State, the daughter of a small-town businessman. Now she occupied the first tier of society in the Northwest's largest city, a member of the opera and symphony boards (as well as the board of the Metropolitan Opera in New York City). She selected her clothes from wares brought to her home by salesmen from the finest designer shops, paying up to $5,000 for a single dress. The Seattle papers announced her plans for vacations and parties, and Vice President Hubert H. Humphrey was among the guests who frequented the McCaw mansion. The McCaws "played with the big boys," as a family chef put it.

Marion McCaw's sons enjoyed tremendous freedom. From age twelve they were driving cars or boats. They could be up and away at dawn, so long as they had their breakfast first. Their mother was organized, meticulous, and calm, seemingly never rattled by a household of boys and their friends. Once, when their Great Dane, Duke, fouled the floor of the mansion, the family housekeeper fled, repulsed by the stench. Marion McCaw calmly cleaned up the mess. "I do this all the time," she said.

The entrepreneur who sustained the family's exuberant lifestyle was J. Elroy McCaw.

Elroy McCaw "was not an impressive-appearing fellow. He looked like a bank teller," recalls Les Keiter, a former employee. Just five feet nine, with dark, receding hair, Elroy peered at the world through round wire-frame glasses. He was careless of his appearance—people said he looked as though he'd slept in his suit—but he was self-conscious nonetheless about a scar on the side of his face, the result of a childhood accident with boiling water.

Elroy McCaw was born in Idaho, the son of an engineer. He worked to put himself through college, where he dabbled in radio, then in 1937 bought into his first radio station in the small town of Centralia, Washington, where Marion Oliver had grown up. Almost from the moment that station went on the air, Elroy McCaw was buying or starting other stations, then buying bigger stations, then collections of stations. He quickly built a broadcasting empire, typically making deals with small down payments and heavy debt. Some called Elroy's borrowing reckless, but it was grounded in his faith that the businesses he bought could be turned around—that he could make money before others discovered the value they had overlooked.

"Elroy was very bright. He was ahead of his time in terms of leveraged buyouts and debt finance," says friend and former broadcaster Les Smith. "He was a deal maker, not an operations guy." But in at least one case, Elroy's broadcasting instincts proved sound: He made a killing when he changed the programming format of a struggling New York radio station to rock 'n' roll just in time to ride the new music's sudden popularity to huge profits.

Craig McCaw didn't see much of his father. Most months, Elroy spent half his time in New York or Washington, D.C. His days at home were spent closeted in his office in the mansion, speaking with his secretary or working the phones. But Elroy did make time for family cruises on the yacht. More important, he tutored Craig in business, brought him to an occasional board meeting, and, when the boy turned eleven, gave him some shares in the Ford Motor Company.

Craig may have wondered why he knew so little of his father. Others felt the same way about Elroy McCaw. He was secretive by nature; he kept odd hours, and his whereabouts were often unknown. Elroy had served in army intelligence during World War II, and rumors of some kind of clandestine career—with the CIA?—always dogged him. Years later, his own family would hire a researcher to get the facts about Elroy's hidden life. Had he refused to answer their questions, or had they been reluctant to ask? That remains unclear. But Elroy's personality was one of layers and compartments, like that of his son Craig. To this day, Craig feels that he was closer to his father than were any of his brothers—not because of any long, intimate talks they had, but because they had played chess together in the mansion.

Craig treasured those games. Chess was a way for him to get inside his father's mind, to share his instinctive feeling for complex relationships and strategy. Like business, chess was a game of recognizing opportunities, removing or avoiding obstacles, developing a plan, then moving into position for the kill. Eventually, it got to the point—so claims Craig McCaw—where, when his father secreted a black pawn in one fist and a white pawn in the other for the traditional random choice for first move, Craig was able to guess which hand held the more desirable white pawn "nine times out of ten."

This window into his father's restless genius opened a mental link between the teenager and the tycoon. Craig, who would later build some of the world's great businesses with his intuitive ability to read people, still defers to Elroy on that score: "My father had an ability to think in a complex way that was different than in other people," he says. "There was a trust and optimism about him that is unique in people I've known, and, of course, something I don't possess—an ability to convince people of things that was uncanny."

In August 1969 the protected world of the McCaw family seemed as secure as ever. The family was united, their finances appeared solid, their lifestyle was insulated from the strains that threatened the rest of American society. Even big government, a favorite target of complaints for most entrepreneurs, seemed more a friend than an enemy. To broadcasters like Elroy McCaw, the Federal Communications Commission could be a nuisance, but the airwave licenses it distributed were like tickets to one of the world's most enjoyable, colorful, and profitable industries. A successful TV or radio station could boast profit margins of 60 percent. For the lucky ones like Elroy McCaw, the profits seemed unimaginable and unending. And in the late sixties, the FCC seemed to be continually trumpeting new ideas—for cable TV systems, satellite systems, and wireless systems—promising new frontiers for the industry. There was no greater apostle of the future of broadcasting than Elroy McCaw, a future in which Craig's place was assured. The only question was which of his father's companies he would someday run.

Maybe young Craig was hoping for a game of chess that August morning when he went looking for Elroy. It was almost noon, but Craig had no reason to worry about his father; Elroy had been up till midnight entertaining guests, so a late morning in bed didn't seem unusual.

(Marion was off in France on a luxury barge tour.) Craig headed upstairs toward his parents' bedroom.

Only Craig McCaw knows the details of what happened next. He has never spoken about it publicly, and even the McCaw brothers claim to have never discussed it among themselves. But Craig later told officials from the county medical examiner's office that he found his father in bed, completely motionless. Elroy was rushed by ambulance to Northwest Hospital, where he was pronounced dead on arrival. A massive stroke had claimed his life at age fifty-seven. Craig quickly summoned his brothers, and they set about trying to contact their mother with help from Senator Henry Jackson's office.

Elroy's sudden death was only the first shock. Within weeks, it became clear that the McCaw family finances were in tatters. Elroy's death had triggered dozens of claims and lawsuits from creditors. A family friend and business associate who studied the family's accounts concluded that Elroy McCaw's last deals were mostly bad ones. He had died broke.

Instantaneously, it seemed, the expanding world of the McCaws had collapsed.

When the claims reached $12 million, the family's bank declared the estate insolvent. Feeling besieged by lawyers and judges, Marion McCaw tried to fight back. The McCaw companies were not broke, she said—just short on cash. She asked for time to reorganize them. But the creditors wanted their money, demanding immediate payment even on long-term obligations. The family mansion, the yacht, a TV station that had just purchased new color-broadcasting equipment, and other assets were sold to pay creditors. Proud Marion McCaw was forced to petition a court to release funds so she could pay basic household bills.

The trauma, the embarrassment, the shock at discovering the truth about Elroy's business affairs devastated the McCaws to an extent they never revealed. The family had always been protective of Elroy's eccentricities. Now they had to endure the gossip and snickering of those who claimed they had foreseen his downfall. A file at the Seattle courthouse began to fill with previously unknown details; creditors told tales of broken promises, unpaid bills, fraudulent practices.

Craig McCaw's friends could only guess at the depth of his anguish.

Later, he would say simply, "A lot of bad things happened to my family." Subject closed.

As for the future, the McCaw family, it seemed, was certain to fade from prominence, like so many other clans whose fortunes had withered with the death of the family founder. Rarely does a family regain its lost wealth. In such cases, there is typically little or no money left to invest; the willingness to work hard has been spoiled by a life of comfort; optimism has been soured by decline.

Craig McCaw would later call the family disaster triggered by his father's death "a very defining moment in my life." He never elaborated. But it is evident that the trauma caused him to take stock, to reshape his plans to follow in his father's path, and to vow never to repeat Elroy's mistakes. He could draw energy, intuition, and interests from his father, but would avoid his excesses.

Elroy was the raw McCaw. Craig McCaw would become, in many ways, more baffling and eccentric than his father, but a far more talented businessman. Where Elroy disregarded or overlooked risk, his son would focus on it as a problem to be analyzed and managed—and transformed, ultimately, into a road to success. Potential disaster would often shadow Craig McCaw, and many predicted he would go the way of Elroy. Yet if people misunderstood what he was doing, that was fine with Craig. It even became a part of his strategy: *Let the other guy think I'm nuts.* A shrewd manager of his own image, he would turn a seeming weakness—his quirky personality—into a strategic asset, with results no one could question.

* * *

In 1987, within a week of the eighteenth anniversary of Elroy McCaw's death, McCaw Cellular Communications went public. The initial public offering catapulted the family into the ranks of the nation's richest people, with stock holdings worth close to $2 billion. They had gone from broke to billions.

Craig McCaw himself was riding a crest of fame. McCaw Cellular Communications had risen seemingly out of nowhere to be the largest cellular telephone company in the nation. McCaw was being called "the king of cellular." Most businesspeople in the same position would have relished their years on the throne, but Craig McCaw's bag of surprises was far from empty. Just six years later, in 1993, he stunned the telecommunications industry by selling his company to AT&T.

As he walked away from the business he had spent years building, he said he had no idea what he would do next. McCaw had one of the world's largest yachts, a jet capable of crossing oceans, several palatial homes, and more money than anyone could spend in a lifetime. None of it seemed to matter very much. McCaw went kayaking and thought about life. The business world waited and watched.

Before long, McCaw had started over yet again. He founded NEXTLINK Communications, a provider of telephone service to businesses, and took it public. He bought Nextel Communications—a nearly bankrupt wireless telephone company—fixed its management problems, modernized its technology, and turned it profitable.

After selling out to AT&T, McCaw had vowed to work less hard in the future. His new ventures apparently paid better than most part-time jobs. Exact figures are elusive, but it is clear that McCaw has netted as much as $9 billion from his stock in NEXTLINK and Nextel—his second staggering fortune made before reaching the age of fifty.

Who is Craig McCaw? How does he do it? And what's his next billion-dollar idea?

The story of Craig McCaw is one of tragedy and triumph, an amazing personal and business tale. But it is also a mystery, because the man at its center is so opaque.

McCaw is no Howard Hughes, the eccentric airline pioneer who made a fortune, then retreated into a bizarre world of untrimmed hair, uncut fingernails, and elaborate hygiene rituals. To all appearances, Craig McCaw is a normal northwesterner. He strolls the streets of Seattle typically dressed in casual Lands' End–style khakis and sweaters, attends parties, and remains close to a few old friends. He likes to fly his float plane into Canada and camp in the woods or water-ski on Lake Washington. It's a good life but an unpretentious one.

Though McCaw doesn't court media attention, he can't help attracting it. He's interesting, charming, and quotable; he makes good copy because he's so refreshingly different from the typical executive. But whenever he can, he lets subordinates speak for him. "I'm extremely boring," he claims. As far as he's concerned, what he did yesterday is ancient history; what he's doing today is too personal to share; and what he'll do tomorrow is a strategic secret.

McCaw's penchant for privacy is no false facade. "Shy" doesn't begin to describe his personality. Once, before a speech at a university, he sequestered himself for an hour to avoid mingling with the school officials. And he is genuinely uninterested in what the public thinks about him; he never reads his clippings. He would rather stay "focused," one of his favorite words. He agreed to cooperate with this writer, but after a few interviews got bored and quietly shut that door.

McCaw runs his companies in a style that reflects his personality. "I want to be the Wizard of Oz," he once said, leaving others to interpret his words. Here's one reading: Dorothy's Wizard empowered those who sought his help, granting them courage (the Cowardly Lion), wisdom (the Scarecrow), compassion (the Tin Man)—clearly a role McCaw seeks to play with those who work for him.

McCaw also needed a kind of magic to make McCaw Cellular a business success, wriggling through seemingly impassable regulatory straits, overpowering the deep-pocketed major phone companies, and extracting cash by a kind of leveraged alchemy from the vaults of banks and other lenders.

And like the Wizard—an unabashed master of humbug who, when unveiled, has the nerve to command, "Pay no attention to that man behind the curtain!"—McCaw dissembles when it suits him, conjuring up an exaggerated, almost mystical, image of his intellectual and intuitive prowess, which serves to intimidate allies and adversaries alike.

The longer we study McCaw, the more the contradictions pile up. He is a fierce competitor with no ego. A dyslexic who sees what others miss. A visionary who communicates clumsily. A gifted leader who avoids people. A fitness nut who looks frail. A near recluse with a talent for reading the motives of others. A billionaire who wears a cheap digital watch. A tireless strategist who tries to be spontaneous. A business celebrity whose office security camera is a fake. A soft-spoken man with the look of a seminarian who shoots Nerf balls at visitors. A futurist immersed in the study of history. A wallflower who wagers billions on risky deals.

Craig McCaw bows when he sees you, or calls up and addresses you as "Kemo Sabe." A health food advocate, he chose eggplant sandwiches for the menu at a company retreat, prompting some attendees to sneak off to McDonald's. Many tell stories of odd encounters with the boss. One executive ran into him in the hallway. McCaw paused, held up his hands, fingers spread, and signaled for the executive to do likewise. McCaw pressed their fingertips together and consulted some inner gauge. "Hmmm," he said finally, "pretty good," and walked away. *What the hell did that mean?* his deputy wondered.

"He's weird," one of his top aides says. The boss isn't always pleasant. He can be moody, demanding, and disdainful of those who displease him. "For a lot of folks, McCaw's like the sun," says Scot Jarvis, a former aide who admires the man. "You don't want to fly too close, because you'll get burned. And he's hardest on the ones closest to him."

McCaw's executive style is difficult to label. Microsoft's Bill Gates—a neighbor of McCaw's on Lake Washington in Seattle—has emerged as the most dynamic businessman of his generation, but his command-style management is basically a variation on conventional business leadership. McCaw is something else. Engaged only on issues he sees as critical, he is increasingly remote from details and is often unseen except by a handful in his inner circle. Bill Gates apparently can't slow down, while Craig McCaw grows more nomadic; he is frequently absent from the office, yet constantly gathers the information necessary to monitor his businesses. His closest aides often have no idea where he is. They leave word on his voice mail and wait. He might call back from California, Alaska, Europe—or down the hall. McCaw personally embodies his own vision of the modern worker freed from his desk by global wireless communication services.

Behind his back, some of McCaw's deputies grumble about his taking frequent yachting trips while they toil without vacations. They say he's the nomad, pondering the desires of average folk, while they remain at their desks, keeping a furious pace set by his companies. Ironically, McCaw is the first to say he could never survive in a typical business environment. He avoids meetings, dislikes paperwork, speaks in parables, and sometimes gives orders he never expects to be followed. If he worked at IBM, "they'd throw me out," he admits.

* * *

Today, looking for even greater challenges, Craig McCaw has persuaded Bill Gates to join his latest dazzling project: an array of hundreds of low-orbit communications satellites expected to cost at least $9 billion. Currently scheduled to begin offering service in 2004, the Teledesic system will deliver high-speed data access, including voice, video, and sound, to every part of the globe.

The idea is so far-fetched that few took it seriously at first. No one in history has launched so many satellites, much less received regulatory approval for such an enormous project from world agencies that typically spend years just deciding on agendas for their meetings. Teledesic will need to seek permission from government departments in each country, one by one, an overwhelming task in itself. And will it work? No one knows for sure how to make so many satellites cheaply enough. No one has written the software to link them. Many scientists and communications analysts call the idea preposterous.

John Pike of the nonprofit Federation of American Scientists was among the early doubters: "I think it is extremely unlikely that Teledesic is going to happen or make any money," Pike said in 1996. But he added:

> On the other hand, if it does happen and does make money, it will make a preposterous amount of money. It will make an amount of money the likes of which no one has ever seen in recorded history, because basically they will have established an impervious monopoly in whatever markets they manage to penetrate. They'll be in the position that AT&T was in before Judge Greene got ahold of them.

Because the visionary behind the Teledesic plan is Craig McCaw, the naysayers are beginning to give way to the believers. Embracing a seemingly impossible idea—taking huge risks and going for a huge payoff— has been the pattern of McCaw's career. He knows no other way.

McCaw would be uneasy about too many comparisons to his father. Elroy did deals on the backs of envelopes, lost track of details, hired too few good people, tried to do too much by himself. His son has vowed to avoid those mistakes. But though Elroy left behind many secrets, Craig McCaw clearly learned important lessons from him, especially the wisdom of the unconventional path. The father is one key to understanding how the son made himself a multibillionaire . . . and where he first got the urge to monopolize the heavens.

2

"A Bit of a Loose Skipper"

The Elder McCaw and the Origins of an Empire

I f Craig McCaw had followed the conservative path, he probably would have lived out his life in Centralia, Washington, running the little cable TV system that ultimately constituted his father's sole legacy. But doing the sensible thing isn't Craig McCaw's style any more than it was Elroy's. McCaw inherited from his father a sense that business could take alternative forms. It could be run formally, like the offices of Boeing/McDonnell Douglas or one of the other corporate behemoths of Seattle, or it could be run informally. Growing up around Elroy, the right choice was obvious: Informal was more fun.

As Craig McCaw built one company, sold it, and built another, always extending his reach and increasing the size of his bets, he thought often of his father, the extraordinary deal maker whose early death had left his wife and children in pain and their family fortunes in disarray.

The relevant portion of Elroy McCaw's career began in 1937, when radio station KELA first warmed up its tubes and announced itself to the world. At 500 watts of power, KELA couldn't broadcast far beyond its base in a soggy corner of southwest Washington, but the event thrilled the folks of Centralia, a town of fewer than 8,000 people that had been shrinking throughout the Depression. The men of Centralia— those with jobs, that is—made their living cutting trees in the hills around the county, digging for coal, or farming the region's rich soil. A generation earlier, the town had played a prominent role in the history of northwest radicalism. In 1919 a famous gunfight broke out in Centralia between American Legionnaires and members of the left-wing union, the Industrial Workers of the World (the Wobblies). By the late 1930s, however, politics in Centralia had become quiescent. The launch of KELA was the biggest news in town.

KELA's owners, car dealer Arthur St. John and theater owner Cecil Gwinn, picked twenty-six-year-old J. Elroy McCaw to run the station and be their partner. The men wanted an aggressive promoter to get people's attention. Elroy filled the bill. He had gone to high school in nearby Aberdeen and studied radio at Washington State College, where he ran the student station, hosted some shows, and did some acting. But while other students were captivated by the romance, fun, or technical challenges of radio, Elroy saw it primarily as a wonderful business. Sentiment never kept him from selling anything (which is also true for his son); a radio station was always for sale for the right price.

Elroy used KELA as a springboard for connections with national figures in broadcasting and with politicians and government regulators, especially those of the Federal Communications Commission. Thanks to his efforts, Centralia's station won an affiliation with the Mutual Broadcasting System (though Elroy failed to get a CBS affiliation) and won FCC approval to boost its broadcasting power to 1,000 watts.

By 1941 KELA's owners had sold Elroy a piece of the station as an inducement to stay on, but he was already thinking of bigger opportunities. "He was eager. He wanted to climb, that's for sure," recalls Elaine Gwinn O'Toole, Cecil Gwinn's daughter. Les Keiter, who joined KELA in 1941 as assistant sports director, felt something close to awe in Elroy McCaw's presence. "When you were in conversation with him, he'd always be five jumps ahead of you," says Keiter. "So many times he wouldn't say good-bye. He walked out on the conversation. Some thought he was rude, [but] he wasn't. His thought process was in another area." Neither man nor nature could stop him. When the Chehalis River overflowed and spilled around KELA's offices, as it often did during winter rains or spring runoff, Elroy told his engineers and DJs to row to work. One such day, a frog hopped onto a control panel and became a radio celebrity, dubbed Blinkey by KELA's charmed listeners.

At a picnic hosted by the Rotary Club, Elroy met his future wife, Marion Oliver, the attractive daughter of the owner of the Lewis & Clark Hotel and a hardware store. She came from money, at least by the modest standards of a small Washington town.

If opposites attract, Marion was the perfect match for Elroy McCaw. Where Elroy was rumpled, brash, and loquacious, Marion was tailored, elegant, and well spoken. She was warm but not chummy with new acquaintances. She was meticulous about details and gifted with a retentive and accurate memory: When Marion quoted a dollar figure, you could be sure it was correct to the penny. If Elroy was the type of person to jump over cliffs, Marion would make certain the altitude was measured first. Lawrence Minard, a schoolmate of Craig's who later became managing editor of *Forbes* magazine, calls her simply "one of the smartest people I've ever met."

In a later era, Marion Oliver might have enjoyed a successful career in business. Not in the late 1930s. Though Marion did well in her accounting classes at the University of Washington, advisers warned her that the men who called the shots wouldn't accept a woman CPA. Her father, however, advised her to experience business firsthand so that later she would understand the world of her husband. So shortly after graduation, she took a stab at real estate development. In 1939 Marion built a forty-acre subdivision north of Centralia, handling all the permits, financing, and contract negotiations. She had no trouble with the men who worked for the county or the power company: "I knew what I was talking about," she explains. She made a tidy profit, then quit business until she met Elroy McCaw.

After their marriage in 1942 she served as Elroy's adviser and accountant: "I was sort of a right hand for Elroy." It was an often exasperating job. Marion kept records; Elroy did not. He avoided lawyers, sealed deals with a handshake, and preferred to trust people's memories rather than documenting deals in writing—even deals that involved complex contingencies and different classes of shareholders. Elroy's style reflected his sunny outlook and clever mind, but also his recklessness. "I was always a great believer in paper. Elroy was not," Marion said later. For most of their marriage, she unsuccessfully tried to get him to slow down, watch details, and be more careful. She pressed him to bring order and method to his impulsive dealings. Friends say she worried that his high-wire schemes would bring them to ruin. In this, of course, Marion was prophetic.

During World War II Elroy served in the Army Air Corps (the predecessor of today's Air Force), working in intelligence, mainly with radio systems. Exactly what he did remains murky even to family members and close friends. One unproven story has him making a secret journey to Russia to install a weather station to assist British pilots. If true, perhaps this would explain why he was decorated with the Order of the British Empire.

After the war, Elroy and Marion had their first child, Bruce, in June 1946. Craig came next, in August 1949, followed by John and Keith. Elroy resumed his business career and quickly began assembling a radio empire, acquiring full or partial ownership of stations from Hawaii to Texas, including effective control of KELA. He spent little of his own money. His friend Les Smith, longtime owner of Seattle's KJR-AM, calls Elroy one of broadcasting's first leverage artists, for whom a network of financiers was the critical asset: "Elroy had every banker. He had zillions of bankers."

Elroy's eccentric personal style didn't change. He often traveled on business without a razor, a hat, or even a change of clothes. He would show up at a friend's hotel room, bed down on the couch, and scrub his wash-and-wear shirt in the bathroom sink. He constantly bummed cigarettes and cigars from friends and developed a habit of stepping away from the dinner table to make an urgent phone call just before the check arrived. If not for Elroy's energy and charm, he would have been just plain obnoxious.

Craig McCaw's later interest in the liberating power of the cellular phone was foreshadowed in his father's business style. Talk was Elroy's currency, and he spent it freely. He was always on the phone, about to make a call, or just completing one. He often juggled multiple calls. The pace of his talk amazed friends. Les Keiter remembers Elroy's calls from Seattle to friends and employees on the East Coast at any hour of the day or night. "Elroy, do you know it's three in the morning?" an awakened Keiter would demand. "Not here," Elroy would reply. Not even Elroy could maintain such a schedule indefinitely. Sometimes he would call people and fall asleep on the line three minutes later. "I'd yell '*Elroy!*' and he'd wake up," recalls Jim Adduci, a friend in Washington, D.C.

Elroy believed he could talk his way into anything, and the stories suggest he may have been right. He was famous for getting into places he didn't belong. A Republican, he crashed John F. Kennedy's inaugural ball and a Democratic powwow with Lyndon Johnson. More significantly, Elroy could talk his way into any banker's vault.

Joe Clark, an old family friend, describes Elroy as a kind of Mr. Magoo, the nearsighted cartoon character who blunders cheerfully—and with impunity—through an endless variety of unlikely adventures: "He'd walk right past a secretary. People would never stop him because he had that air that he was supposed to be there." One time Elroy agreed to buy a Learjet from Clark's airplane dealership. Later that same day, Elroy walked into Peoples Bank, cigar in mouth, in search of the money to pay Clark. "Howya doing, Ken?" he said to a vice president. "I've just got a minute. I need a hundred thousand dollars."

"I don't think we can do that," replied the banker, explaining that a loan committee would need to review the request.

"Wanna bet?" replied Elroy. "I keep a substantial amount of funds on deposit in your bank. Check it out. I'll be back at one P.M.—an hour from now." Elroy got his money and his plane.

According to family legend, "Mr. Magoo" caused his greatest stir in 1962 by appearing, wholly by accident, inside the White House during a top secret briefing for President Kennedy on the Cuban missile crisis. Kennedy's press secretary, Pierre Salinger, disclosed the incident in 1971. A colonel in the Air Force Reserves with a security clearance, Elroy had been a member of the Air Force National Defense Council, a booster group for the Air Force. One day Elroy showed up late for a council meeting at the office of General Curtis E. LeMay, who had been called away to an urgent meeting at the White House. Elroy explained that he was late for a meeting with the general. LeMay's confused secretary, thinking that Elroy meant the National Security Council, said the meeting was already under way. She called the White House to notify aides that Elroy was coming. Elroy followed her directions and found himself entering a darkened room where slides of Soviet maneuvers in and around Cuba were being projected.

Accounts of what happened next differ. One version has Elroy sitting right next to President Kennedy, who reportedly said to Elroy as the lights came on, "Tough damn situation, isn't it?"

Wherever Elroy sat, it soon became clear to the FBI, Secret Service, and Pentagon security officials that he was in the wrong place. After some explaining, the FBI called Elroy's friend Jim Adduci, who ran the Air Force office that sponsored the advisory council. Several hours later, a grinning Elroy was released to Adduci. "Hey, Jim. Wait till I tell you what happened to me!" Elroy said.

The White House was not amused by this security breach during one of the most dangerous crises of the Cold War. Several people were fired and security systems were overhauled in what Adduci called "the biggest damn security shake-up you ever saw at the White House."

*　*　*

Like many radio owners, Elroy McCaw showed an early interest in broadcast television (controlled, like radio, by the FCC), as well as cable, a means of extending the TV signal into distant areas poorly reached by broadcasting.

Beginning in the 1950s Elroy bought television stations in Tacoma, Washington (KTVW), and Denver, Colorado (KTVR). He also unsuccessfully sought a television license to serve Walla Walla, Washington. He managed the TV stations in his typically eccentric way. He would often call Roger Rice, the Tacoma station manager, late at night and open the conversation not with "Hello" or "This is Elroy" but with a brusque "What's new?" Rice enjoyed working for McCaw despite the fact that one of his duties was to face down angry creditors. Elroy often managed debt by waiting till a creditor threatened to sue, then offering to pay fifty cents on the dollar. It worked—sometimes.

Financially squeezed, the Tacoma station faced entrenched competitors in Seattle with more powerful signals and attractive network affiliations. But in 1968 Elroy came up with an idea to lure viewers who shared his enthusiasm for business information. He turned Tacoma's KTVW-TV into a twenty-four-hour financial news network, much like those launched nationally by CNN and NBC decades later. Elroy set up a studio in Seattle and aired business news with a stock ticker running continually at the bottom of the screen. He tried syndicating the show to other stations, but no one else thought the idea had a future.

Ultimately, it became clear that the TV stations were dogs. Elroy told *Broadcasting Magazine* in 1960 that his losses for both stations had totaled $2.5 million that year.

Meanwhile, Elroy was dabbling in the nascent cable TV business. In 1952 he won the bidding for Centralia's tiny cable franchise on the basis of a foolish promise to cap monthly subscriber rates at $3.65. This amount doomed the company to small profits and too little capital to deliver quality service. Nonetheless, Elroy expanded service into the nearby town of Chehalis, renaming the company Twin City Cablevision, and eventually built a customer base of 4,000.

Late in his career, Elroy used his contacts in the New York radio market to break into the nation's largest potential cable TV market. According to author Rick Sklar, Elroy convinced Mayor Robert Wagner that cable TV would allow him to address every convention in town without leaving his office, and used this notion to gain permission to use city conduits to wire every major New York hotel. Elroy didn't stop with hotels; he wired all of midtown Manhattan, creating for himself a free cable TV franchise. This system, then called Channel 6, would eventually become Manhattan Cable Television.

Elroy McCaw's most profitable deal cost him almost nothing. In 1953, already owning interests in eight radio stations, Elroy and a minority partner bought the money-losing WINS-AM in New York from Crosley Broadcasting Corporation for a sale price of $450,000, nearly all of it borrowed. "Somehow, he survived with smoke and mirrors and friends who helped him," says Bill Daniels, a friend of Elroy's and principal of a Denver-based communications brokerage firm (and later an important player in Craig McCaw's company).

The bargain price tag on WINS—a fourth of what Crosley had paid for the station seven years earlier—reflected the apparently gloomy outlook for the radio industry, which was losing advertising dollars to television. Elroy was determined to make the deal work. Rather than rent an apartment at Manhattan rates, he converted a portion of the WINS premises into living quarters and began flying to New York from Seattle every week—often using his Air Force Reserve status to cadge free flights on military planes. He started slashing the station's operating costs. According to Rick Sklar, a WINS program director who later became vice president of ABC Radio:

> He locked out the studio orchestra. He ordered the lightbulbs changed to sixty watts. To save paper costs, he switched the United Press teletype machines from costly multicopy carbon-paper rolls to the free single-paper rolls that came with the service, and he

issued a directive to single-space the program logs. . . . If, through natural selection, a new humanoid species were to evolve that could instinctively survive without any money of its own, Elroy McCaw would have been the progenitor.

In Rick Sklar's words, "Elroy believed that there was virtually no reason to have to pay for any goods or services in this world." It was inevitable that Elroy McCaw and the powerful broadcasting unions would clash. In 1958 the American Federation of Television and Radio Artists briefly struck WINS. Later, when the engineers struck, Elroy had secretaries running the booths in the studios, and he gave a mailroom boy a crash course in engineering and sent him to produce remote broadcasts. During subsequent negotiations, Elroy tried to win sympathy by arriving on crutches he had earlier used to recover from a car accident, but the ruse was exposed when he slipped, dropped the crutches, and walked away. The stunt failed, but Elroy had the last laugh; the engineers got only a token raise.

Desperate to raise ratings and so attract greater advertising dollars, he accepted the station managers' suggestion to try a new musical format called rock 'n' roll. WINS hired two veteran announcers, already nearly legendary in New York, Alan Freed and Murray "the K" Kaufman. The station staged numerous goofy publicity stunts. To attract crowds on the street, disc jockeys interviewed employees in gorilla suits and camped inside the subway. Advertisers were induced to take "free" late-night slots (the catch was a modest "service charge"). Ratings soared and money started pouring in.

When the New York Giants baseball team moved from New York to San Francisco in 1958, Elroy decided to borrow an idea from the 1920s and re-create the games live using play-by-play accounts received over the Teletype. He wanted Les Keiter, his sportscaster, to do the plays, complete with staged sound effects—ball striking bat, crowd reactions, and the like. Keiter told McCaw he was crazy—that the broadcasts would be a joke. (Actually, Keiter feared *he* would be the joke.) Elroy countered that not only would the games be a ratings success but Keiter would be the biggest name in New York. Elroy was right. During the 1958 baseball season, hundreds of thousands of New Yorkers in apartments, taverns, and taxis followed every hit by Willie

Mays and a rookie named Orlando Cepeda (the "Baby Bull") through Keiter's re-creations.

"The whole idea was a masterstroke from a master broadcaster, Mr. J. Elroy McCaw," Keiter wrote in his memoir, *Fifty Years Behind the Microphone*.

One of Elroy's schemes landed him in hot water with AT&T, which then had a monopoly over local and long-distance phone service and essentially controlled all hardware connected to its network. It charged radio stations a premium to rent high-quality long-distance lines for remote broadcasts. Eager to avoid the higher tariff, McCaw asked WINS engineers to devise a system of amplifiers and attach them to an ordinary long-distance telephone line. The system worked, but when AT&T found out, they shut it down in the middle of a live WINS broadcast. According to Sklar, McCaw later sued the phone company and persuaded a judge to order AT&T to make such systems available at reasonable cost. "Dad was always trying to get one step ahead of the phone company," Bruce McCaw says.

AT&T also looked askance at Elroy's plans to operate a long-distance reselling service from Seattle. Launched in the late 1960s when few thought it possible to compete with Ma Bell, the plan went so far as to have Elroy building a switchboard and renting WATS lines to be offered to businesses at cut rates. Elroy eventually dropped the project, though son Bruce has no idea why.

Even at home, Elroy McCaw enjoyed tweaking the Bell monopolists. The McCaws had two or three phone lines and more than a half-dozen phones, most unauthorized and technically illegal. Once in a while, the phone company would send an inspector to the McCaw house to hunt down the suspected phones, but Bruce always managed to yank the wires and hide the evidence in time.

In 1961 Elroy faced the biggest threat to his career. The FCC accused WINS employees of receiving payoffs from record companies in exchange for airtime for their artists—all with the knowledge of station management. Ominously, the FCC also announced it would hold hearings on whether to renew Elroy McCaw's New York broadcast license, which was about to expire. The so-called payola scandal and the shadow it cast over Elroy's broadcasting rights killed a pending sale of WINS to Storer Broadcasting. The New York district attorney,

Congress, the FCC, and Elroy himself launched investigations. Though Elroy was never personally implicated, the episode put a terrible strain on him. In self-defense, he pleaded ignorance of station operations—a credible claim for those who knew about Elroy's hands-off (not to say disorganized) management style. In late 1961 the FCC announced that it would renew the WINS license after all. Elroy immediately began looking for another buyer for the station and sold WINS the following April to Westinghouse Broadcasting Company for $10 million, at the time the largest sale in broadcast history. He then exercised an option on WINS property at 7 Central Park West, selling it to a skyscraper developer for nearly as much money. All in all, Elroy McCaw had cleared nearly $20 million on his seven years of WINS ownership—not a bad return on a $60,000 down payment.

Elroy had to do something with the $10 million check from West-inghouse. An inveterate prankster, he thought it would be fun to have painfully introverted twelve-year-old Craig, then visiting his father in New York, deposit the check. Elroy sent his son to the local Chase Manhattan branch. As instructed, the boy handed the check to a teller, saying "I want to put this in my account." At a safe distance, Elroy watched, roaring with laughter as the teller gasped and hastily summoned a senior bank officer.

Back in 1953, the same year he had bought WINS, Elroy had found another bargain in The Highlands, just north of Seattle. A seven-bedroom, seven-bathroom mansion had been built by the Boeings and was owned by Children's Orthopedic Hospital, which was eager to unload it. But the house had been on the market for years; vacant for more than a decade, it was badly dilapidated. Neglected shrubs had nearly swallowed the driveway; vines covered the house; rain blew in through broken windows. To Elroy, it had exactly what he saw in broken-down radio stations: hidden value.

"Don't tell anybody," Elroy told his friend Les Smith after buying the house. "Marion doesn't even know."

"What the hell do you need that big a house for?" Smith recalls asking. "I'll work it out," Elroy replied.

Marion didn't want the mansion. To her, it was just too big—nearly ten times the size of their Centralia home. In time, however, she grew to love the house because of what it offered her sons: room to roam and play. The McCaw boys made friends in The Highlands, though perhaps not as many as they would have found in the city. The isolation kept the family together, as Marion wanted: "My feeling was if they grew up being friends, they could always have each other and they could make friends later on."

The mansion was both home and headquarters. Elroy would be gone as much as two weeks a month, and on his return he often disappeared into his home office to talk on the phone or dictate to his secretary. Marion, too, worked nearly full-time, not cleaning or cooking but managing the numbers for Elroy's empire, working in her own office with a small staff of accountants. The dining table was often piled high with IRS forms and reports, which Marion pushed aside when the boys got hungry. Though Marion was meticulous about her work, her office door was always open for her sons. Interruptions never bothered her, Bruce says.

While Mom and Dad were working, the boys prowled the wooded grounds in go-carts, motorcycles, and old cars, chased by their enormous dog, Duke. Bruce McCaw was driving by age eleven. They shot off guns in the backyard or in a range Bruce set up inside the garage. (Neighbors were too far away to be bothered by the noise.) A family cook made meals for the boys and their buddies. Friend Matt Griffin marveled at the mansion: "The only time I've seen anything like it was on *The Beverly Hillbillies*," he says. "Exploring the house, for a kid like me, was a major event," says Lawrence Minard, whose own grandfather had founded a successful car dealership in Seattle.

At Elroy's command, the boys would play pranks on unsuspecting visitors. Departing dinner guests would start their cars only to hear a loud bang followed by puffs of white smoke from one of the exploding gizmos Elroy bought at novelty shops.

Craig, as a teenager, realized that his father was different from most businessmen. It wasn't just Elroy's freeloading habits or his appetite for juggling numerous deals; it was also his zest for life, his dazzling gift of blarney, and his ability to convince others to agree to his schemes. An introvert, Craig envied his father's easy way with people.

"There was a trust and optimism about my father that is unique in people I've known, and of course something I don't possess," he said later:

He had an ability to convince people of things which was uncanny, plus his absolute sense of innocence. You've probably heard the story about him getting into the briefing for the Cuban Missile Crisis. That was actually how he would do it. He could talk his way through and into anything. But you know, you can't do that simply as a matter of dishonesty. There's something about your soul that people read in your face. He had an optimism about people that could be misplaced, but he believed anything was possible and didn't worry about how you were going to do it.

From Craig's perspective, his father's most powerful strength was also his greatest weakness. Despite his own irresponsibility, Elroy McCaw trusted business partners, eschewed formal contracts, and spent little energy monitoring his subordinates or partners. That freed Elroy's people to work as they saw best. "If the trust is blind enough and the expectations high enough, you can get extraordinary results from your relationships with people," says Craig McCaw. But Elroy wasn't careful about whom he trusted, and some people took advantage of him in ways that became apparent only later.

Meanwhile, his success provided a princely lifestyle for his family. While Elroy scrimped on business expenses, the money flowed freely at home. In 1970, for example, Marion spent $7,000 a month on household expenses: part-time cooks, housekeepers, and gardeners; flying lessons for the boys; European travel for Craig; dues to the Seattle Gold Club and the Seattle Tennis Club; charitable, religious, and cultural donations; orthodontia for the boys; tuition at private schools in Seattle, Menlo College, and Stanford; and cars, including a Cadillac and two Porsches for the boys.

Elroy would take his sons, their friends, and Marion's nephews for cruises on the family yacht, the sixty-three-foot *Sumarlee*. The boys and their friends learned bridge on yachting trips down Hood Canal or up to British Columbia. It was a carefree life. Afloat, Elroy was as eccentric as he was on land. "Elroy was a bit of a loose skipper," recalls Steve Oliver, Marion's nephew. "He'd always manage to go aground on a sandbar. His favorite saying was 'Don't worry, boys. We've got plenty of water.' A few minutes later, we'd run aground." But the goal was fun, not expert seamanship.

Elroy wasn't satisfied with the WINS success. He kept looking for the next killing. He tried to buy the ABC radio network, but ABC wasn't selling. He cofounded Jet Air, which leased a helicopter and some airplanes, including one of the Northwest's first Learjets. Jet Air didn't make much money, but it helped the boys pursue their interest in flying. Elroy bought control of a large moving company and made many other investments, including a 200-acre industrial park in Kent, Washington; a shopping center in Sacramento, California; an apartment building in Florida; and a Canadian steel manufacturer that went bankrupt. Publicity about the WINS sale brought a flood of other investment proposals. "He had so many opportunities, he couldn't make up his mind," Homer Bergren, a friend and business associate said later.

Marion knew as well as anybody that Elroy was spreading himself thin. She knew the numbers. She urged him to slow down and to be more careful about recording transactions in writing. He wouldn't. "There were times," she said later, "when I think he paid a lot of attention to what I had to say, but when he was caught up and interested and intrigued with something, he was just inclined to go ahead with it."

In August 1969 Marion and Elroy were due to travel to France for a barge trip. At the last minute, he backed out, saying he wanted to spend more time with the boys. Marion left with a female friend in Elroy's place. He died early the next Saturday morning.

When word of Elroy's death spread among his business associates, no one knew what to do. There was no clear record of the myriad transactions, commitments, collateralized deals, promises.

A curious Homer Bergren visited the King County courthouse, where he picked through the listing of Elroy's assets and investments, thinking there might be something he could buy. The papers shocked Bergren. There was nothing worth having, he concluded. "He was flat-ass broke," said Bergren.

For future executive Craig, his father's death carried a profound lesson. He needed to take the best from his father while remembering the advice of his mother, who had long preached the need to manage risk and control the variables that can wreck a company. When Craig McCaw began his own business career, he kept his mother by his side, where he could seek her advice on business and people.

Craig proved to be the ideal blend of his mother and father. Like

Elroy, Craig had a passion for deal making, a willingness to take risks and try unconventional approaches, and an easy-to-overlook shrewdness. But Craig also had his mother's moderation. He avoided aggressive transactions unless every possible outcome had been examined. Like his mother, he chose friends, employees, and business associates with care. Though impatient like his father, he had his mother's well-bred manners. Craig loved to have fun, but always kept his mother's seriousness and sense of focus.

He himself viewed his first great company, McCaw Cellular Communications, as an outgrowth of his parents' blended influence. "I think of the company today as half my mother and half my father," he once said, "my mother in terms of the embodiment of greater systemization and broadening; my father in terms of sensitivity to opportunity."

He made a similar point in an interview with the American Academy of Achievement:

> My mother was an interesting role model. She gave us a lot of benefit of that precise thinking that came from accounting. My father, on the other hand, was an extremely creative, almost wild-eyed visionary, and we saw the balance of the two. If anything came of that, it was that my mother added the anchor to my father's creativity. I learned fairly young that if you didn't do the precision part, the creative part would evaporate. You had to have the foundation under the creativity.

3

"Money Was Not the Issue"

A College Boy Takes Charge

In the fall of 1969 twenty-year-old Craig McCaw went back to Stanford—reluctantly. He had wanted to quit school and help his mother handle his father's estate. Perhaps Elroy's old chess partner felt he sensed the order underlying his father's maze of dealings, but Marion insisted that he finish school first.

After Elroy's death, Marion McCaw spent the next seven years trying to sort through her husband's tangle of oral promises, contracts, scheduled payments, and collections, and a grab bag of investments. Many of the lawsuits filed against the estate were bogus. Some of Elroy's partners had cheated him and were now trying to take advantage of Marion.

No charges of fraud against Elroy were ever proven, but for several years after his death, the family had no idea of their net worth. A court agreed to put the family on a generous allowance as the claims were sorted out. For help, Marion turned to one of Seattle's most prominent lawyers, William Gates, whose son of the same name would later cofound Microsoft.

The trauma surrounding the estate enormously affected Craig McCaw's evolving sense of himself as a businessman. It taught him the importance of carefully selecting people to trust, because no agreement, however lengthy, could anticipate everything or eliminate the dangers of dealing in bad faith. Finding good people, McCaw decided, was key to the type of company he wanted to run. He didn't want a traditional company where everyone waited for the boss to issue directives. He wanted employees who knew the company's overall goals and didn't need the boss around to do their job.

McCaw would spend hours with an applicant for a key position.

Keen intelligence was one requirement, but the right values were more important. He wanted people who would respond to his trust, work even harder in his absence, innovate, and be ethical in their business dealings. In McCaw's system, trust would be both a burden on the employee and tremendously liberating.

One of Elroy McCaw's acts saved the family financially. Shortly before his death, Elroy had walked into an insurance office and bought a $2 million policy on his life, naming Marion and the boys as beneficiaries. Elroy always avoided paying cash, and this deal was no exception: He had merely signed a promissory note to pay the premiums, which the family later paid. Marion had to press the insurance company to honor the policy, but eventually it issued $1 million to her and $1 million to the boys—a fabulous return on another no-money-down deal. Elroy's last deal may have been his best.

It was no surprise that Craig wanted to quit school. He had been raised to make his own choices. As a student at Lakeside, an exclusive prep school for boys near Seattle, McCaw had enjoyed a system that had few rules but high expectations. Built for the elite and designed to resemble a prosperous New England college, Lakeside offered small classes of twelve students or fewer. Most of the students came from comfortable backgrounds. "They were golden retrievers. Everyone's teeth were straightened by age twelve," says Gardiner Davis, a former Lakeside teacher.

The school assigned nightly homework of three to four hours and assumed that its students would do schoolwork without much supervision. In Lakeside's privileged environment, the self-motivated could flourish, but the unmotivated could escape penalty. Some Lakeside boys talked about future careers in business, but most wanted to make their own paths, says Mick Deal, a graduate. Some viewed their successful fathers as a tough mark to beat. Others relished the challenge. Among the most notable Lakeside graduates were future Microsoft entrepreneurs Paul Allen, son of a university librarian, and Bill Gates.

McCaw set himself apart at Lakeside with an early focus on his goals. While many seniors chatted during study hall about bets on football games, "Craig was dreaming of products and business ideas," says Mick Deal. With his slender build, McCaw played a forgettable role in school sports, especially after breaking a leg during an eighth-grade football game. After that, he mainly played intramural games.

McCaw struggled in his early school years, burdened by the dyslexia that made it difficult for him to read. (The family says Elroy's odd hand-writing and aversion to paperwork suggest that he had dyslexia, too.) To work around the problem, McCaw took special training in reading from the fifth grade on. He hated the lessons, but they helped. School friends never knew about the disorder. Although McCaw was once reluctant to discuss his dyslexia, today he speaks openly about how it forces him to think hard about what he wants to say or write. Rather than reading a document, he will usually put it aside for later, and then he listens—really listens—to the person who handed it to him.

Perhaps as a result, McCaw's listening powers are legendary. Once he tunes in, he completely absorbs what one says, and he often remem-bers years-old conversations verbatim. Generally, McCaw doesn't want memos; if any are written, they'd better be concise.

McCaw, through his dyslexia, sees patterns where others see details; he sees goals where others are focused on increments. Forced to keep more in his head, he has learned to absorb an entire situation. He has had to think more about *thinking,* a process that eventually helped him become a talented business strategist.

"A dyslexic tends to be more conceptual and does things that other people wouldn't see as obvious," McCaw says:

And that's part of the thing where people don't exactly figure where I'm trying to go. You see the world differently because of [dyslexia]. I have no idea as to why, but I understand that, and I've seen a certain number of dyslexics who are that way. So maybe it's a strategic asset, though it makes detail and organization more difficult. I can't go to a piece of paper and organize things as most people would and come up with a plan. I have to explain concep-tually what we want to accomplish and then somebody else has to translate that into a concise, organized plan.

As McCaw's business empire grew, he found a variety of people to serve as his translators.

McCaw first joined the business world in 1966, when, at age sixteen, he accepted a summer job at his father's Centralia cable company, then still owned by KELA. When Elroy suggested the job, Craig was not excited. The thought of leaving Seattle for Centralia didn't appeal to him. Centralia was a drab, depressed timber town almost two hours by car from Seattle. Little had changed there in decades. For a teenage city boy, there wasn't much to do but hang out at the A&W hamburger joint and watch cars. Centralia "was three degrees past awful," McCaw said later. But McCaw cut a deal with his father: He would take the job if Elroy paid for flying lessons.

McCaw persuaded a Lakeside friend, Steve Countryman, to spend the summer with him. Countryman liked the idea of working away from home; his parents didn't mind that the boys would be sleeping and taking meals at the old Lewis & Clark Hotel. Since Elroy owned the hotel, they would never see a bill, and cousins on Marion's side would be keeping an eye on the boys.

McCaw and Countryman arrived in high style, swooping down from the sky in a Learjet. Owned by Elroy's friend Bill Lear, it was probably the only one in Washington State at that time. McCaw and Countryman stepped out and were greeted by the slack-jawed pilots and mechanics of the humble Centralia-Chehalis Airport. It was McCaw's only flamboyant act that summer. The boys were sent door-to-door in blue blazers to sell subscriptions for the tiny cable company. In 1967 cable television had scarcely developed from its beginnings in the late 1940s: small systems that captured broadcast signals and piped them to homes, with reception weakened by distance or obstructions such as hills.

At first, broadcasters made no objection to cable systems reusing their signals without paying; local TV stations welcomed cable as a means of reaching a larger audience for advertisers. Only later, when cable began to carry original programming that lured viewers and splintered the audience, did broadcasters begin to see cable as a threat.

Building a cable system involved erecting a large antenna or microwave receiver to capture the broadcasting signal, then installing amplifiers to boost the signal, which ran through wires hung from poles controlled by city or county governments. Cable systems tended to be a spotty patchwork, often launched in small towns by appliance store owners as a means to promote sales of TVs.

Elroy McCaw's system in Centralia imported TV signals from Portland to the south and from Seattle to the north. It provided five channels—unreliably. Ever the tightwad, Elroy kept the system underfunded and poorly equipped. Customers called to complain of faulty reception and were fobbed off with vague promises of repairs. Knocking on doors that summer, Craig McCaw experienced firsthand the result of poor customer service. He didn't like it. It was not only personally embarrassing, but also bad for business. People spread the word of their unhappiness to one another and to the town councils that regulated cable companies. McCaw later vowed to make quality a mantra for all his companies—one step that set him apart from the rest of the cable TV industry, which was notorious for poor service.

For $100 a week, McCaw and Steve Countryman spent the summer calling on almost every home in the region, seeking orders for new cable service. It wasn't easy. Many people didn't know about cable. Despite his natural shyness, McCaw was an enthusiastic salesman. He saw himself as offering something people already wanted: sharper TV pictures. McCaw would never have trouble talking to people about ideas that excited him. Fellow salesman Steve Countryman says, "If he believes in a product or service, he doesn't have any trouble talking to whoever he needs to, whether they're customers, bankers, or the media."

After hours, the boys sometimes drove go-carts, McCaw's old Peugeot, or company trucks, or just walked around town. "There wasn't a lot to do in Centralia," says Countryman, who sometimes went off to flirt with the local girls. McCaw wasn't interested. Instead, he would visit KELA or Twin City to ask questions about business operations.

"He was much more mature and focused than I was," says Countryman—and far from being a typical teenager. One day, Countryman opened the desk the two boys shared and found a stack of McCaw's paychecks—uncashed. Though Countryman himself came from a comfortable background—his mother was a physician, his father a successful pharmaceutical salesman—it was his first hint that the world was divided into two groups of people: those who worked by the hour for a paycheck and those with different motivations. The former, he would soon discover, usually worked for the latter.

It was also a discovery about his friend McCaw. "Money was not the issue [for McCaw]," Countryman says. "Earning money was not the reason he was there."

* * *

McCaw's visits to KELA and Twin City became a kind of summer session at the Centralia school of business, where Elroy's theories were put into practice and where Craig got his first glimpse of the culture of an organization. A keen judge of people and situations, he could take the measure of Elroy's choice of managers, what employees thought of the owner, and what customers thought of the company.

The summer also gave the company employees a chance to meet their future boss. Royce Hull, the cable company's chief engineer, liked young McCaw, though he found him too serious for his age. McCaw was curious about every aspect of the cable business, down to how accounts were handled and what was done if somebody didn't pay. He went out with installers and wired houses; he traveled with construction crews. When McCaw visited Hull's laboratory, he asked questions, wanting to know how things worked not just in general terms, but precisely. He wanted to know the technical terms engineers used. He listened and remembered. McCaw might not have decided yet what his career would be, but his effect on those answering his questions was clear.

"He wanted to learn from the bottom up," Hull says. "So later, when he talked to people, no one could bamboozle him. He was different than his dad." Of course, Hull's impression of Elroy differed from many others':

> His dad was very aloof. He wouldn't mix with people lower than manager. Craig could do that. . . . Once Elroy came down [from Seattle]. Elroy and I ate at the Lewis & Clark Hotel in the bar, so Craig couldn't join us and had to wait outside. Elroy loved his boys, I'm sure he did. But Elroy was all business. I wouldn't do that to my son.

Of the four McCaw boys, Craig McCaw showed not only the deepest interest in business, but also the most serious personality. Bruce, the eldest, had a taste for fast cars, hunting, and the excitement of the television industry. Bruce worked for Elroy's TV station and later cofounded an insurance company that specialized in aircraft. John showed his father's ability to talk his way into people's graces, but seemed self-absorbed to some; he would later work for Craig. Keith, the youngest, who had hardly known his father and struggled to find a role for himself, would also work in minor roles for his brother.

Craig never severed his business relations with his brothers; the family always owned things together. In a sense, business became another bond between the brothers and with their mother. The four sometimes squabbled, but there was a clannishness to them, perhaps because they had grown up in a rural setting, sometimes with only one another for company. One business associate likens the McCaws to the Japanese, presenting a single face to outsiders and rarely revealing their disagreements.

The McCaws truly functioned as a group. When Elroy was alive, he would gather the clan for formal board meetings to discuss family holdings. After his death, the family gathered to consider Twin City Cablevision, whose status was uncertain given the claims against the estate. No one was afraid of staying in business, however; the fiasco of Elroy's estate did not convince the family that business was bad, only that some situations could go wrong. Far from being overwhelmed by fear of failure, the McCaws shared an abiding belief that they knew how to start businesses. If some failed, they could start some more. Bruce McCaw says it this way: "If you learn how to understand how to make something happen, you don't fear failure so much, because you can make it happen again. Some people never understand how to do it."

So the McCaws weren't ready to quit. But who would take responsibility for the cable company? Bruce didn't want the job. Then making $400 a month running Jet Air, he didn't think the cable company could "afford" him—perhaps his way of saying he wouldn't accept a pay cut. John and Keith were too young.

Craig saw an opportunity. He quickly asserted the leadership he would show over the rest of the family. Craig McCaw wanted a career in business and felt cable was something he understood, an asset his father's friends had described as a potential gold mine, though profits then were modest. The company employed ten people, served 4,200 customers, collected $8,000 a month in gross revenue, and turned a small profit. But it kept growing because anyone who moved into town eventually wanted cable TV, which by 1970 had become a widely known and generally understood commodity. Unlike other products that had to be explained, positioned against a competing product, and sold to the customer, cable pretty much sold itself. Thus, McCaw reasoned, there had to be a future in this business.

McCaw also preferred cable to broadcasting because it seemed simpler. Broadcasting used on-air performers who could be hard to manage, and there were other complications. Yet broadcasting and cable had much in common. Both broadcasters and cable operators sold programs that traveled invisibly until they were amplified and converted for home use. As receivers of broadcast signals, cable operators had to be familiar with the technical aspects of the airwaves. Many in broadcasting also worked in cable. Both businesses tended to use the same lenders.

Later, McCaw would say that he had no idea that cable would become highly profitable; getting into the business just seemed like a natural evolution. "Maybe it was dumb luck," he says.

With permission from his mother and his brothers, Craig McCaw took over the cable business. He kept the company's manager and began making weekly telephone calls from Stanford to monitor budgets and policies. There was no guarantee that McCaw would be able to keep the cable company after graduating from Stanford. As creditors pressed claims on Elroy's estate, it became clear that nearly all of the assets would have to be sold. But soon after Craig took over the company, the boys learned that they, not their father's estate, owned Twin City Cablevision.

It was the result of a typically complex Elroy McCaw deal. A few years before he died, Elroy had reorganized the cable company in Centralia. In this deal, Elroy created two classes of stock, a preferred class for himself and another that he "sold" to his sons. The dividends went to Elroy, but the sons got the company and could buy out the preferred stock. Elroy also set up a $50,000 trust fund for each son. He never bothered to tell Marion or the boys.

The boys learned of their good fortune from a study of the Centralia system for possible sale to The Seattle Times Company. The Times Company had urged Elroy to sell and now wanted the boys to do a deal. In 1970, the newspaper company sent Marion a $25,000 check as earnest money and offered a deal that would have netted each brother $180,000. To Craig's brothers, the offer must have been tempting. None of them showed interest in cable or excitement about the idea of moving back to Centralia. But Craig, who could be stubbornly determined, wanted his brothers to leave their money in the company.

"I said 'Don't sell,' " McCaw recalls. "I had worked there . . . that was the only thing I'd ever done in my life, my only job." Marion recalls that Bruce backed Craig, arguing that it would be good for the family to own something together. They quickly agreed not to sell.

Craig soon pressed for another decision. Believing that the company would be choked if the family took large dividends, he argued that the company needed a stream of revenue to service debt and fuel expansion. The family agreed to forgo some dividends, turning the money over to Craig as Twin City's chief executive. Soon, they further deepened their commitment by personally guaranteeing company loans.

This proved to be the smartest decision ever made by Bruce, John, and Keith McCaw. By agreeing in this way to trust Craig and subordinate their egos, they eventually joined the ranks of the world's wealthiest people.

*　*　*

McCaw presented an image of discipline and maturity to his family, but not to his friends at Stanford. Back in Palo Alto, he was known as one of the chief party organizers at Delta Kappa Epsilon—the Deke house. McCaw never impressed anyone as a scholar at Stanford, says Fred Morck, a Deke fraternity brother who later became a lawyer. McCaw eventually settled on a major in history, which allowed him to analyze how people succeed or fail. (Napoleon and Hitler launched major campaigns without adequate contingency planning, McCaw now likes to point out. McCaw has never been one to start Plan A unless Plan B is in readiness.)

McCaw's desultory college career and reputation as a party animal seem out of character. Perhaps he was reacting to the death of his father or presenting a persona that helped him fit in. His natural shyness wouldn't have lasted twenty-four hours in most frat houses. McCaw later explained that he viewed college as a time to have fun and that he

felt no hurry to finish his studies; he also worried about the draft. And
though McCaw personally was not drawn to radical politics or the coun-
terculture, Stanford overall was a wild place, filled with drugs and booze
and frequent anti–Vietnam war protests that sometimes provoked tear
gas attacks by police. In any case, McCaw at Stanford showed the
clownish side to his personality, one he has never fully abandoned.

"Craig was one of the chief Animal House guys," says Fred Morck.
"When I met Craig, he was one of the most engaging people I ever met,
very outgoing, magnetic almost. You were attracted to him. He was
extremely friendly and charming." Morck recalls parties in McCaw's
room, equipped with an elaborate stereo system and a fancy blender.
McCaw was an eager bartender, at times opening the bar before lunch.
He liked to stroll through the fraternity house spraying people with the
fire extinguisher, says Morck. McCaw and others launched water
balloons from a rooftop catapult.

McCaw drove an old truck and a Porsche Targa sports car. As a
member of Stanford's flying club, he invited friends to join him for trips
around the Bay Area in a single-engine Cessna. He started dating Wendy
Petrak, the daughter of a Hewlett-Packard manager, who helped him
with his history studies.

Despite his frivolous reputation, McCaw itched to get on with his
life, to get going in business. He hated the parasitic idea of living off the
family-owned company. He wanted to expand Twin City, to start
making acquisitions, to be creative—like his father. So even before his
graduation from Stanford, McCaw contacted Bill Daniels, a communications broker who had worked with Elroy, and said he wanted to buy
another cable company—something small and affordable that he could
seize upon, make his own, and begin growing.

Looking for deals in northern California, McCaw says, he almost
pushed one broker to the point of exhaustion. McCaw came close to
buying the Palo Alto, California, cable system, but that deal collapsed.
The owner of a small system in Shelton, Washington, was interested in
selling, but only for full payment, literally, in gold.

In 1971 McCaw finally found the right deal, a cable system south
of Centralia serving the hamlet of Winlock, Washington. The town's
mayor owned and operated the system, which served just 204 homes. In
his sixties, the mayor wanted to retire, and word got back to McCaw's

employees in Centralia. Marion, ever cautious, worried about the deal but bowed to her son's wish. He would always remember the terms of that first deal: a $50,000 purchase price with 25 percent down and the rest paid over eight years at an 8 percent interest rate.

That same year, McCaw went to Washington, D.C., for his first national cable convention. Discovering that someone had stolen his wallet from his room at the Hilton, McCaw called the front desk. To McCaw's shock, the security officer didn't believe that the skinny college kid was a businessman. Instead, he suspected that a prostitute had robbed McCaw.

But straight-arrow McCaw wasn't looking for a call girl. He was looking for more cheap deals on cable companies. Within a year he found a low-money-down sale on a company serving fewer than a hundred homes in Tenino, Washington. "We sweet-talked our way into that one," he said later, a line that his father might have used with pleasure.

McCaw's empire building had begun, though no one at Stanford had any inkling of this side of his life. McCaw quietly ran his business by long-distance telephone, calling managers in Centralia and checking with Marion on estate litigation and creditor negotiations. His penchant for secrecy would ultimately become a tremendous business asset. "He put a helluva mask on," says Fred Morck. Jeff Ruhe was a close friend at Stanford but always knew that McCaw maintained a private zone. "He's a great listener," says Ruhe, who later became an executive with the ESPN sports network and is still a friend of McCaw's. "He doesn't give away much, but he takes in a lot."

McCaw was succeeding his father not only in running the business, but also in creating what others saw as a layered, enigmatic personality. It's hard to tell whether the sense of mystery about McCaw is the result of a deliberate style of business, or of a fragment of DNA inherited from his father. The young man making margaritas in the Deke house was keeping secrets, planning his next chess moves, running two companies, and itching to run more. There would be even bigger surprises once McCaw left Stanford.

4

"How Can We Build Our Dreams on This?"

The Small-Town Origins of a New Management Style

I n 1973 Craig McCaw graduated from Stanford. He went straight from sophisticated Palo Alto to rural Centralia, where he set up an office at Twin City Cablevision in a converted gas station that looked out on a small concrete island stripped of its pumps. Three women worked with McCaw in the office, plus the company's manager, Tom Elder. Three men worked in the field, making repairs and stringing wires.

The characteristics of Craig McCaw's management style emerged almost immediately. People found him a refreshing departure from Elroy McCaw: friendly, humane in his dealings with people, curious and actively engaged, but also set apart and different in a pleasantly interesting way.

McCaw was younger than nearly everyone else, but those who worked there recall a certain aura about him. It was more than the atmosphere around any boss: McCaw conveyed a gentle authority that immediately established him as a genuine leader.

Tom Hull, who started with Twin City as a commercial painter and later worked as a cable installer, was fascinated by the young executive. "He was much more refined than I, much more mannered, very calm," says Hull. "You'd go in to talk to him and sometimes he wouldn't say anything for a while, and you'd have to say something because it was too uncomfortable. I don't know if that was a trick or something, but he was just a really mellow guy."

Outwardly, McCaw was confident and pleased with the people working for him. Inwardly, he was stunned at what he had inherited. Though he had run Twin City for more than a year, he hadn't fully comprehended its disorganization and substandard practices. McCaw was almost obsessed with the idea of focus, being locked on a goal, and shedding extraneous baggage. After a period of absentee management, Twin City was adrift. "The operation was a mess," he said later.

There was a host of unaddressed business problems. The town councils of Centralia and Chehalis were hostile to the company. Some employees were rude to customers. Others just weren't professional. One employee sold real estate during office hours. One employee questioned customers about their marriages or other personal details: How's your girlfriend? Have you paid your bar bill? It wasn't unusual for friends in a small town to talk that way to one another, but McCaw cringed at such talk. It hardly reflected his view that customers had to be treated professionally and with courtesy.

McCaw was passionate about that point. It was almost a moral issue for him. He knew that the cable TV industry had an awful but largely deserved reputation for shoddy service and abuse of customers. He didn't want anyone lodging that complaint about his company, or about him. Perhaps, at a much deeper level, he also wanted to distinguish himself from Elroy. Up in Seattle, his mother struggled almost daily with the consequences of his father's casual practices. McCaw may have wanted to establish the highest standards to help restore the family name. He didn't care if people thought he was crazy in business. But he cared deeply whether business associates thought he was fair and honest.

McCaw set about putting his stamp on the company. He told employees to treat each customer as the only one they had. He held morning staff meetings at which he rallied employees to a vision of growth and shared rewards. Work with me and everyone will make more money, he said. Despite his mother's aversion to spending money before Elroy's estate matters were settled, McCaw authorized immediate improvements. Trucks got fresh paint—red, white, and blue stripes. Field employees got uniforms. Office employees were taught to answer customer calls promptly and courteously. McCaw made plans to build a new company headquarters. Led by a twenty-one-year-old with no formal business training, Twin City soon became a professional operation.

Even before the company spent money to end outages and improve the signal, customers thought they detected a better TV picture. "A lot of it was just superficial things," McCaw said later:

It worked beautifully. People liked you, everybody said, "Boy, the pictures are a lot better." They saw the trucks were painted, they were clean, the employees were professional, they were nice to the customers. "Oh! The pictures got better. I get it." I mean, the more you did, the more you realized that respecting the customer paid back dividends. It was good business.

McCaw made employees happy by raising salaries. He also showed that he was willing to do menial work. For the Tenino system, McCaw desperately wanted another channel to make the system attractive enough to gain another hundred customers. So he and Royce Hull, a senior engineer and Tom Hull's father, trooped around a hillside, carrying an antenna in the hope of finding Portland's Channel 12 in the airwaves. "Royce, we're going out to that hill and walk around until we find some signal," McCaw said. They did.

What had been a distantly managed company under Elroy McCaw became a friendly place with a family atmosphere. Craig by now had married Wendy Petrak, his Stanford classmate, whom he brought to company meetings. Attractive, with shoulder-length blond hair, Wendy took an interest in the business and, though not generally outgoing, hosted occasional receptions for employees. When installer Roy Budde was injured, she visited him at a Seattle hospital. Budde and others felt lucky to be working for Craig McCaw. Later, when he worked for other cable operators, Budde sorely missed his first boss. "I told everyone that I was going to sue Craig because he spoiled me on private enterprise," Budde joked.

From those early days, Craig McCaw tried to build a management system that blended Elroy's approach to business and the life Craig and his brothers had enjoyed as children. Elroy had delegated responsibility because he was too busy with new deals; at home, Marion had allowed the kids to come and go, drive the boat, and shoot their guns, so long as they ate regularly, did their homework, and stayed out of trouble. Craig felt that he acted more responsibly because he had been trusted by his mother. Now, as a young boss, he trusted others to run their jobs.

McCaw deliberately tried to decrease his involvement in routine matters and small decisions. Although the office needed dramatic change, he avoided giving too many direct orders. Instead, he appealed to people's better instincts. "To me, the American Dream is what happens if you give people freedom and accountability," McCaw once told an interviewer. "Anything is possible if you allow people the rope with which to do things, either hang themselves or climb higher."

In short, McCaw's approach let people figure things out for themselves. He didn't want to be a preacher or a taskmaster. To break an established practice of installers' hanging out at a coffee shop, where idling trucks damaged the image of quick customer service, McCaw simply asked that they not all go to the same shop at the same time. "He didn't say, 'Don't stop for coffee,' just that it didn't look good," recalled Roy Budde. "He was such a nice guy that we stopped going out for coffee. It showed he was thinking."

Few ever saw him get angry, raise his voice, or curse. Since he treated everyone with respect, there were few tests of his authority. But Tom Hull vividly remembers one incident involving a recalcitrant manager of a system. The manager came from a construction background and was very muscular. McCaw took the manager into an office and closed the door. The office staff expected a dustup. No one heard a raised voice, but the drift of the conversation soon became evident. Finally, as Hull tells it, the manager appeared, "the sick look of sweat beads popping out of his macho head after the closed-door discussion with McCaw. [But] McCaw came out as if he had just had a cup of coffee." McCaw had no trouble with the manager after that. (In a later interview, the manager involved confirmed the story and declined to reveal the issue, other than that he had done something wrong and McCaw had been right.)

To Tom Hull, McCaw could be aggressive or gentle, whichever best suited the needs of his company. McCaw promoted Hull to a management job in another part of Washington State, where he worked fourteen-hour days overseeing construction. Once that step was completed, however, the job really needed someone with training in office management. When Hull resisted a move back to a lower-paid job, McCaw repeated back to him, word for word, how Hull had once said he would rather be an installer than do certain tasks as a manager. Hull thought to himself, *Gee, what does this guy have, a photographic memory?*

Hull agreed to return, impressed with how McCaw had handled him. "He managed me in such a way that I wasn't a disgruntled employee," says Hull. "Some bosses would just say 'Get your ass over there. You're going.' " Not McCaw.

Years later, Hull came to recognize McCaw's central motivation: to find people whose skills matched the jobs to be done. Throughout his career, McCaw showed a remarkable ability to pick people suited for the tasks ahead. "He recognizes people's strengths and weaknesses," Hull says.

Hull remained a huge admirer of McCaw's, but for all their time together, like many of McCaw's employees, he never felt he really knew the boss. Contrary to the usual learning process, the more Hull saw of McCaw, the more he realized he did not know the man. Throughout McCaw's career, his employees not only enjoyed telling war stories but also had fun talking about the unique qualities of their boss.

Tom Hull remembered one dinner he had with Craig McCaw that featured long and, for Hull, painful silences. Hull wondered what McCaw was thinking during those spells. Why didn't he fill the time with chitchat like other people? How about that football game? Or even the weather? Anything but the clatter of forks on plates.

"I think Craig does that as a technique," Hull says. "It gives him the upper hand to find out about you, not you about him. Through that silence, he puts pressure on you to talk, and he's going to learn something about you."

Focused on what he needed to learn, McCaw fully engaged himself in operations. When he traveled with engineers looking at cable systems for sale, he asked questions about antennas, microwave receivers, signal interference, amplifiers, customer preferences. He asked for advice. He listened. "He sponged up information," says Royce Hull.

McCaw paid especially close attention to town council members and their motivations, for they held power over cable TV companies. City or county councils typically restricted each market to one cable provider, whose rates were controlled by the council. McCaw knew an unfriendly council could choke a cable system by capping its rates. Thus no cable company could replace equipment or create cash flow to fund acquisitions. Low rates doomed a company to inadequacy.

More important, they limited the dreams of a company's owner. Under Elroy, Chehalis and Centralia had never approved increases sought by Twin City. For a time, they resisted Craig McCaw as well. He saw their resistance as not just a personal insult but as an obstacle to his personal ambition to grow the company into a collection of cable systems, just as his father had acquired a string of broadcasting properties.

"After [Elroy McCaw] died, we tried to get the rates up, and the cities wouldn't do it," Craig McCaw says. "I mean, they were very hard on us. I was very involved in those things, and you know, they were going to treat us like a utility and all this stuff. Geez, I mean, life is too short, you know; this is not the way to run a business, where you ask for a dollar and you need a dollar, and they give you twenty cents. It's not going to work [I thought]. How can we build our dream on this?"

At that point, many on Wall Street viewed cable TV as a stagnant business facing long-term problems. First, most systems needed major improvements that seemed unaffordable to their mom-and-pop operators. Many owners were approaching retirement and did not have the stomach to lobby councils for rate increases necessary to pay for improvements. Owners also usually lacked the sophisticated financial knowledge to obtain bank loans and manage a large capital program. Moreover, in some cities it was hard to budget for expansion because landlords demanded payoffs to enter their property.

Second, many customers were dropping cable because of improved broadcast signals and more sophisticated home antennas. A homeowner could climb his roof, install a new antenna purchased from a hardware store, and cut the coaxial cable.

A third problem was theft. A homeowner could easily steal a signal by cutting into the cable wire and attaching his own wire purchased from Radio Shack. Other customers stole converter boxes. As a result of these problems, some cable companies lost money. Even in Manhattan, one of the world's most densely populated regions, the two companies serving the island were each facing operating losses of $3 million a year.

As a result, values of systems dropped. Sales fell to an average of about $100 per subscriber annually, and revenue from subscribers seemed stuck at $6 or $8 per month. Smart investors looked elsewhere. McCaw, however, wanted to buy. He focused on small, deteriorating systems that were poorly run and judged hopeless. His sense of hidden value turned not only on his own evaluation of a company, but also on his faith that cable TV would ultimately grow in popularity. Other executives would analyze depreciation, customer counts, and cash flow, and perhaps shrink from the difficulty. McCaw had a driving faith in his own sense of what could be done—by him. "Craig was very aggressive at a time when lots of people thought cable had no future," Royce Hull says.

While others fretted, McCaw set a goal of 10,000 customers—more than twice what he had inherited from his father. When it came time to find a logo, he asked employees to comment on the choices. He picked an image of four blue lines that formed a rectangle and abruptly turned arrows that pointed in four directions. The design cost McCaw all of $510. Roy Budde remembers what McCaw said: "I'm going to pick this one because it shows expansion, the arrows going off in all directions."

McCaw's business aggressiveness worried his mother, who knew the peril of debt and gambles gone bad. McCaw did value her opinion. She was not only his mother, but a smart, trained accountant with years of experience from substituting at board meetings for her husband. She knew the cable industry, and she had significant institutional authority within the family company. She served as Twin City's president and became chairwoman when McCaw moved to Centralia.

McCaw eventually overcame her concerns about risk, but he did make one major concession. He agreed that all four brothers would receive dividends from the company, even though that ate up some of the cash flow he needed to grow. To strengthen their identification with the company, McCaw gave his younger brothers jobs. John McCaw climbed poles and installed cable and later worked as a manager, ultimately becoming one of McCaw's most trusted lieutenants. Youngest brother Keith later took a variety of jobs at company franchises.

With Twin City on a sound footing by 1975, McCaw hunted for opportunities, believing that he could run several cable systems with a common staff. He saw two ways to grow: He could buy an existing cable system or bid against others for an open franchise. He searched ads in trade publications, told cable brokers to look around, and asked employees to let him know what they heard about systems on the block. One day, he spotted an ad for a 700-customer system in Burney, California, near Shasta Lake not far from the Oregon border. The seller wanted $400 per subscriber, which McCaw thought was too high—but he still wanted to buy.

Unfortunately, the system had already been sold to a young cable operator named Gordon Rock, who ran a Kirkland, Washington, company with his brother, Greg. Losing to Rock proved to be a stroke of luck to McCaw—the first of several occasions when he picked someone's brain, absorbed the lessons, and refined his own strategy as a result.

Curious about how he had lost, McCaw called and discovered that Rock was doing exactly what McCaw wanted to do. Rock had negotiated a deal that worked out to $300 a subscriber, a low sales price, as well as generous terms: Rock hadn't put up a nickel but had borrowed the entire amount. Moreover, Rock had structured the deal so he hadn't bought the company but only its assets, an approach with tremendous tax benefits. Under current tax rules, a buyer could record the assets at a low value, so the seller avoided a big capital gains tax. The savings to both meant the sale could go for a lower price.

McCaw soon tried to buy another system in Coeur d'Alene, Idaho, from The Seattle Times Company, but McCaw sensed that as "a punk kid" (his words, years later) he wasn't being taken seriously. Rock got that one, too, in a seller-financed sale under terms so favorable that McCaw was astonished. "He stole the system from the Times," McCaw says.

McCaw admired Rock, whose company eventually held cable TV systems in rural areas in Alaska, the Northwest, and California. "I learned so much by just watching him. He was very creative," McCaw said later.

By this time, John McCaw had graduated from the University of Washington and become a full-time employee in McCaw's company as general manager in Centralia. Of the four McCaw boys, John and Craig bore the closest resemblance to each other. John Elroy McCaw, Jr., had graduated from Lakeside one year behind Craig. John had his brother's thin build and the same penetrating eyes, which darted back and forth when he was thinking. He loved boats and cars and planes, like Craig, but he was far more skilled than his brother at befriending people. Marion considered him the warmest of her four boys. When he chose, John McCaw could approach a stranger, establish common interests, and talk for hours.

John would serve Craig well in establishing bonds with potential sellers of cable TV systems. But there was another side to John, some say. He could be temperamental or indifferent about work. John didn't properly work a deal in Yakima, Washington, recalls a disgusted Craig McCaw, "because he wasn't in the mood." Yet when John wanted to, he could do excellent work. John "redeemed himself in Alaska," says Craig, referring to John's skillful lobbying of politicians during an important franchise battle.

"John had his strengths," says Wayne Perry, who later became Craig McCaw's number-one lieutenant. "To a lot of people, he was selfish. John was like a fighter pilot: If he had you on lock-on, he'd stay with you. [But] sometimes he'd just fly away and not have lock-on. John wasn't for everybody." But Craig McCaw put a premium on loyalty, and John, in turn, bowed to his older brother's judgment.

In 1976 McCaw moved his company headquarters north to Seattle. In the tradition of his father, he picked a cheap location in a drab building far from downtown. What was soon called McCaw Communications Companies occupied a small suite in a two-story building in the Greenwood District, a neighborhood near the Woodland Park Zoo mainly known for its used furniture stores. About a quarter of the suite was consumed by Marion's desk and the stacks of paperwork and boxes from Elroy's estate disputes, still a year away from resolution. In the back half of the suite, three or four desks were used by McCaw, a receptionist/bookkeeper, and whomever else happened to be around.

The least appealing feature of the office was the smell. The office was above a first-floor Chinese restaurant and a beauty parlor. On some days, the smell of hair being dyed or permed would mingle with the exotic odors of Cantonese cooking and, through some sort of perverse chemical reaction, produce what the McCaw people would later describe as the most awful combination of scents ever encountered. "It was a horrible place," McCaw says. Fortunately, they quickly outgrew it.

CHAPTER

5

"There's This Crazy Kid . . ."

McCaw Becomes an Apostle of Debt

I n 1975 Wayne Perry was one of thousands of attorneys in downtown Seattle pursuing a safe, predictable career in tax law. Then one day in July, a senior partner stopped by, somewhat apologetically, with an assignment that would change Perry's life and eventually make him a wealthy man.

"There's this crazy kid down in the conference room who's got this nutty idea," the partner told Perry. "Go down and spend some time with him, but don't take too much time. You're too busy. But don't piss him off, because his family's been a client of the firm for years."

Perry went down and met "the kid." It was Craig McCaw, who was close to Perry's age, twenty-six. McCaw described how he had taken over a small company, put it in good order, and was ready to do deals. "I want to grow," McCaw said.

The nutty idea happened to be a scheme for using one cable system as leverage to finance the purchase of another. Perry saw it had nerve: a combination of tax write-offs and losses for years. It was a brilliant scheme, says Perry, because it kept the two systems under separate corporate structures but washed the gains of the first against the losses of the second. It was like using the equity from an old home to buy a new one, saving real estate taxes in the middle.

Perry suggested a small change in the plan and helped McCaw make his next acquistion: the Selah, Washington, cable system, with 600 customers.

Freeze that moment. Craig McCaw and Wayne Perry are both in their mid-twenties. McCaw is just two years out of the Deke house. People that age are usually too young to know what they don't know; or, more relevant to this story, too young to know what they can't do.

Craig McCaw, with no formal business training, has happened on a brilliant financing scheme. He wants Perry to make sure the idea will pass legal and IRS scrutiny. The Marion McCaw side of Craig is paying attention to the details; the creativity comes from Elroy McCaw; but the guts is pure Craig McCaw.

While Elroy had been seemingly indifferent to or unaware of the risks of his highly leveraged transactions, Craig thought through every awful consequence. If he borrowed big, the lenders would require strict adherence to financial performance. He would have to reach so much profit, have so many customers, use the dollars to build so many assets. If the economy turned down, if a manager failed, if a town council proved stubborn about rates, he could get in trouble. Because his system would be built on the promise of ever larger cash flow, he worried about combinations of bad events wrecking his plans.

McCaw mulled over every possible turn for the worse and considered his options—his future chess moves. Competitors and business associates marveled at his guts, but it was never simple daring. McCaw saw fear of failure as another motivation to plan well and think hard. "There are the times when you really have to become good because you're scared to death and you know what can happen," McCaw says. "It's like walking on a tightrope. In the good times, you can only fall six inches. In the bad times, you can fall a hundred feet. So you know that, at those times, you can't fail."

Debt was a tool to get where he wanted. Another was the right people to execute his plans. Wayne Perry was one of those people. Within two years of meeting McCaw, Perry was working full-time for the company. Others would come and go, but Perry remained, even after the McCaw siblings had left the business.

Born in Olympia, Washington, in 1950, Perry quickly became the second most important presence at McCaw Communications, more important perhaps than any member of McCaw's family. A Mormon married to his high school sweetheart, a hiker dedicated to the Boy Scouts, Perry had the ethics sought by Craig McCaw, but much more: a photographic memory, a total grasp of tax laws, phenomenal energy and enthusiasm, charisma, humor, a salesman's ability to push ideas or contracts, and a choirboy's face that masked his business wiliness. He loved to outfox and outwork his rivals. He thrilled at maneuvering against the big, the pretentious, the powerful. He wrote complex agreements containing understated language which gave his clients latent powers or maneuvering room—what he called "back doors"—the kind of language that gave McCaw Communications an escape or jujitsu leverage over other parties if problems developed.

Perry's idea of fun was walking through mud and snow to a 10,000-foot plateau in Wyoming to track big game. On cross-country trips in the McCaw jet, he devoured hunting magazines, a sight that offended Wendy McCaw, an animal rights supporter. "Wendy and I had a détente about hunting," Perry says. "She didn't ask and I didn't tell."

Equally important, Perry's personality balanced that of his eccentric chief executive. Whereas McCaw could be moody, odd, or even absent, Wayne Perry would interpret the leader's confusing pronouncements and rally everyone to a practical plan. If McCaw Communications was a religion, Perry was the Greek oracle who explained the riddling pronouncements uttered by the deity. McCaw thought in curved lines; Wayne connected the dots. Don't focus literally on what McCaw says, Perry told people: "Listen to his heart."

McCaw could be subtle, elliptical. Wayne was direct, blunt. McCaw played shy; Wayne played the ham.

Perry also functioned well among the big egos eventually attracted to the McCaw company. He served at times as a bridge among the McCaws, listening to them, counseling, guiding them as a group in a direction that best served the company. When friction would erupt between McCaw and a brother, Perry would help them find common ground. "Craig would sometimes forget some sensitivities," Perry says. "I would remind Craig that it is not easy being [his] younger brother."

McCaw trusted Wayne Perry completely, which gave Perry power and responsibility. He could tell the boss that a "dumb-ass idea" wouldn't work without being considered personally offensive. Though he wasn't always consistent in his own behavior, McCaw put a premium on courtesy in part because he himself was sensitive to slights.

Few handled Craig McCaw as well as Wayne Perry, though their relationship sometimes baffled the second tier of aides. Much later, when Perry's stock holdings had made him a very wealthy man, aides wondered why he stayed with McCaw, who, they said, was sometimes impatient and harsh. "Wayne took some pretty heavy abuse over the years," says Scot Jarvis, a longtime company executive:

A lot of [McCaw's] frustrations get expressed on those closest to him. You have to have a remarkable personality to sustain that, come back, and not take it personally. Some of us have talked about Wayne and wondered, What is it? Did he have a hard relationship with his father, or whatever? What is it that makes him want to come back? . . . [Perry and McCaw have] had a long relationship. When you've known each other a long time, you get more comfortable speaking your mind—that's just a guess.

From Perry's perspective, the relationship has been beneficial. "You measure fairness in a continuum of time," he says:

After twenty-five years, have I had a good time? Challenging things to do in a great industry? And made lots of money? Were there times when I think he was wrong or unfair or made mistakes? Damn straight. But you get mad at your wife, too. . . . Some people get with Craig and think it's all going to be perfect and everything's going to come out Moses-like in tablet form, and it's all going to be easy. I've always known Craig makes mistakes and isn't always on, but on balance I think I've been treated extremely fairly.

Perry felt that the foundation of their relationship was his loyalty to McCaw. "Craig understood that I had the interests of the company at heart," Perry says. "It was very easy for me to move the company's goals down the road. I found it fun, exciting, and rewarding."

Wayne Perry wasn't the only brilliant man jockeying for position and power within the McCaw empire. Occasionally, deputies would compete for credit or embellish tales of the company to enhance their own roles. McCaw sometimes worried that all the egos would hurt the company, but in the end, the competition among them was a situation for him to manage. Above all, he had no doubt about Wayne Perry's complete loyalty to him and to the company.

"Wayne was the brilliant consigliere," McCaw says. "Not a good leader, but a brilliant inside guy. . . . As people would tell you, he was the Steve Ballmer [Microsoft chairman Bill Gates's right-hand man]. What would I have been without him? He was as good as anyone I ever worked with."

McCaw was in a hurry to grow, at a pace some rivals regarded as rushed, even reckless. But to go where he wanted, he needed people who could find ways around obstacles, who enjoyed defying conventional wisdom. He wanted people who would toil relentlessly in pursuit of a goal, without regard for public recognition or approval. His favorite models came from the classic caper movie *Butch Cassidy and the Sundance Kid*. No—not the handsome bank robbers, played by Robert Redford and Paul Newman, but their relentless pursuers, who toiled on, night and day, never giving up, never seeking approval. McCaw wanted frustrated rivals to marvel at the trail marks left by his people—to wonder, "Who *are* those guys?"

McCaw didn't want toadies on his payroll. He said he wanted "invigorating, interesting, and dangerous people who cause trouble" for the industry and even for the company, if need be.

"We're not looking for a purely cohesive group," McCaw said later:

There's the IBM person in a white shirt or a Ross Perot person who came from the military. We want people who are not absolutely conventional. Who cause trouble because they are willing to break some of the boundaries and challenge us or someone else, or challenge an idea. You need a certain amount of brewing in the pot. [Otherwise,] the tendency for people is, well, let's all just get along. I don't want the organization to settle in to lattes and talking about what we did over the weekend.

McCaw saw Wayne as the sort who didn't let corporate structures get in the way. "Wayne is the kind of guy that you'd just never put in a big company," says McCaw. Perry was blunt, irreverent, impatient. "And yet he's a prodigious worker, very efficient, and very bright. And I know that at IBM, they'd throw Wayne out. They'd certainly throw me out."

* * *

Wayne Perry joined Craig McCaw at a critical moment. The McCaw company was about to exploit a quickening transformation in the cable TV industry triggered by satellites, which would play a huge role later in McCaw's career. At this phase, the change they brought to the economics of cable TV favored McCaw's expansionist dreams.

As Les Brown recounts in his *Encyclopedia of Television,* the cable industry grew slowly until the mid-1970s, then caught fire chiefly for the appeal to consumers of pay cable channels that delivered uncut, commercial-free movies. The transformation was led by Home Box Office, which began distributing its programs by satellite in 1975. HBO brought a monumental change to the cable industry because it demonstrated, for the first time, that people might be willing to pay for television.

The following year, Ted Turner's WTCG in Atlanta established its national presence as a "Super Station" through distribution by a new RCA satellite. Over the next decade, many other services were launched, including Entertainment and Sports Programming Network (ESPN) in 1979, Cable-Satellite Public Affairs Network (C-SPAN) in 1979, and Cable News Network (CNN) in 1980. Meanwhile, the Federal Communications Commission and the courts were moving to relax rules that had limited cable companies' expansion, especially moves into larger markets, as well as their right to carry network signals and movies.

Satellite reception created new costs for a cable operator. Each of the enormous satellite receivers, called earth stations, cost up to $100,000 initially. However, the cost for the thirty-foot-diameter dishes began to fall quickly after TelePrompTer Corporation, then the largest cable operator, announced in 1976 that it would buy an earth station for each of its systems. Other cable companies followed suit, and the price of earth stations fell to $25,000 by 1979. The cost fell again when the FCC halved the required size of satellite receivers to fifteen feet.

The impact of satellite programming on cable systems' revenues was enormous. Many customers were willing to pay twice what they had before. Cable operators had to split the added revenue with HBO and other providers, but the new revenue boosted cash flow—that is, income after expenses and before depreciation and taxes—the standard by which banks lent money.

Since banks loaned at a multiple of cash flow, every new dollar of cash flow expanded a cable company's borrowing power. At first the multiple was 4.5, so a bank would lend $450,000 on cash flow of $100,000 a year. The multiples grew, eventually reaching eight times cash flow. An operator could increase his cash flow, and thus his borrowing ability, by consolidating costs such as billing offices and maintenance crews and obtaining volume discounts from HBO, CNN, and other providers. A company with 500,000 customers paid CNN 7¢ a household per month, while a company with 2 million paid 5¢, for example. In other words, the bigger you got, the bigger you could get. At McCaw, "we understood we had to grow or leave the business," says Perry.

Steve Halstedt, an investment banker with Daniels & Associates, met with McCaw and explained the new economics of cable—how a growing cash flow created tremendous buying leverage.

"Wow, is that all we have to do?" McCaw asked.

"That's just how it works, and it's all you have to do."

Suddenly, McCaw knew he could grow as fast as he could hustle. The revelation was as powerful as hearing "there was life after death," McCaw said later. If bankers were offering life after death, McCaw became an apostle of that religion. He started a simple process: buy a system at its undervalued price; bring in professional management to improve service; raise rates and find more customers to goose cash flow; then get a new loan and use that new money to buy another system.

The process was not difficult or unique to McCaw. Because a professional manager could easily boost cash flow by 50 percent, a large collection of cable systems could be accumulated rapidly.

"You literally were able to grow exponentially off a very meager beginning," says Gordon Rock, the friend of McCaw's who bought cable systems in Alaska and the Northwest. Rock thought his company was aggressive when it bought a cable system a year. But when things got clicking, McCaw was buying twelve a year. McCaw "is a master of leverage," Rock says.

Well-financed companies such as Atlanta-based Cox Communications were buying cable systems, but few in the Northwest could match McCaw's pace. He was gutsy about buying, but also smart about creating the right system for supporting rapid growth. Unlike Rock, who personally spent time at a system to improve its operations, McCaw found more productive uses for his time. He created an organization that functioned, as Wayne Perry described it, like an efficient predator. Always hungry, it kept moving, kept buying. Perry's description of the future McCaw cellular operation fit the cable business perfectly: "We were constantly in search of money. There were so many opportunities and we were so acquisitive. We were like a shark—eat or die."

To strengthen his ability to buy cable companies, in 1976 McCaw hired Joe Liebsack, a thirty-year-old executive with TelePrompTer. Liebsack had been buying systems for TelePrompTer, but left because he appreciated Craig McCaw's vision. McCaw Communications had little money, almost zero organization, and an office smelly from the hairdresser downstairs. The corporate dining room was a nearby hamburger joint, and the chief executive drove a shabby Pinto wagon. But McCaw Communications had a commitment to grow as fast and go as far as it could.

McCaw and Liebsack agreed that satellite and pay-TV would soon transform cable. "Craig could see much further. He was looking ahead at what future values [of cable] might be," Liebsack says. As the new director of operations, Liebsack had a humble start, sharing a phone and desk with John McCaw. They raced each morning to see who would get to the phone first. Disputes escalated into rubber-band fights, Liebsack recalls with a laugh. Liebsack became Craig McCaw's principal operations expert: he would visit a potential cable acquisition, size it up, and kick it into shape if purchased.

At each field office, McCaw essentially made two points: Keep customers, and hit the targets for revenue growth. "This system's yours," McCaw told manager Larry Manthey, who operated in Whatcom County, near the Canadian border. "You run it. This is what I expect out of it. If you hit the targets, I'll fly you and your wife to Tahoe." Manthey made the goals, and McCaw was as good as his word; Manthey and his wife found champagne, flowers, and other gifts waiting for them at the hotel.

With the industry poised for growth, financing getting easier, and the first members of his team in place, McCaw soon escalated his goal of cable subscribers in breathtaking fashion. He set a goal of 100,000 subscribers—ten times larger than the goal he'd set just a few years earlier.

To get that big, the shark needed to feed—and fast.

In the summer of 1976 McCaw Communications went after three cable franchises that were open to bid: two in the Washington State towns of Yakima and Wenatchee, on the eastern side of the Cascade Mountains, and one in Fairbanks, Alaska. The company generally disliked franchise competitions. "We didn't like franchising because it turned on the ability to promise more than you can deliver," Perry says. Councils used their leverage to demand services that had nothing to do with cable, such as new police firing ranges and trees for parks, Perry says. The public notices also drew the bigger cable companies, who mounted sophisticated campaigns that could dazzle small-town council members. The gleam sometimes came from gold; councilmen, especially some in the East, often expected bribes, Liebsack said later.

McCaw didn't have much taste for politics. He supported some Republicans and a few Democrats, liked free-market ideas and later opened his home for a few political fund-raisers. Otherwise, he tried to stay clear of politics and the associated influence peddling. In franchise applications, McCaw refused to pay bribes to anyone and went to extreme lengths to distance himself from even the hint of scandal.

In one Oregon town near the Columbia River, the McCaw company paid a big price to keep its name clean. One night at eight, Wayne Perry got a call from a McCaw attorney there who said he had heard a consultant claim she'd paid a bribe to win the franchise for McCaw. The story was false, yet Perry knew the rumor could gain a life if the company won the competition. Perry told the attorney to go to the next town council meeting, formally withdraw the McCaw bid, and walk out without an explanation.

"God, that hurt," Perry said later. For a company scrambling for nickels to improve its cash flow, the loss of $250,000 in development expenses hurt badly. "It hits your financial statement, ga-zow. [But] I didn't even have to check with Craig [before making the decision]. I knew what Craig would do."

McCaw vowed to run a company that was ethical but tough. He knew that the rougher aspects of business would test his standards of conduct. "Your integrity is always challenged in business," he once said:

I have long believed you have to assess your options in a very military way. You have to decide what the possibilities are, and then
you have to decide whether you're going to use them. The people
around you will bring you options which are amoral or question-
able or aggressive. For the benefit of the people around you, you
have to know what the alternatives are, what the other person
might do to you, and how to respond to it. You have to know what
evil to put on the other person, as it were, to prevent them from
doing it. You have to have your guard up. You have to think almost
as a chess player. If they do that, what will I do[?] What could they
do to me, and how do I defend against it?

So you're constantly coming to grips with the morality of it,
because you are looking at all the evil you could do and then deciding what you will do. Mostly, when you make it clear that you've
got something bad you can do to the other people, they behave,
because they recognize that you are not namby-pamby. You're not
akin to Jimmy Carter trying to deal with Iran, where our American
sensibilities were incompatible with their sensibilities and they view
you as weak if you haven't thought out the consequences. You have
to demonstrate strength in order to be good.

For most of that summer of 1976 McCaw, Wayne Perry, Joe Liebsack, and Steve Countryman, McCaw's friend from Lakeside, would
meet at a Denny's restaurant, then make the three-hour drive to eastern
Washington to campaign for a franchise. John McCaw split his time
between Yakima and Fairbanks. The McCaw people would form a partnership with a local group of civic leaders, woo the council members,
and interview and lobby the public, door-to-door, to generate a positive
climate around the McCaw application.

In Wenatchee, McCaw allied with Clyde Ballard, who owned a
medical supply company and later became Speaker of Washington
State's House of Representatives. Ballard thought highly of Craig
McCaw. "He was a very nice guy," Ballard says. "I was always
impressed with him. I always thought they [the McCaw people] were
real straight arrows with lots of guts."

In Yakima, McCaw brought his mother along to some meetings
with potential franchise partners, including the publisher of the *Yakima*

Herald-Republic. Although she always made a good impression, Marion was just the first of many "gray-hairs"—veterans whose visible presence reassured bankers and others that the youthful McCaw company hadn't been formed at a schoolyard.

The long drives across the Cascades did not pay off. The company lost in Yakima and Wenatchee. The defeats meant losses of money and momentum. The Yakima application cost at least $150,000. McCaw put some of the blame for that loss on John McCaw, who was supposedly keeping an eye on Yakima.

On the other hand, the winning bidder, a large national company, won so easily that it appeared the process had been greased. By payoffs? There was no evidence, but the McCaw people had their suspicions. "Somebody was passing money under the table," Marion later speculated.

McCaw also lost Wenatchee, where the winners had characterized the McCaws as slick rich kids from Seattle. Ironically, the opponents themselves were allied with a national cable company.

Fortunately, the company found other prizes. McCaw was about to buy a small system in Omak, Washington, a deal Liebsack had brought to the company. But the big victory was winning Fairbanks, Alaska. The contest had gone on for months, at one point costing as much as $4,000 a day. Overall, the company racked up some $400,000 in transportation, engineering, and legal costs. But John McCaw, along with a Fairbanks lawyer, worked very hard and won the franchise, despite opposition from the Teamsters, who complained that McCaw was antiunion.

That deal turned out to be a fabulous investment, Perry says. They took the simple system, added pay channels and other services, and doubled the cash flow. Within three months, the company used Fairbanks's assets to borrow more than twice the purchase price. Of course, the loan fueled more acquisitions.

The word went out: Anyone in the Northwest and Alaska with a cable system to sell should call the McCaws. Soon a predictable pattern emerged. The company would find a system, figure out how to boost cash flow, and buy it under the cheapest terms possible. Sometimes the seller agreed to finance the sale. Other times the company managed to borrow more than the sale price by persuading a lender that the improved cash projections were reasonable. Credibility was key. Once McCaw said it would expand revenue, it had to make good on its projections or lose the confidence of lenders and risk future deals.

While Liebsack improved the operations of the new systems, the job of lobbying town councils for needed rate increases fell to John McCaw, the champion schmoozer. John was a careful dresser, even when he wanted to look shabby or needy. Those worn-out shoes he sometimes wore? Gagsters at the company called them his "rate-increase shoes."

Good service not only matched a family philosophy of doing right by people, but it also made shrewd business sense. Providing good service made it easier to get rate increases approved by city councils. In comparison to other cable operators, McCaw had some of the highest rates in the nation, but among the fewest complaints. McCaw customers were relieved they could watch an entire Super Bowl without an outage, and they were willing to pay more for more channels.

Happy customers meant more grist for the borrow-and-buy cycle. Cash flow rose eightfold to $16 million between 1981 and 1984, twice the growth rate of revenues, which reached $36 million. "We got better rates and better returns than anybody else by being nice to people," McCaw says.

McCaw soon perfected the acquisition machine. Once anyone showed interest in selling, the McCaw team went manic, comparing a system's balance sheet to its business models, crunching numbers, analyzing risk, often working twenty-four hours or more without rest, fueled only by bags of cheeseburgers and milk shakes.

Their goal was to reach what Perry calls "ninety percent of comfort." They couldn't get every single question answered or eliminate all the unknowns in the limited time available, but they felt they knew enough about the essentials of all cable systems to make an informed, quick judgment about what they would pay and whether they could later get financing. And their financial analysis sped up every time the computer industry released new hardware or software; the McCaws started with Apple IIs, moved on to Apple IIIs, and felt they had reached unbelievable sophistication in 1982 with the Compaq portable, which allowed them to do complex calculations on location.

With the analysis complete, they would swoop in to visit the potential seller via company plane, moving to negotiate terms as rapidly as possible. Whoever was on the scene had full authority to make a deal. If the seller wanted a sweetener—say, another $50,000 on the purchase price or a promise to keep someone's brother-in-law on the payroll—the McCaw buyer had the authority to say yes. "Here's the contract, we're ready to sign," he would say. "We're ready to go."

That speed and autonomy gave the company a big advantage over rivals who had to seek approval from headquarters for every decision. The McCaw motto was "Sign 'em quick, close 'em slow": Get effective control of the franchise fast, but delay the moment when you have to pay precious cash to complete the sale. The delay before closing could serve an important purpose; sometimes the company lacked money to pay for the purchase and had to scramble for cash.

Even before closing the deal, the company would often get the seller to turn operations over to the McCaw team, which immediately began lobbying regulators for transfer of the franchise. Sellers usually were getting more money than they expected, so they were happy to walk. Occasionally, the owner would see the first signs of the growing profitability of the system he was selling. In one deal, McCaw took control of a system sold at $21 million and negotiated a loan for $10 million more than the sale price because of the increased cash flow. The extra $10 million went toward—what else?—the next purchase.

If any sellers tried to back out, they discovered the steely side to lawyer Wayne Perry. Look at the papers you signed, Perry would say: Read 'em and weep.

Sales didn't always happen fast. Liebsack remembers Wally, a reluctant seller in Alaska, who had to be wooed over three years. Wally never wanted to meet at his office, only at bars, where he insisted on greasing the conversation with pitchers of martinis, usually past midnight. Liebsack had a hard time remembering what they talked about, but eventually Wally agreed on a price for his 4,000-customer system—not the only McCaw deal negotiated in a bar. (The Alaska system performed poorly, one of a few labeled for lenders as "deferred development accounts"—a euphemism McCaw used to describe a bad investment.)

By September 1980 McCaw Communications employed about 200 people and was serving nearly 30,000 customers, as compared to 15 million by the entire cable industry. Despite the rapid growth of his company, McCaw wanted to preserve a family atmosphere, and he launched a company newsletter to help. *Comline* recorded the purchase of new systems, welcomed new employees, and, in "Happy Happenings," congratulated employees on their marriages and births. "We are earnestly striving to remain a closely knit, friendly company that makes itself a great place to work," the young McCaw wrote. "When we fail at this, I ask your forgiveness with the hope that we can correct the errors of our ways."

Those following McCaw's career were amazed at his skillful use of debt, his shrewd sense of timing, and his willingness to take huge risks. "They were having fun. I don't think they had fear of failure. So they were willing to push things to the max," says Gordon Rock, McCaw's friend in the cable business.

Maybe that's how it looked to outsiders. But Craig McCaw felt otherwise. He had talked his brothers into pledging everything they owned to finance purchases by the company. They had agreed to receive few or no dividends so that company cash could be used to fuel rapid growth. Any one of them could have pulled out at any time, which would have broken the company.

Wayne Perry, the rare outsider to attend family meetings, swears there was no family strife. The brothers trusted McCaw totally, he says; McCaw was their leader. But they recognized the downside. The disastrous end of Elroy's deal-making career had taught them what happens when mistakes are made.

Craig McCaw knew the truth. "We were always scared to death," he says.

6

"Always Have a Back Door"

The First Major Partner Comes on Board

Since 1969 the McCaws had run the company as a committee. Craig McCaw suggested the direction but consulted with his mother and three brothers before acting. "Craig was the strategist, but his mother and brothers had to approve it," says Steve Countryman, McCaw's close friend. "He had to manage by consensus."

Most observers say the family functioned well together. If they had any conflicts, outsiders rarely saw them. "Certainly we've had our squabbles at one time or another, but we never fought," Bruce McCaw says. "We always believed in what we were doing and where we were going."

But much as he loved his family, consensus did not suit Craig McCaw's style. In all his other business dealings, there could be no question about control. He could be shy about the limelight, indirect in his communication, and deferential in personal dealings, but no one working for him or with him could ever doubt who was boss. Now he had to change the business structure because it was too cumbersome to gather his family members to approve each financing or other key decision. Bruce was often on the road with his insurance business, and John was courting people to buy their cable systems. So in 1979 Craig gathered his mother and brothers and sole outsider Wayne Perry for the most important meeting to date in the family's history.

"Craig told his brothers, 'I either get control or . . .' I don't remember if the rest of the sentence was implicit or explicit," says Perry. "The implication, if not the exact statement was, 'I'm going to go alone. I want control.' That was a meeting where it was discussed very frankly."

As McCaw recalls the meeting, he said he would not stay unless certain things were agreed upon: Specifically, everyone had to dedicate himself to the company and agree that McCaw was in charge. "This is what I want to do," McCaw told them. "I want to grow the company; I want to make it as good and as big as it can be. I'll live by that standard and be measured by that standard, and so will all of us."

McCaw's little speech brought his family to its most significant decision since the death of Elroy McCaw. First they had decided to keep the Centralia cable company; now came the moment to decide whether they would hang together. Through their shared equity, each family member had cash on the table. Each could have grabbed some and walked. But none did. They all stuck to the principle of what was best for the company.

"The brothers have never fought because of that basic issue," Craig McCaw says. "They knew I cared more about the company than my selfish interests, and I expect other people to live by the same standards." Bruce McCaw claims that ceding authority to his younger brother wasn't difficult: "Craig was sensing more than the rest of us what needed to be done," he says.

The family formally designated Craig as the decision maker for their interests in McCaw Communications, and the company was reorganized as a holding company controlled by a family trust. Until a later refinancing, the brothers' personal guarantee for the company's debt remained in force, as did their equal shares in the company. In time, the arrangement significantly enriched all of the McCaws, including Bruce, who never worked full-time for the company, and Keith, who never held a significant position. Only through employee stock options did Craig and John gain greater wealth.

Blending caution and nerve, McCaw used the 1979 meeting to establish ironclad controls over his brothers. The agreement he forged prevented them from ever creating mischief for the company—by supporting a hostile takeover, for example. "We had them tied up four ways till Sunday," says Perry. "We had layers of defenses."

McCaw's move to consolidate his authority coincided with a move, after three years in Seattle, to offices in a two-story wood-frame building in suburban Bellevue, not far from the offices of a young software company called Microsoft. The new headquarters remained a family affair. Bruce McCaw's company, Westar Insurance Group, occupied the ground floor. Near Craig's office on the top floor, his mother, now remarried to real estate developer John L. Scott, arranged her files and desk in front of a large collection of photographs of her four boys. Despite Craig's distaste for memos, she issued a regular flow on topics ranging from investment strategies to the latest IRS rulings. ("She probably wrote thousands over the years," says Bruce McCaw.)

The atmosphere remained informal. Marion, who served on the financial-advisory boards of the Seattle symphony and opera, shared tickets with employees. McCaw's wife, Wendy, would arrive in a white pickup truck (soon replaced by a red Mercedes 450SL), greet employees, and offer redecorating tips. (One of her ideas was hanging framed Hermès scarves on the walls.) John McCaw would put his feet up on his desk, call potential sellers, and arrange squash games. Keith McCaw came around sometimes, but employees wondered what he did. Everyone went by first names—except Marion, who was always "Mrs. McCaw."

As McCaw's operations boss for the cable companies, Joe Liebsack kept in daily contact with employees through a direct line to each franchise. Steve Countryman, friend, had been part of the McCaw executive team from the beginning, though he says he never got over the feeling that he was an outsider working for the family. Now he found that he didn't get along with Liebsack, who seemed protective of his turf. Countryman figured he'd rather leave and remain a friend than stay and be an employee involved in discord. He quit and took a job with Boeing.

Craig McCaw worked in an office whose doors rattled when knocked. He often apologized to employees that the company was getting too big. At least during the early years there, he personally ran staff meetings and made a practice of letting employees speak their minds. Sylvia Padgett, who oversaw purchasing, appreciated McCaw's letting employees work without excessive supervision. At one meeting, a senior manager worried about Padgett's handling of large accounts. But McCaw said she could do it. "He had a tremendous amount of faith in his employees," Padgett says. She responded as most employees did— by working harder to make sure that his faith was well placed.

Lyn Pawley joined the company in 1980 as Craig McCaw's executive assistant. Because McCaw was away on Pawley's first day, no one would let her tackle one obvious problem: the heaps of documents and newspapers stacked on his desk, bookshelves, and credenza. "Craig was a slob. He never seemed to throw anything out," Pawley says. On McCaw's return, the two cut a deal. Pawley could neatly file everything so long as she could retrieve his papers when he needed them.

Like others who worked for Craig McCaw, Pawley found him fascinating. Sometimes she would look in and see him leaning back, feet up on the desk, hands joined, his eyes fixed on some distant point. He wasn't daydreaming, but thinking through a business issue. Later, he would drop on her desk "an extraordinary document he had scribbled and wanted me to type up for the next day"—an announcement of some strategic adjustment or a solution to some problem that no one else had been able to solve. "I don't think he ever stopped dreaming or thinking," she says.

Typically, McCaw arrived at the office at 9:30 A.M. and started the day by greeting Pawley with an exaggerated salute and bow in deference to the office sahib. He relied on Pawley to keep his schedule clear of time wasters. He once caused a flutter of talk when he issued a memo to employees—including members of his own family—insisting that there be a purpose and an agenda for every meeting with him. Pawley, McCaw joked, operated an imaginary stoplight above his office. "He didn't want interruptions. He needed time to strategize and study," Pawley says. McCaw refused to be drawn into battles over small matters. "I don't need to know that," he'd say. "I'm the big-picture guy. You take care of it." He would usually leave the office around 6:30 P.M., often armed with yellow legal pads for more work at home.

Pawley spent six years with Craig McCaw, working on his daily schedule and fielding calls from him at all hours. Affectionate as she felt toward him, she always respected his desire for privacy. When McCaw looked exhausted, he would wave off her solicitous questions as if to say, You're not my mother. He never volunteered details about his childhood, his vacation plans, or the other routine personal chitchat of most offices. That part of McCaw's life remained behind an invisible wall.

* * *

Throughout the 1970s McCaw was always prospecting for cash to buy cable properties. In 1980 he hit his first gusher. Tim David of Daniels & Associates in Denver helped McCaw Communications obtain its first large financing, $8 million from The Bank of New York—twice what the company had borrowed earlier from Seattle First National Bank. The deal removed the family's personal guarantees, reduced the interest rate on their borrowing, and helped modernize company finances. It also meant that the pace of the company's acquisitions could accelerate even further. McCaw was delighted.

McCaw and his management team flew to New York to sign the loan agreement on May 18, 1980—the same day Mount Saint Helens in Washington State erupted with the force of an atomic blast, killing fifty-seven people and spewing volcanic debris 70,000 feet into the air. As ash fell throughout the state, transforming lush hillsides into gray moonscapes, the McCaws and their bankers sat together in New York, tracking the news reports and wondering about possible damage to the company's cable systems. They tried to reach Keith McCaw in Yakima, 100 miles east of the volcano, where the ash had fallen especially heavily, but phone lines were jammed. The McCaw people and the bankers canceled their planned celebration. "It was a very short and quiet lunch," says Bruce McCaw. As it happened, the company had actually suffered little damage.

Almost as fast as Saint Helens blew ash, McCaw Communications consumed cash. Buying cable systems as soon as they were found, the company quickly burned through The Bank of New York's money and began leaving deals on the table. McCaw needed money to fuel more growth. Or, to use Wayne Perry's metaphor, the company had captured territory across the front like General Patton's tank corps only to run out of gas.

* * *

Craig McCaw had to find an investor who would fund his aggressive growth strategy. Ironically, the fuel was to come from one of the most conservative companies in America. In 1981 Affiliated Publications, which owned *The Boston Globe* and ten radio stations, approached Tim David, a broker with Denver-based Daniels & Associates. Affiliated wanted to match the success it had seen when other newspaper companies had invested in cable. But with no background in that field, it wanted a share in a cable company, not control. An owner of radio stations in Seattle and Sacramento, Affiliated was also thinking about expanding its West Coast presence. David told them about a rapidly growing company in Bellevue, Washington, named McCaw Communications.

The two companies were an unlikely match. With a century-long history, Affiliated was a formal, stuffy organization that had been controlled for generations by the Jordans and Taylors, two old-line New England families. Where Affiliated's style was elegant and polished, the McCaw company was mainly a ragtag group of tieless boys who didn't sleep much. At McCaw, people joked that Affiliated had more people on its board of directors than McCaw Communications had on its total payroll.

Yet the two groups meshed well. Affiliated liked McCaw's growth strategy and its financial results; and, as a family-run company, Affiliated liked the idea of a company where the chief executive consulted with his mother. "The McCaws believed in honesty and trust, which was compatible with our philosophy," says Dan Orr, Affiliated's vice president for acquisitions. Craig McCaw's boyishness didn't bother William Taylor, Affiliated's chairman and chief executive. "I'm interested in the brains, not the looks," Taylor says. "We had pretty good confidence in what they could do."

The fact that Affiliated did not want management control suited Craig McCaw. As others would learn, McCaw would discuss anything with a potential partner—except control. Affiliated agreed to put $12 million into McCaw Communications' expansion and in return got 45 percent of the company. The transaction significantly boosted McCaw Communications' borrowing power and enhanced its credibility.

Affiliated's investment eventually reached $85 million, and the payoff it yielded staggered the Jordan and Taylor families. Within seven years, the investment's value hit $2 billion—more than the value of the *Globe* itself. The investment illustrated another recurring theme of the McCaw saga: Big players that do business with McCaw habitually underestimate—often drastically—his cleverness and ambition. "At the time, they thought they were just making a peekaboo investment to buy part of the company and buy the rest later," McCaw later said. "[But] our intentions were to buy *them*." As it happens, he never did—but not because he couldn't afford it.

Given their trust in McCaw and their relatively small initial invest-ment, Affiliated felt content to let McCaw run his company without interference from Boston. Although occasionally astonished at the pace of the McCaw company's acquisitions, Affiliated never required heavy reporting, which fit with McCaw's too-busy-to-write style. Affiliated did make one serious mistake. At the beginning of the relationship, it picked the wrong person as its representative. Apparently acting on his own, the young executive decided he would use the McCaw company as a showcase for his talents. On his first trip to Seattle, the young executive met with McCaw and his staff and began announcing new things McCaw Communications would do and what it would stop doing.

Joe Liebsack vividly remembers what happened. McCaw was deeply enraged, but did not betray his emotions. In the middle of the meeting, he politely excused himself and phoned Boston. Liebsack followed McCaw and overheard him talking to William Taylor. "We've got a problem," McCaw said. As of that moment, he said he wouldn't continue to deal with the Affiliated executive. Taylor agreed, and the troublesome executive quickly disappeared.

In his place, Taylor sent Dan Orr, a congenial former circulation director for the *Globe* who seemed to know every newspaper publisher in Oregon. Orr and McCaw got along famously. (Orr thinks McCaw may have considered him a bit of a father figure.) McCaw introduced Orr to the McCaw company staff members, saying, "If there's any infor-mation he wants, you give it to him—including the combination to the safe."

Affiliated's money helped McCaw make its largest purchase to date, a cable TV system in southern Oregon owned by the irascible Bill Smullin. The deal would more than double the company's cable subscribers to 92,000 and would make Craig McCaw a large regional player in the industry.

Smullin was a pioneer in cable and broadcasting. Starting with a small radio station in Eureka, California, he had built a communica-tions company based in Medford, Oregon, that included seven televi-sion stations, four cable systems, and three radio stations. In 1981, however, the FCC barred ownership of cable systems by broadcasters in areas where a company's broadcast signal overlapped its cable territory.

Smullin had to sell, though he didn't want to, which made for difficult negotiations with Craig McCaw and his staff.

Some say Smullin tended to annoy or offend people. Tim David, for one, viewed Smullin as a bully. The Smullins had their own view of the McCaws. "They were very tough negotiators and they were raising a lot of minutiae," Patricia Smullin, Bill's daughter, said of the McCaw team. "There were several times when my father was ready to walk away." But it helped somewhat that Smullin and his wife had been acquainted with Elroy and Marion McCaw.

The McCaw team on the purchase included Craig McCaw, John McCaw, Wayne Perry, and Joe Liebsack. Despite Craig McCaw's youth and his self-effacing style, he established his authority. "Craig handled himself very well," says Carl Brophy, a Medford attorney who represented Smullin. "Craig tended to be . . . *reserved* isn't the right word . . . less vocal, but it was clear he was in charge. Craig was clearly in command but quiet. It was clear he was very bright."

McCaw wanted those southern Oregon cable systems badly. Smullin wanted $1,000 per cable subscriber, which worked out to about $60 million, a very high price. Normally, McCaw would try to secure any deal with as little money down as possible. This time McCaw told his team to offer $1 million as a down payment. McCaw believed that would swing the deal, Liebsack says. But Smullin's lawyer dismissed the offer as too low. McCaw raised his offer to $3 million down, and Smullin agreed.

Though Liebsack fervently believed in cable's future, he worried about the price Smullin had won. "I didn't like the deal," Liebsack says. Tim David agreed. Most cable deals at the time were for $700 per subscriber. "They overpaid, big time," David says.

"Craig wanted it very bad," David adds. "He was convinced that it was just a matter of time before you started to make money on [cable subscribers]. It was hard to overpay for cable because revenues were constantly going up. HBO was going up on the satellite, Ted Turner was adding content, and court decisions were going our way. So revenue was going up fifteen or twenty percent a year regularly. You could add a channel and raise [monthly] rates by a dollar and do it again the next year and raise rates again."

The deal underscored McCaw's nerve and his faith that, with cable's bright future, the numbers could be made to work. Yet even with Affiliated's cash, he still didn't have enough to pay Smullin. So McCaw struck a deal in which Affiliated agreed to put up more money and help arrange loans through banks in New York and Boston. The arrangement meant that Affiliated owned 72.5 percent of the southern Oregon system. The entire deal rested on McCaw's making loan payments that could not be paid without substantial changes in the Oregon systems, producing far more cash flow than Smullin had seen. But as the McCaw team had learned, the systems were giving poor service, and Smullin had alienated many of the town councils in Oregon that set cable rates.

John McCaw remembers this period as the most perilous in company history. Many difficult tasks had to be performed quickly. The Oregon system was in shambles and needed cash for improvements. At the same time McCaw needed to pull cash out of the systems to service debt. But to raise rates, the company needed the approval of eleven different county and city councils. Persuading them fell largely to John, as the designated "relationship guy."

To run the southern Oregon systems, McCaw brought in Cal Cannon, a thirteen-year manager with Viacom. Big and sociable, Cannon had the personality of a friendly bear, the perfect symbol of how the McCaws wanted to deal with council members and the public.

Cannon's hiring reflected McCaw's unusual style of business. McCaw took extreme care in filling senior positions, often subjecting an applicant to an exhaustive meeting where he would spend hours asking about personal history. He would pose questions about how an applicant had handled problems or how he would manage a hypothetical situation. He might ask: Have you ever hired anyone smarter than you? Have you ever taken a complex process and made it more simple? By the time an applicant had survived this process, he would have truly earned any job offer.

In this instance, McCaw spent six hours with Cannon, wanting to know how he could upgrade the Oregon systems from twelve channels to thirty or more without the huge expense of completely rebuilding them. McCaw showed him the financial targets that the systems had to meet and introduced him to John McCaw, Wayne Perry, and others.

When John McCaw walked in, the two brothers put their arms on each other's shoulders. Cannon took their obvious affection as an auspicious sign. "This is a real family," he thought. "It felt good. Coming to the company was like being accepted into a family."

Cannon sensed that he was being measured not just for his professional talents but also for his ethics. At one point, McCaw stood up and announced, "I have to make a phone call. I'll send my mother in." Cannon thought he was joking, but in walked Marion, who subjected Cannon to her own battery of questions.

Even Patti Cannon, Cannon's wife at the time, got a call from McCaw. It was ostensibly a mere courtesy call, but Patti suspected that the purpose of McCaw's questions was to determine whether anything in Cannon's home life might create problems for the company. Patti Cannon took no offense; she saw it as smart. "Craig cared about your family, your whole life, because it influenced how you could produce at work," she says. "That's how he succeeds. He thinks about the entire package."

Cannon passed the test. He got such a good feeling about the company that he didn't feel a need to record his compensation deal in writing. He chose to trust McCaw and the others. "They usually do more for you than you expected," says Cannon. "They're very fair and honest people."

Cannon and John McCaw began lobbying the town councils of southern Oregon. Cannon was amazed at John's talent as a communicator. "He was very smooth," Cannon says. "You'd like John. You trusted him. You believed him. Somebody would spend five or ten minutes talking with him and you'd believe him. And if he said it would be done, it would be."

In Ashland John dealt with Brian Almquist, the city administrator. Almquist was no small-town rube; he was fully briefed on the cable industry, and he felt relieved to see Smullin out of the picture. Ashland was overdue for improved service, fewer outages, and more hookups for people in lightly populated areas, Almquist thought. He also believed that the cable company should set up a public-access studio and share its revenues more generously with the city, paying not just the usual 2 to 3 percent but 5 percent, and to press his point he reminded John McCaw that Congress had been talking about regulating cable industry rates.

Almquist found John McCaw a tough but fair negotiator. In the end, McCaw Communications agreed to Almquist's demands, but it also won a major concession. Instead of the usual ten-year franchise, McCaw got a twenty-year deal.

Cannon invited all the council members to visit their city's cable system and see how things worked. Lou Hannum, then mayor of Medford, Oregon, praises Cannon's style and substance. Cannon gave Hannum and his colleagues a detailed briefing on cable TV technology, made himself available for questions and complaints, and kept council members informed of scheduled improvements. When one homeowner called the mayor's office to complain that promised cable service hadn't been installed, Hannum called Cannon, who put that installation at the top of the schedule. The homeowner got cable service within a week.

When Medford's Pear Blossom Parade needed a celebrity to serve as parade marshal, McCaw Communications arranged for a visit by a Disney character, a tie-in to the debut of the Disney Channel in Medford. Cannon "never tried to pressure or hassle me," says Hannum, but "if he could do something to make me more comfortable, he would do it. I always enjoyed my conversations with him."

McCaw Communications got the rate increases it sought, and cash flow soared. McCaw made good on its promises to customers. Service did improve. Cannon added new programming—though not the Playboy Channel, which he saw as needlessly controversial and a poor use of precious spectrum on the cable. The company handled the public with respect, and most people were happy. "The complaints dropped to near zero after McCaw took over," says Almquist. "It was a breath of fresh air after having dealt with the previous operator."

But it wasn't all sweetness and pleasantries. From Elroy, Craig McCaw had acquired an aversion for unions. McCaw felt that employees shouldn't need a third-party negotiator if they were treated well, and he always tried hard to avoid unionized workforces. But when he bought southern Oregon, he inherited Local 659 of the International Brotherhood of Electrical Workers, which had represented Smullin's employees for thirteen years. Oregon had a long history with unions, but this was a first for McCaw Communications.

The company quickly moved against the union in a campaign coordinated with a Seattle law firm. According to Walt Conner, Local 659's assistant business manager, McCaw gave the workers new trucks and uniforms and said they would do better without a union. The company did nothing illegal or underhanded, Conner concedes, but they "did a real slick job of convincing people they didn't need a union." Cal Cannon says employees decertified their union because it hadn't been doing a good job, but Conner says wages never did rise as fast as employees expected.

Having now swallowed a company as big as his own, McCaw did not rest and digest. Instead, he raised his sights. The target of 100,000 subscribers was increased to 400,000. If this goal was met, it would make McCaw Communications one of the nation's largest cable companies.

To travel within his expanding territory, McCaw bought a twin-engine Beechcraft King Air E-90, which carried eight passengers and could fly nonstop from Seattle to Anchorage. He offered the plane to employees for personal use at $205 an hour, though hardly anyone took the offer. Bigger, more powerful airplanes, including jets, would come later, all personally flown by Craig McCaw as well as by corporate pilots. In fact, McCaw became one of a very few chief executives to take the time to go through the intensive training required to earn a multi-engine pilot's license.

A company joke had it that McCaw grew his company to justify ever bigger airplanes. In truth, McCaw needed to grow—or the house of debt would collapse.

"We always leveraged future growth," explains Wayne Perry. "We would go to a programmer and we'd say, 'We're at a hundred thousand subscribers today. We want you to give us the discounts equal to two hundred and fifty thousand subscribers and we'll promise to be there by the end of the contract. If not, we'll have to rebate you all the money.' " Programmers liked the idea because of the prospect of increased revenue from a larger subscriber base. "It was a gamble, but in effect we allowed ourselves to get the discounts equal to the bigger players," admits Perry. "Therefore we could compete in both acquisitions and our current financial performance. We had to grow."

McCaw also knew he needed financial management to match his ambitions. In 1982 he lured Rufus Lumry from Seattle First National Bank, where Lumry had served as senior vice president and was said to be on track to become chief financial officer. Landing Lumry was a major effort, four months of what McCaw called "the toughest hire we ever had." Lumry was meticulous about details and contingencies, which is exactly why McCaw wanted him. But as a job negotiator, he exhausted McCaw with his requirements, such as a provision for more money if his pregnant wife gave birth to a sickly child.

But after McCaw landed him, "I couldn't have been happier. Rufus was a godsend," McCaw says. After a pause, he adds, "Not that there wasn't a price to that."

Bearded, thin, and delicate-looking, Lumry was a driven personality. A perfectionist, he would go without sleep to analyze numbers in preparation for a presentation. Some saw him as a negative personality: He fussed, he complained, he worried. He expected his staff to work seven days a week and had a habit of leaving messages at 3 or 4 A.M.

Unlike McCaw, who chose to trust people as a matter of philosophy, Lumry was "a little bit suspicious by nature. He was a product of the bank and the navy. He's nervous about things he can't control," McCaw says. Furthermore, unlike others at McCaw who always seemed to be having fun, Lumry couldn't seem to fully enjoy his work. His presence rubbed some people the wrong way—apparently including the office pet, a brilliantly colored macaw with a saber-shaped tail and powerful jaws, which began to squawk and carry on whenever Lumry walked by.

But no one ever minimized Lumry's importance to the company or doubted his genius at raising money. For the increasingly high-flying McCaw company, Lumry was the airborne tanker supplied with financial fuel. He took the company's meager financial results and blended them with talk of McCaw's vision and the future of cable into a tale that won the support of bankers and other investors. He knew what to tell the bankers and what not to tell them, and how to give them bad news that sounded good. If losses ran bigger than the company projected, Lumry gave them a happy spin. That red ink, he would say with feigned pride, was a "tax shelter ahead of schedule." Lumry led the bankers to the only logical conclusion: that McCaw could walk on water. In the end, they would be eager to lend $85 million on $4 million a year of cash flow.

McCaw executives would sometimes chuckle over how much money they could raise. And the chief technician of the famed McCaw smoke-and-mirrors machine was Rufus Lumry. Craig McCaw says merely, "He was a financing dynamo, to say the least."

The company hired another Seafirst banker, Steve Hooper, to serve as Lumry's aide. On his first day of work in 1982 Hooper showed up early at the Bellevue office, where about twenty people worked, and discovered that he had no desk and no computer—not to mention no office. Having left a big downtown bank, with its luxurious offices and fancy equipment, he wondered *What have I done?*

Hooper spotted a little wobbly-legged desk in a hallway, apparently destined for the trash, and fetched tools from his yellow Volkswagen to secure the legs. He pushed the desk into Lumry's office and began attaching clamps and wires to stiffen its parts. As people drifted in, a secretary approached Hooper with a message from Marion, the chief executive's mother (who by then had remarried): "Mrs. Scott would like you to be careful with that desk. Don't write on it too hard, because the wood is soft." Hooper dutifully went out to buy a blotter to cover the desk.

Only later did he learn the reason for Marion's concern: He had salvaged an old student's desk that McCaw or one of the other boys had used during the Lakeside years, a cheap Swedish-style item worth less than $40. "An utter piece of junk," McCaw later recalled. But junk or not, it belonged to the family, not the company, and Marion McCaw didn't want to see it go to waste.

This wasn't Hooper's only chance to glimpse the McCaw frugality in action. Hooper was asked to share an Apple IIe computer with Lumry and to use cardboard boxes for his files. It was not an encouraging start. "I was about to get back into my car and go back to Seafirst," Hooper says.

For some reason, he stayed. He quickly learned that the casual dress of the McCaw employees belied a heavy workload. Hooper worked at least six days a week, twelve hours a day, for the next six years—nine months of it without an office of his own.

Hooper also found out why two other Seafirst bankers had declined a chance to work under Lumry. "Rufus is a wonderful human being, but he is a driver," Hooper says. "He absolutely would be hard to work with. I just didn't know. He calls at all hours of the day and night. Saturdays and Sundays. . . . It changed my life more than I had ever imagined."

Hooper later rose to significant operating positions in the cable and cellular divisions, but at that point one of his main jobs was tightly controlling spending so the company could service its debt. In the world of Craig McCaw, no dime was spent before its time. Hooper used to joke that McCaw dollars stayed locked away so long that they blinked in the sunlight when they finally came out.

As controller, Hooper signed all the payroll checks, often at home at night while his wife folded diapers. Payroll and bills from small vendors were always paid on time, but other payables could be "managed." McCaw regularly owed money to HBO and to a construction company that did most of the cable installations. The accounting department would issue a check and Hooper would toss it unsigned into his desk drawer, where it would remain until the last possible moment in part of the company's unorthodox but effective cash management system.

HBO and other large creditors frequently became upset and demanded payment. At one point, the McCaw company ran up a debt so big that it offered a construction company equity in some of the cable systems as payment. The company insisted on cash—one of many occasions when people underestimated the future of McCaw Communications.

As another cash management technique, Hooper would send a check in the wrong envelope or matched with the wrong invoice. So the irate creditor would get a payment, all right, but addressed to someone else—which Hooper would explain over the phone as an innocent mix-up. "Oh, dummy me. I botched another one," Hooper would exclaim. He would ask them to send back the wrong check and offer to send the correct one, a process that bought another two weeks.

This kind of fancy financial footwork typically happened only near the end of a quarter, when Hooper and Lumry were struggling to ensure that cash flow would meet the targets set in loan agreements. (Hooper says the practice only lasted a year.) The company took great pride in never violating a loan covenant. McCaw aimed to set the highest ethical standards, but there were times when it was necessary to push the envelope—so to speak.

The need for revenue was relentless. The bank covenants required cash flow from southern Oregon to triple by the end of the third year.

Lumry and Hooper built computer models of revenue flowing from the company's many cable systems, including the jumps in revenue from planned rate increases. After a while, the company could accurately forecast how many customers would quit if rates rose. "You could predict the growth in cash flow pretty well. It was always growing," says Hooper:

> You knew if you had a $2 rate increase going in across a base of 20,000–30,000 customers, somewhere, boom, that would fall right through to the bottom line. . . . It was very stable down in southern Oregon, which was half of our base—pretty consistent penetration level. We never got it to grow a whole lot. But every year we were able to get another couple-buck rate increase and, across 50,000 customers, that's $100,000 a month times 12 months is $1.2 million, times five is $6 million more borrowing capacity.

To further sweeten the picture, Lumry and Hooper did everything they could to shift costs from daily expenses to capital accounts, where spending would not count against cash flow (that is, revenue left after operating expenses). Nearly everyone in the organization focused on CFAM, cash flow after marketing. Was that dollar spent on just maintaining something—an operating expense—or on extending its useful life—a capital expense? If a plausible case could be made for the latter, then that's where the money would be slotted.

For example: Didn't Cal Cannon spend a lot of his time overseeing construction of that new plant? Sure. So 30 percent of his salary became a capital expense, and CFAM looked rosier. How about Cal's staff and their expenses? Same thing. Independent auditors accepted the shifts. "We got to know the accounting rules very well. We really stretched the definition of 'expanding the useful life of an asset,' " Hooper says with a laugh.

Moreover, as the McCaw organization did more borrowing, Wayne Perry, Rufus Lumry, Steve Hooper, and others carefully worked over the loan agreements to give the company wiggle room. The McCaw team fogged definitions of debt or capital expenses, built "back doors," and otherwise structured agreements to follow Craig McCaw's oft-repeated dictum, "Flexibility is heaven."

McCaw would often gather his managers and force them to sort through every possible future scenario, from the most obvious to the most bizarre. He would throw out provocative possibilities to be analyzed: Could we take the money for cable system X and spend it instead on cable system Y? Or not on any cable system, but on some other kind of business altogether? Maybe we don't want to do that today, but who knows about tomorrow? McCaw's moral: Don't let the bank make our decisions. In the next loan agreement, let's define "authorized spending" as anything for a "communications business" as opposed to a "cable company," thereby creating options, openings, possibilities . . . in other words, back doors.

The emphasis on flexibility would prove to be enormously important as McCaw's attention shifted from cable to other arenas in the burgeoning communications universe.

"I have a principle I live by," McCaw said later:

> Never go through the front door unless you've got a back door, and the hardest thing to get people to do is to not commit themselves to one course of action . . . [to think] about what you're going to do next. Playing chess with my father, I give him credit for that. I mean, if you haven't thought three moves ahead and what if he does this, and what if that happens, and what if that happens, in today's world you can't predict what's going to happen. . . . You can take chances, but you never, ever play the game without an out. Maybe that's from being a history major, [studying] everybody in history who has failed to have a back door, whether it's Hitler, Napoleon, and down the list. If you take a chance, always have a back door. That's the fun of it.

Drafts of McCaw lending agreements were written and rewritten, studied and lengthened, a tedious process usually done without McCaw's direct involvement. The agreements became very complicated—which is exactly how the McCaw teams wanted them. They wanted long, intricate, crushingly ornate loan documents. "The more complicated it was, the more I enjoyed it," says Hooper, who had to do the required reporting on the agreements. "I thrived on the chaos. We loved complexity, because in it we found flexibility."

This is a paradox of Craig McCaw, the prophet of simplicity (simple vision, relentless focus on task) whose tactical strength flows from stupefyingly complex agreements—crafted by McCaw's deputies under his guidance but without his personal involvement. McCaw "never really appreciated the detail that went into loan agreements," says Hooper,

> [but] he understood the mechanics of how to grow his business as well as anybody in the cable business. He understood the tax game of getting some of these tax carryover losses and how to leverage that to his benefit in acquisitions. But the details of the loan agreements that we put together? He never saw to that.

As McCaw Communications continued its breakneck expansion, most industry observers offered two reactions: first, astonishment that such a small company could grow so quickly while taking on such debt; second, predictions that the company would eventually collapse under the weight of that debt. These twin reactions would always dog McCaw. People who knew the family history often assumed he would follow Elroy down the path to ruin. Only the real insiders knew about Elroy's wife and her enduring, moderating influence. In the earliest days of McCaw Communcations, she oversaw the accounting personally. Later, as a longtime board member, she always pushed for "good paper."

"She was a voice of conservatism," Perry says:

> Marion always believed in the paperwork. That attitude of having good paper, strong paper, documenting things, making sure you're very careful. . . . Marion instilled in us one of the McCaw attributes, which was to outdocument people. Be smarter in documentation of everything, things like programming agreements and acquisitions agreements. . . . A lot of people think that a highly leveraged company is an out-of-control company. What they don't understand oftentimes is that the companies that are highly leveraged have the most control. People assume that a company that is wild and woolly in its acquisition strategy and moving along at a breakneck pace, that the rest of the company is like that . . . [that]

nobody is keeping track of the operation, nobody has good accounting, nobody has good management information systems. [But at McCaw] it's just the opposite. McCaw had a very aggressive growth strategy. But we had a very sound system of managing the business, keeping track of the organization and certainly paying attention to our contractual sides. That was a big part of [the growth strategy]. It wasn't just me as general counsel. McCaw was a stickler for making sure we had things protected, had thought things through.

McCaw didn't want only one exit if a deal went sour, for example. He wanted multiple exits tied to different scenarios. Since the McCaw holdings were an intricate web of corporate entities and debt, if problems erupted in one end of the company, McCaw wanted mechanisms "to blow up a deal," Perry says. Ordinarily aloof from particulars, these were the granular details that McCaw examined and discussed speck by speck.

And so the shark kept eating. Wayne Perry quit his law firm and became a full-time employee of McCaw Communications. Even that move generated another incredible deal, a testament to the personal trust McCaw and others wanted as the foundation of the company. As Perry recalls:

When I became an employee of the company, I said, "Craig, we're going to have one deal: We're never going to have a conversation about compensation." Everything I've got, all the salary I've got, all the stock options, everything, have been solely because Craig has said, "That's what it's going to be." That gives you a sense of how much trust I had in Craig and his leadership.

McCaw Communications built or bought systems throughout the Northwest, plus in Alaska in 1981 and Texas in 1982. Outsiders presumed that McCaw's prime motivation was money. But the former chess player had another, more childlike motivation. As he looked into the future of cable television and his own company, McCaw began making side bets in a new technology derived—of all things—from the oldest form of electronic communication: radio.

Cable kept growing, but for McCaw the new radio gizmo had strong appeal. It faced long odds, was attracting little public attention, and would require players with phenomenal nerve. For a gambler like Craig McCaw, this new game would prove irresistible. The money was nice, but he wanted fun even more.

7

"What Would Be in Their Best Interest?"

McCaw Discovers a Revolutionary Telephone

One day in the fall of 1979 Craig McCaw sat in the cab of a mobile home, riding south on Interstate 5, traveling toward his future.

McCaw was heading to a conference near Portland, Oregon, with several men from Seattle who shared his curiosity about a new kind of service being developed by AT&T: cellular telephones. The group included Ace Feek and Gordon Kelley, whose family owned small paging companies in Seattle, as well as Charlie Desmond and Jim Bellamy, who worked for paging companies.

Kelley, who was driving the mobile home, was typical of many businesspeople in paging. In 1936 his family had started Kelley's Telephone Answering Service, a twenty-four-hour service using human operators. The Kelleys got their first radio license for two-way contact with drivers in another family business, automobile towing. They got into paging after they realized that the same radio airwaves could be used to enhance the telephone answering business.

Though the public knew nothing about cellular in 1979, many operators in paging considered it a logical next step in the radio business, though not necessarily a rival to the telephone. The freedom of mobile communication offered by cellular service looked like something the public would want, but the costs to build a system were daunting and apparently out of reach for any small, independent company. Who could afford to spend millions of dollars to build a host of transmission towers and switches? Who could persuade a customer to spend thousands of dollars for a single phone? And who would be crazy enough to compete with Ma Bell—even assuming the government would allow competition?

The risks scared nearly everyone, but they attracted thirty-year-old

Craig McCaw. Something about his personality made him zig when everyone else zagged; perhaps the chaos that frightened others made him calm. But the men riding with him that autumn day were not going to benefit from his thinking. "Craig always had a mystique about him," says Desmond, then vice-president of Pacific Paging in Portland. "You'd go out for drinks with the others, but never Craig. . . . He wasn't one to give you insight into what he was going to do."

All the men in that mobile home were operators of small paging companies who, by virtue of their relationship with the Federal Communications Commission, were well positioned to hear about new radio technologies.

McCaw had entered the paging business almost by accident when a Centralia paging business sought permission to attach a small transmitter to one of Twin City's antenna towers. McCaw already knew about pagers from Elroy McCaw, who in 1962 had carried one of Seattle's first pagers. It was connected to a direct-dial system, a technology showcased at that year's Century 21 Exposition. But Elroy, a volunteer vice president of the fair, did little with his pager; he mostly left it at home to beep till its battery went dead. Staying in touch was not Elroy's strong suit.

But Craig McCaw could see that cable TV and cellular had much in common. Both were regulated by the FCC. Both involved transmitters and towers, assigned radio spectrum, and had common engineering issues such as signal interference; and both businesses were often supported by the same lenders and brokers.

Furthermore, the business fundamentals of paging appealed to McCaw. Pagers sold easily to physicians, salespeople, and others who needed to stay in contact with an office. The devices, McCaw figured, would become even more attractive as the units shrank and volume drove prices down. A company could offer regional service by accumulating several licenses for different markets with compatible frequencies. No powerful competitor dominated a market. It represented the sort of quiet, steady backwater business with strong growth potential that appealed to a personality like McCaw's that avoided the spotlight.

Helped by the Washington, D.C., law firm of Haley Bader & Potts, which specialized in representing companies before the FCC, McCaw won a paging license in Centralia and started service in 1974. He spent

$50,000 on hardware and did little marketing other than to run a picture of a pager on his cable TV system. Even so, the Centralia system attracted a few hundred customers and soon made a profit.

That established McCaw as a licensee of radio spectrum. More important, it gave him a taste of how paging, as another source of cash flow, could fuel his larger ambitions. If he managed paging as he had cable TV, both could grow separately, expanding his ability to borrow and buy.

So what was McCaw doing in that mobile home? Why would he want to look at a third business when he already had two that consumed his time?

For openers, McCaw always hunted for new technology. Years later, some people would assume that the Craig McCaw vision was to lock on to one technology and ride it. Not true. McCaw always attended presentations of new gadgetry. You could always find him playing with some new kind of phone or betting a few dollars on promising technological ideas that might flop. Most did flop, or didn't succeed soon enough. McCaw liked AT&T's EO Personal Communicator, a small device that read handwriting, and Steve Jobs's black-cube NeXT computer, which featured an operating system to rival Microsoft's Windows. Both failed. But McCaw kept watching changes in technology, measuring each innovation against his sense of the future.

If McCaw had a vision of his role as a businessperson, it was to imagine what people would need in the future to make their lives better and then provide it. As he told the American Academy of Achievement:

> It's your job [as a businessperson] to think almost anthropologically about humanity and say, "What would be in their best interest?" And then try to get there first, and know that eventually they'll learn what you have is worth their while. If I ever got a vision in business it was that, the *Field of Dreams* mentality, and that's how I've really operated in my career. I've never worried whether somebody else thought it was the right thing. If I believed it was the right thing, then I was prepared to build it and hoped that "they would come" based upon [the fact that] if I were that person and I were in their circumstances, that I would appreciate what product was being created and it was worthwhile.

* * *

To fully understand how Craig McCaw looked at cellular telephones, it's useful to recall a bit of the history of radio.

Radio has been around since the early 1900s, and mobile two-way radio communications began in 1921 in Detroit police cars. In 1946 AT&T began offering mobile telephone service. Three years later, the FCC set aside spectrum for Radio Common Carriers (RCCs) to sell mobile phones and service in competition with AT&T.

Because of price, spectrum, and technology limitations, mobile telephones appealed to only a tiny percentage of car owners. The phones had to be custom-built, cost as much as $5,000, and required bulky equipment loaded into the trunk. They were also inconvenient to use: The caller had to contact an operator and request a clear channel and a specific phone number. However, by 1969 newer systems allowed a caller to push a button, hear a beep when a channel was clear, and simply dial a number.

Mobile telephones used various parts of the spectrum, depending on the transmission system. But no system for mobile phones provided much capacity or efficiency. The most commonly used system provided twelve or fewer channels and hogged a wide swath of spectrum. In order for both parties to hear each other simultaneously—full-duplex, as the technicians called it—the mobile phone system needed two frequencies, one to send and one to receive. Thus, a single mobile telephone conversation consumed a whopping 60 kilohertz of bandwidth over an area of 10,000 square miles or more. By comparison, an AM radio station might use a sixth of that spectrum width—10 kilohertz.

Customers typically waited a long time, sometimes hours, before a channel opened up. They found it nearly impossible to receive a call during peak hours. In some large cities, thousands of people couldn't get the service because of spectrum limitations. New York City's system could accept only 700 customers, and even that group experienced constant problems in getting a channel.

By the late 1970s an estimated 143,000 customers nationwide were using mobile telephone service, compared with an estimated 16 million using citizens band (CB) two-way radios. Carried over forty channels,

CB offered only scratchy voice quality, limited reception, and erratic service, but transmitters were cheap and airtime was free. Compared to CB, mobile telephones were a market failure, serving just one tenth of one percent of the nation's 160 million trucks and cars.

However, McCaw saw that the idea of the mobile telephone had promise. He knew that despite the obvious frustrations of mobile telephone service as it then existed, people appreciated the convenience when the balky systems worked. Everyone liked making calls from their cars. Equally important, McCaw himself used a mobile phone and loved it. For a free spirit like Craig McCaw, who preferred to come and go without schedules or interference, the liberating effect of wireless communication was exciting. He was impatient to see the devices improve. He knew they would—it was just a matter of a breakthrough. Eventually technology would catch up to the dream.

By 1974 cellular looked like that breakthrough.

AT&T's work on cellular had begun in the late 1940s, when Bell Labs came up with the idea of dividing a mobile telephone-service area into segments, or cells, that could be served with many low-powered transmitters rather than one big tower. The idea vastly expanded the potential number of users per channel. Capacity could grow by adding more cells with transmitters. As a single cellular telephone traveled across a service area, the system kept track and "handed" the call from one cell to another, thus allowing different cells to use the same frequencies. That meant a system in New York City, for example, could have thousands of simultaneous telephone conversations instead of the twelve allowed by the old mobile telephone system.

As Bell Labs improved its designs for switching the electronics of the cellular telephone, the system offered other benefits. A cellular telephone consumed much less power and could travel farther than a mobile phone, which relied on a single radio transmitter that covered an area up to twenty-five miles. And theoretically, a cellular phone could "roam" from city to city, crossing the nation without losing calls.

However, the cellular telephone relied on complex technology: a system for constantly monitoring the identity and whereabouts of each cellular telephone; a means of integrating the mobile phone with the switching system of the wired telephone network; and a reliable method of assigning the mobile phone from one cellular transmitter to another without signal interference. Each posed a technological challenge to be met before cellular would be truly practical.

Bell Labs tested its first cellular system in Newark, New Jersey, in 1974, and tried again with 100 Bell employees in Chicago in 1978. Still, no one at Bell Labs yet saw the cellular telephone as a major product, says Amos Joel, a key company scientist—they considered it a niche business. Nonetheless, in 1971 AT&T asked the FCC for permission to launch Advanced Mobile Phone Service (AMPS), a cellular service built around the company's standards, and to take a broad band of spectrum, including Channels 70 through 83 of ultrahigh frequency (UHF) television.

It would take a decade for the agency to sort through a host of spectrum issues, complicated by its continuing scrutiny of AT&T's monopoly over telephone service. These debates coincided with lobbying efforts by Microwave Communications of America (later known as MCI) to promote competition in telecommunications and with the 1974 Department of Justice antitrust suit against AT&T.

The FCC had several choices. It could award a monopoly over cellular service to AT&T, perhaps the quickest path of getting the service to consumers. It could disperse the service among many competitors, a route that might lead to patchy systems of poor quality. Or it could pick a middle ground.

Naturally, AT&T wanted the biggest slice of everything. It wanted all the licenses and hoped to act as a wholesaler for paging companies, which would serve as resellers of cellular service to customers. AT&T also expected to get a big share of the cellular equipment manufacturing business through its Western Electric subsidiary, a competitor with Motorola and Japan's Oki Electric.

The FCC was inclined to reward AT&T for its pioneering R&D efforts in cellular, yet it was reluctant to award an open-ended monopoly to any company. The resulting high-stakes battle illustrates how little-known government regulators can powerfully influence an industry. The news media gave scant attention to the early debate about cellular, and the public at the time knew little about decisions being made that would ultimately affect pricing of services for millions of consumers.

As the FCC issued conflicting statements about its intentions, everyone in the communications industry was confused. Until the agency announced how it would carve up the airwaves, no one knew how or whether to launch a cellular business to exploit the new opportunity. Would the process favor AT&T, newcomers, partnerships, or experienced communications companies? How many licenses would be issued for a given city? Would the cellular business look more like radio, with many competitors in a city, or like TV, with the field restricted to a few? The uncertainties made it difficult for Craig McCaw and others to raise money or make plans.

Finally, in 1979 the FCC issued a "Notice of Proposed Rulemaking" that revealed its tentative cellular policy.

The FCC would issue two licenses for each market, each with 20 megahertz of bandwidth. But the FCC still didn't know what to do and declared itself "not confident" that it had sufficient information to make a final judgment. Perhaps the entire 40 megahertz should be equally divided among applicants in each market, it said. Let consumers decide which provider survives.

Telocator, a publication of the paging industry, reported that paging companies were impatient with the FCC's slow process. As pioneers in wireless messaging, paging operators felt they deserved at least a share of the business, just as the market for earlier mobile telephones had been shared.

Thus, on that fall day in 1979, as Craig McCaw and nearly all of the Northwest's other paging operators arrived at a hotel in Tualatin, near Portland, Oregon, for a crucial meeting on the future of cellular, there were more questions than answers about the new business.

The assembled businesspeople listened to a presentation by representatives of Motorola, who were eager to claim a piece of the emerging industry. Many in the audience were impressed to hear about what cellular could do but were dismayed by what it would cost. A good paging system for a city like Seattle might cost $500,000 to build, but cellular would be several times more expensive. A system for Seattle would need at least eight cellular transmitters at $250,000 each. Adding a switching system and other costs would bring the total to $5 million or more—perhaps five times the gross annual revenue of a large paging company. "With cellular, it was hard to start cheap," Charlie Desmond says. "You had to spend tremendous amounts up front, plus there were no known lenders."

But the key question just hung there. Was everyone willing to let

AT&T get this business to itself? Someone at the Oregon conference suggested that the paging companies should band together, each contributing $10,000 to start a partnership. It might not lead to a license; it would be only a first step. But toward what? others asked. A $5 million start-up with no guarantee of profit? No one knew what the FCC would do. No one was certain exactly which technical version of cellular would be adopted. The entire field was fraught with uncertainties.

Many of the companies pondering the future of cellular were small, family-owned businesses; most of the owners were fearful of debt and risk. So many of those present at the Oregon conference said "No—forget it," and left, abandoning cellular to those with more nerve and a greater belief in cellular. A few others said they wanted to think it over. McCaw didn't hesitate. He committed his $10,000 for the partnership concept immediately.

Of course, in retrospect, it's easy to say that Craig McCaw always knew cellular would be a hit. Gordon Kelley, a paging operator who became one of McCaw's partners, insists it's true.

As they rode back to Seattle, the older men in the mobile home chatted about tidbits from the conference: what a cellular system would cost, which companies might enter the field, the technical issues. The money problem loomed above all others: Who could raise enough money to make a real impact in this new business, and where would the cash come from? Craig McCaw let them talk; he said little. Gordon Kelley remembers feeling that McCaw had locked onto something beyond the initial problems and issues; he was already energized towards a goal.

It seems likely that McCaw was thinking about the problem the way Elroy McCaw would have: How can I get started without putting much money down? "There was a sense about him that he was going to make something happen," Kelley says. McCaw's silence was perfectly reasonable. Does the magician explain his tricks? "He was always quiet . . . like a submarine," says Desmond.

8

"We Were Dreaming of Dick Tracy"

A Fraternity of Independents Takes on Ma Bell

In March 1980, even before the FCC decided how it would issue cellular telephone licenses, Craig McCaw formed a partnership called Northwest Mobile Telephone (later Interstate Mobilephone Company). Its purpose: to grab McCaw's share of those licenses.

McCaw had four partners: Gordon Kelley, the Tacoma *News Tribune* in Washington, John Raptor, and Charlie Desmond. Members of the group owned paging companies in Portland, Oregon; Tacoma, Seattle; and Centralia, Washington. Because the FCC had given conflicting accounts of the licensing rules, the group had no idea what they needed to do to win. But they knew they wanted licenses for Seattle and Portland. Just as paging companies tried to serve contiguous markets, Interstate Mobilephone planned to exploit cellular's roaming ability by providing service from Washington State's Canadian border south to Salem, Oregon.

Certain features distinguished Craig McCaw from the others in the partnership. Coupled with some lucky breaks, his talented staff, and other factors, those differences would make him a billionaire. The others would do well by their investments in the cellular frontier, but nothing like what McCaw did.

First, McCaw possessed an unshakable faith that cellular had a future. It wasn't just that the service seemed a likely hit with the public. His faith started with a fundamental belief in the value of spectrum. Though it was too early to know how much spectrum would be given to the lucky winning companies, everyone assumed it would be a sizable chunk, probably 20 megahertz to nonwireline companies. This was a gift of virgin territory, free from the government—something for nothing. If it had any value at all, it would be money from thin air.

"It's got to be worth something, for God's sake," McCaw said. "Look how much there is."

Second, the idea of cellular service connected with McCaw's sense of people's yearnings. He felt that people, deep down, preferred to roam, unrestricted to fixed places. The telephone tied them down. As he would later explain, cellular let humans become nomads, the lifestyle he himself preferred.

"You learn and you see an opportunity—a gap between what is and what should be. If one thinks in anthropological terms, if you go towards what should be, then eventually things will get there and you just have to work out the timing," McCaw says:

> With cellular telephony, in particular, we saw an enormous gap between what was and what should be. I mean, [the fixed phone system] makes absolutely no sense. It is machines dominating human beings. The idea that people went to a small cubicle, a six-by-ten office, and sat there all day at the end of a six-foot cord was anathema to me. If one thing is obvious, people will pay, will contribute something for control of their lives, the right to choose. And I think if we saw anything in cellular telephone, it was that people were being subjugated needlessly to 1890s technology.

Third, McCaw would take risks to deliver on his vision. While his partners were cautious about committing money to cellular, once McCaw saw appropriate controls on his risks, he was willing to put up the money far sooner and in far bigger amounts than his partners then (or his rivals later). McCaw's ability to deliver flowed from his experience in cable, where the smart players were highly leveraged. If spectrum was an asset to be gathered, McCaw would play Monopoly, collecting as many licenses as he could. By borrowing to buy those assets, "he played with other people's money," says Richard Callahan, who ran US West's first cellular operation and closely monitored McCaw's growth.

Fourth, the fundamental structure of McCaw's business empire served the vision. His emphasis on control, flexibility, and focus on essentials rather than details kept him poised to exploit opportunities. For example, although McCaw wanted to get Seattle and Portland operating licenses, he didn't spend much time at Interstate Mobilephone's partnership meetings. McCaw sent his kid brother Keith to most of the early sessions, and other aides later on. Keith was not regarded as a major business figure; he was there to monitor the situation and report back to Craig, who made himself available for decisions.

At times, McCaw's absences annoyed his partners, but his representatives made it clear that McCaw intended to go on protecting his time. "Nobody had a lot of contact with McCaw," says Charlie Desmond. Yet they knew "McCaw would think bigger than the rest of us." That made it worthwhile to put up with his eccentricities.

By 1980 McCaw had made the calculation that the FCC ultimately would issue two licenses in each market. Knowing how government followed tradition, he also expected that the cellular licensing process would resemble the licensing of television in the late 1940s and 1950s—that is, a system of comparative hearings that favored applicants that could demonstrate a combination of financial wherewithal, technical ability, public service, and community roots. To strengthen his own candidacy for a Seattle license under such a competitive system, McCaw bought a feeble Seattle paging company from the Diamond family, which owned a large parking-lot business. It helped that the Diamonds already knew the McCaw family. "We did the deal in about five minutes," McCaw says. This gave him a foothold in the Seattle community.

The Diamonds' paging company served fewer than 600 customers; it transmitted from a condominium without a city permit, and its accounts were stored in an old shoe box. The system was so underutilized that no one noticed when it was shut down for four days to transfer operations. Yet all of that mattered little. McCaw never doubted that he could grow the operation; after all, it couldn't do any worse. He combined his paging companies under a name that suggested he was looking to buy more, Western Telepage. Most important, this tiny new entity held an FCC license and served the primary market McCaw wanted for cellular.

Meanwhile, a separate competition was taking shape on the technological front. While everyone waited for the FCC to get moving with formal approval for the AT&T design for cellular, a rival proposal had surfaced—one with much grander potential and risk.

In 1979 Interstate received a call from one of the most energetic players in radio communications, Peter Erb. President of Millicom, a small New York cellular technology company, Erb was a cocky engineer who spoke with an Austrian accent. Now he was going around the country, urging paging operators to dump AT&T's cellular design. Erb was pushing a digital system that broke voice signals into computerized units, rather than AT&T's analog method, which worked more like old radio-wave transmissions. His alternative system, Erb said, would save cellular companies and consumers huge amounts of money. Digital cellular phones could send and receive both voice and data signals, and they would cost a fraction of AT&T's phones. At $300 to $400 each, these alternative phones would be able to compete in price with pagers, Erb said.

Erb's vision went far beyond what others saw in cellular. His digital systems would be cheap enough to install in rural areas as an alternative to wired telephones. Erb talked about an entire national network of wireless telephones that would completely bypass the regulated telephone network. It was an astonishing idea that ran counter to conventional wisdom, legal precedents, regulatory tradition, and AT&T's powerful influence over the entire communications industry, including the FCC. Erb said he would assign a city to anyone who paid his fee of $100,000.

As Charlie Desmond recalls, Erb made a strong argument, predicting that the FCC would drag its feet for years on AT&T's cellular design. "Go with my system instead," Desmond recalls Erb saying. "Get 2,000 customers and the FCC won't dare shut you down." But paging operators like Desmond were fearful of spending money on Erb's system only to be halted by the government. Disgusted, Erb dismissed the paging operators as small-minded "pants pressers."

By contrast, McCaw was dazzled. He saw himself as a visionary and admired the equivalent scope of Erb's ideas.

"Peter Erb was an absolute genius," McCaw says. But, he adds, Erb had a huge blind spot. "He understood everything but U.S. politics. He [thought he] was going to steal the licenses from the FCC and put [his system] in service and none of the politicians would fight it." McCaw liked Erb's system but knew that the FCC would never allow anyone to launch it on the public airwaves without approval. "That was a bridge too far," McCaw says. So he wouldn't do a deal with Erb. (Years later,

Erb said, the industry moved closer to his vision of integrated nation-wide service, but only after spending billions on an outmoded idea.)

Erb learned an important lesson about Craig McCaw: Much as McCaw enjoyed new technology and unconventional thinking, his sense of the future always had to match the realities not only of the consumer and what he might buy, but also of the regulatory environment. Just as Elroy McCaw had needed the FCC to approve the trading of broadcasting licenses for his enrichment, his son now needed to navigate the city, state, and federal regulators who could bless or doom his initiatives. So although Craig McCaw disdained politics, he took pains to show his respect for the regulators.

McCaw believed he was well positioned in April 1981, when the Federal Communications Commission, after thirteen years of delay and wavering, decided to finally begin the process of licensing cellular telephones. Forecasting a fairly quick process, acting FCC chairman Robert E. Lee called the vote one of the most significant in his twenty-eight years on the commission. "This action promoted communication competition benefiting all Americans," he said. "And this really is the coming of a new era. Dick Tracy comes true."—a reference to the wrist telephone long worn by the jut-jawed comic strip hero.

Eager to get the new technology into the hands of consumers, the FCC picked a process and technical standards that mainly favored AT&T. Ma Bell received an enormous chunk of the public's airwaves, the equivalent of several television licenses for every major city in the United States. The commission allowed AT&T's Western Electric division to manufacture cellular equipment and allowed Bell to build and operate cellular systems through its twenty-three local operating companies. However, it forbade AT&T to use profits from its traditional phone service to subsidize cellular operations.

In giving the established wireline companies (AT&T and the smaller General Telephone & Electronics, or GTE) half of the 40 megahertz of spectrum set aside for cellular telephones, the FCC alarmed critics of the telecommunications giant's clout. The Justice Department called the move "blatantly anticompetitive," saying it locked AT&T into a dominant position in the infant industry. But the FCC said its plan would help competition by guaranteeing that consumers would have a choice in each city.

Others claimed that the FCC's decision to adopt AT&T's technology would doom consumers to a needlessly costly system. The commission had rejected pleas by Peter Erb to assign the full 40 megahertz for nonexclusive use, an approach he said would have lower costs than AT&T's system (whose trial in Chicago had cost the average consumer $155 a month). "By its action, the commission has in effect given AT&T the right to control the market for portable telephones, the only available alternative to the present phone service," said Erb.

Erb threatened a court challenge. But he could not block the AT&T juggernaut, and his alternative system never caught on. Today it is merely a footnote in technology history.

The giveaway to AT&T and GTE came with one condition reflecting the FCC's desire for swift construction of the systems. If the phone company did not apply to operate a system within five years, then any company would be allowed to use the frequency. But AT&T said it would move fast, starting its first cellular system by 1983. By the mid-1980s, it would be operating cellular in seventy major cities, the company said.

The FCC also announced that it would hasten the start of competitive bidding for the other half of the cellular frequency, a process that would involve hearings and the weighing of each applicant's merits. The FCC gave potential applicants less than three months to prepare and submit paperwork, an extremely brief period for such detailed work. GTE, the nation's second largest phone company, said it would file for licenses to serve several cities.

That same year, McCaw hired Edwin Hopper, who proved to be another example of McCaw's ability to find people whose skills perfectly matched a need at a given time. Initially a consultant on the cable side, Hopper soon eased Keith McCaw aside and took charge of the cellular initiative, first part-time, then as de facto chief executive of what Hopper called a "skunk works"—a kind of laboratory for creative ideas—with big ambitions but very little money.

Around the office, Hopper was called "Gray Hair" because he was several years older than McCaw's other boyish managers, who still got second looks when they tried to rent cars. Hopper put in long hours and brought a high level of energy and competitiveness to the business. A maverick who had worked for the Arthur Andersen accounting firm as well as the cable and telephone businesses, Hopper lived in Oregon and commuted to Bellevue for the next seven years. Where the company placed its desks and files made little difference to Hopper, since he spent most of his life in airplanes.

Even before cellular began serving the public, McCaw and Hopper both shared a complete faith in its future, which involved three central beliefs:

First, consumer costs for cellular would fall dramatically. In 1981 Hopper visited E. F. Johnson, a Waseca, Minnesota–based maker of radio equipment, and learned how a simple economics principle would benefit cellular telephones. How cheap can these phones get? he asked. A Johnson executive held up a $69 CB radio and a $2,300 cellular telephone that the company had recently made for AT&T's trials. The only difference between the two, he told Hopper, was a $25 smart chip and a long production run. Stunned, Hopper realized that a cell phone eventually would cost less than $100.

Second, cellular would virtually sell itself. For years, McCaw had used a mobile phone, a bulky precursor to cellular phones. Both he and Hopper were convinced that once people tried cellular phones, assuming a reasonable price, they wouldn't want to give them up. Even apart from all the other arguments of convenience and freedom, that plague of urban life—traffic congestion—would sell car phones to trapped businesspeople eager to connect with distant families and colleagues.

Third, cellular operators would need only a relatively small market penetration to make a profit. A cellular system would not be costly to operate. A study done in the early 1980s by the accounting firm Ernst & Whinney (later Ernst & Young) showed that a system would break even if fewer than 1 percent of the people in a community signed up. That compared with more than 40 percent market penetration needed for a cable TV system to break even.

Hopper and McCaw were amazed at the dimensions of the government's planned frequency giveaway. No one knew the licenses' exact value, but Hopper made a rough calculation based on what TV stations, which used much less frequency, were selling for—about $250 million for one midsize station. He figured that the cellular frequency given to non-Bell applicants in the first thirty markets alone was worth $16 billion.

Others saw money in cellular, but also huge start-up costs and risks, especially in facing an AT&T operating company as a competitor. Lehman Brothers Kuhn Loeb Research estimated that cellular telephone usage would generate $2.7 billion in annual revenues in the top thirty-five markets by 1987. It based its revenue estimate on an average customer billing of $150 a month and on 1.5 million customers in the first full year of operation. It cited an AT&T prediction that cellular telephones would fall in price to $1,200 each within a brief period. Costs for transmission equipment, Lehman Brothers noted, would also fall. Rather than $14 million to build a system to serve 10,000 customers, as AT&T predicted, the cost would likely be $7 million.

Lehman Brothers acknowledged that starting cellular systems was expensive, but it concluded that making money in the top thirty-five systems was "easily achievable." With a system financed half by debt, a company could break even when 1,000 customers on average paid $184 a month.

They cautioned, however, about accepting anybody's estimates. AT&T, Motorola, and *Telocator* all gave dramatically different revenue forecasts. AT&T projected 233,096 customers in the first year of service in New York City. For the same market, Motorola predicted 104,940 by the year 2000, while *Telocator* predicted 54,105 after twelve years of operation. Despite those differences, Lehman Brothers thought cellular would be a good business, even allowing for variances in cost and usage estimates. "We believe that [cellular telephone service] will be a large and growing business in the 1980s," it declared.

But what did that mean for Craig McCaw and others hoping to outduel a Bell company? Tough competition and uncertainty, concluded Lehman Brothers. First, AT&T's subsidiaries would certainly get at least half of the cellular revenue. Then the forthcoming process by which the FCC awarded licenses would be "extremely complicated," likely leading to "comparative hearings, lawsuits and appeal" among many applicants.

By the time 1982 arrived, interest in cellular had expanded beyond the fraternity of paging operators who did business with the FCC. Entrepreneurs arrived who would play different roles in the pioneer days of cellular. Some shared McCaw's excitement about cellular and wanted to bring it to the public. Others simply saw cellular as another good business. Many became allies, partners, and rivals of McCaw's as they sought and later traded licenses. Much more aggressive than the paging operators, these businesspeople would place some of the biggest cellular bets and reap huge rewards. And as McCaw's appetite for licenses grew, their license collections became increasingly important to his eventual goal of building a national network.

The new nonpaging players included New Yorker George Lindemann, who had made one fortune in pharmaceuticals and then another in the cable TV industry. As a big licensee of radio units for cable-service trucks, he had learned about the FCC; Motorola told him about cellular, which seemed to be a service that would sell easily. "Anyone sitting in a car for an hour would want to use it," says Lindemann. "This wasn't hard to figure out."

The portly Lindemann looked and acted like a character lifted from the pages of a Raymond Chandler detective novel. He chain-smoked cigars and in gruff, smoke-roughened tones volunteered blistering assessments of his business rivals. Craig McCaw was an exception. Through shared contacts in cable TV and a lawyer who represented both of them in FCC matters, Lindemann had come to know and like McCaw, whom he regarded as pleasant, brilliant, unique. Lindemann once joked that the only reason he owned a company was to have an excuse to lunch with people such as McCaw. "Whenever you had lunch with Craig McCaw, you'd come away with a new concept or an idea," says Lindemann. To those who thought McCaw was often impractical, Lindemann would scoff, "So we're all dreamers. So what? If we weren't dreamers, we wouldn't be in this business."

McCaw and Lindemann shared a respect for the Bell companies' money and other resources, but they did not fear them in the entrepreneurial game. "They were frozen from the neck down. Or maybe from the nose down," Lindemann says. "They couldn't do anything. They might have thought something, but it never got into reality. They'd write memos to people who wrote the next memos. Nothing ever got done."

Yet when Lindemann asked bankers to back him in cellular, the answer was no. Why would anyone want to buy a car phone, the bankers reasoned, when he could pull over and use a pay phone? Lindemann concluded that he would have to finance his cellular bid without help from the banks. He and McCaw discussed forming a partnership to apply for cellular licenses, but nothing came of it. Instead, Lindemann formed a company called Metro Mobile CTS that became a huge player.

Another influential player was John Kluge, who had already made one of the nation's largest fortunes with Metromedia, a television, radio, and billboard company. After hearing a tip about cellular, Stuart Subotnick, Kluge's partner, went down to Washington, D.C., to ask lawyers who followed the FCC about this new technology. Subotnick came back a believer.

"I thought this was not going to be a high-end business," Subotnick said later. "Anything in technology would come down [in price]. This filled an absolute need for salespeople and business executives and, when the pricing got down far enough, for women drivers in case their cars break down." But Kluge and Subotnick rejected the view that cellular would be a product used only in cars. They believed that the phones would shrink to pocket size and would be carried everywhere. "We were dreaming of Dick Tracy and being able to talk to your watch," Subotnick says. "How many chances in your life do you get to come in as a pioneer in new technology?"

To his surprise, Subotnick found the new industry free of formidable competition on the nonwireline side, where no major corporations were preparing applications. Westinghouse, RCA, ITT, and other technology giants were staying out, apparently assuming that they could not compete with AT&T. Instead, most applicants were small mom-and-pop paging companies. Subotnick liked the idea of facing a field of weak rivals.

Knowing that it had come late to the game, Metromedia decided to buy paging companies that planned to submit cellular applications. In cities where Metromedia wanted to license, Subotnick planned to buy those companies with the best cellular applications. Racing against a starting gun, he began meeting with a series of families who were emotionally attached to their companies. To get a quick sale, he offered as much as 50 percent over the company's value. Many astonished applicants quickly agreed to sell. "He was the smart one," Craig McCaw said later.

Kluge bought paging companies in New York City, Dallas, Boston, Chicago, Los Angeles, and the Baltimore–Washington, D.C. area. He heard that another New York City paging company had an application calling for more cellular transmitters and, thinking it might prove to be important, he bought that company, too. The buying spree cost $300 million and made Metromedia the nation's largest paging company. But this position carried no certain benefit. "We didn't know how the FCC was going to judge all this," Subotnick admits. It was one of many calculated gambles being made in the early days of this New Age gold rush.

Also in New York City, three former officials with the FCC had formed a new company, Cellular Communications Incorporated (CCI), to go after licenses. Their main asset was familiarity with FCC procedures and rules. The group included William Ginsberg, former deputy chief for policy in the Common Carrier Bureau; Thomas Casey, former deputy chief for operations in the carrier bureau; and Charles Ferbis, former commission chairman. All three had helped develop the FCC's cellular rules. Ginsberg, the company president, brought in George Blumenthal, an old high school friend whose family owned a securities firm, to serve as treasurer. Paging companies offering a one-way service had begun to rapidly gain value in the late 1970s, so Blumenthal figured a two-way service would also be attractive to consumers.

Ginsberg, Kluge, and Craig McCaw all knew they had to submit applications with certain essential features. The FCC would want evidence that an applicant knew a given market's needs and could build a quality system. That meant hiring engineers, market researchers, and lawyers to prepare exhibits, as well as proving that money was available to build the system.

But the players had to guess about what the FCC would want beyond these basics. How much proof of financing would be needed? Would an independent company need the participation of a big-name partner? How thorough did an exhibit have to be? Did a company's prior presence in a given market make a difference? Did the FCC favor applicants with experience in telecommunications or new entrants? Could an applicant plan on holding down costs by covering only high-density areas, or should it promise to spend more to immediately reach into the suburbs? No one knew for sure, not even former FCC official Ginsberg, because the process would be handed to individual administrative law judges who could interpret things differently. A process for Seattle could go differently from one for Miami.

Even as the FCC got closer to issuing licenses, its policies remained vague. In its list of "decision-making criteria," the FCC said compar-

isons could include assessments of applicants' "personnel and practices." Potential applicants studied news articles in the trade press to
look for clues, but that proved frustrating. A staff member or a commissioner might give contradictory statements. Anonymous sources
predicted that politics and influence would color the process, leading to
lawsuits and delays. "The rules were so indefinite, no one knew what
the hell they were filing," says George Lindemann.

McCaw, however, felt less worried about the uncertainties. Having
dealt with cities and counties over cable TV franchises, he felt he could
anticipate what regulators would most want for cellular: community
service. Perhaps the trade-offs would not be as specific as requiring a
cable company to plant trees in a local park, as Sacramento had. But
McCaw knew that engineering studies and financing only contributed
to the important point: that an applicant promise service to the broad-
est audience possible. That meant his application should envision many
cell sites covering a broad area. "I knew from cable you had to promise
big dreams," McCaw says. "Take care of people. That's what [regula-
tors] want to see."

As 1982 began, the players in cellular rushed to get their applications ready, certain that the FCC would soon start accepting applications. In March the FCC said it would take applications in just ninety
days, on June 7, for the top thirty markets. To prevent endless amend-
ments, the agency said applications would be accepted only that day,
not before or after. If a party missed the deadline to submit a complete
application, too bad.

By pure luck, John Stanton, who was to be a major figure in Craig
McCaw's future, now knocked on the door. The only child of his Belle-
vue parents, Stanton had attended Newport High School and Whitman
College in Walla Walla, Washington. After graduation from the
Harvard Business School, Stanton had returned to the Northwest and
begun working in Tacoma, Washington, as a consultant with Ernst &
Whinney's telecommunications practice.

Stanton was a restless, driven, and brilliant personality who seized
upon a task and worked straight through, often without sleep. He could
be charming and charismatic or abrasive. He pushed others to match his
pace, but few could. He ran complex calculations in his head. "John
Stanton's idea of rounding is four decimal points," says Wayne Perry,

whose own phenomenal memory ran second to Stanton's in the McCaw organization. Stanton could recall events and facts to an amazing degree. He could recall the date of a flight taken years earlier or the phone number of a casual acquaintance from the distant past.

When John Stanton walked into McCaw Communications, he was a young associate determined to make partner at his accounting firm by finding and seizing an area of expertise. Almost as soon as he heard about cellular, Stanton realized he had found his niche. (He later founded his own national cellular company, Western Wireless.) Stanton now came to McCaw with an idea for funding cellular by adapting a form of lending analysis used in the cable industry. This was key because potential investors or lenders needed a reference point to understand a new business where profits were distant. As Stanton later recalled, he met first with Keith McCaw, who didn't say much in response. "Wait a minute," Keith finally said, leaving the room.

Keith came back escorting Ed Hopper, who looked at Stanton's papers, listened to his pitch, and instantly liked the idea. "You're hired," said Hopper. "Can you have a team here tomorrow?"

The next day, Stanton returned with four people, including an Ernst & Whinney partner with a steep hourly rate. Hopper walked in. Without any chitchat, he got down to business. "I don't need any of your time," Hopper said, pointing to the partner. Then he pointed to Stanton, then the associates: "I'll need all of your time, and as much of their time as you think you'll need." Stanton was impressed by how quickly Hopper had eliminated the largest—and least necessary—expense.

In the final months before the FCC filing deadline, a stronger group of players surfaced, better financed and more aggressive than the local paging companies. Cox Communications, MCI Telecommunications Corporation, Associated Communications, and Communications Industries entered the fray. Then there was Barry Yampol, president of Graphic Scanning, who frankly wanted to dominate the new industry. He told *Broadcasting Magazine* that he had had forty-five people working on cellular applications for three years at a cost of $10 million and that he had $136 million in cash to further his plans. He wouldn't reveal all the uses for his war chest, "but obviously we didn't put in all this effort in order to file one application," he said.

MCI, the self-styled rival to AT&T's long-distance monopoly, announced it would go for a dozen or more licenses and would also buy Western Union International and its Airsignal paging subsidiary, which planned to apply for another eleven markets. "We would like to be in the long lines for the cellular radio business," an MCI spokesman said. MCI publicly revealed its strategy in order to pressure the FCC to favor it over small paging companies. With a $300 million line of credit for cellular, MCI claimed that it alone had the size to effectively compete against AT&T's local telephone companies.

But the two players on the wireline side were strengthening their positions as well. To avoid competition for their side of the spectrum, AT&T and GTE secretly cut a deal. On June 8 AT&T said it had decided to bid on just twenty-three of the major markets, leaving the other seven to GTE. By not opposing each other's applications, they all but guaranteed which markets they would win. It gave them a huge head start in building their systems to start service for the public.

For independents like McCaw's partnership, which would be tied up in application maneuvers before the FCC or in court for months or possibly longer, it was lousy news.

"I Can't Go to Bed Owing Somebody
a Billion Dollars"

McCaw Hangs On While Others Lose Their Nerve

In the wee hours of June 7, 1982, Charlie Desmond, one of Craig McCaw's allies in the war on the cellular frontier, finally went to bed in his Washington, D.C., hotel room. The next day, after a fitful few hours of sleep, Desmond would walk over to the offices of the Federal Communications Commission to deliver Interstate Mobilephone Company's cellular applications for the Portland and Seattle markets.

It had been a hectic week, full of worries about the maneuvers of rival applicants and culminating in a midnight meeting at a lawyer's office to check and recheck Interstate's paperwork. The partnership had left nothing to chance, considering even the possibility of random crime or sabotage. Fearing that someone could break into the Interstate lawyer's office and steal the application, Desmond slept with a complete copy at his hotel room.

Desmond worried, but McCaw did not. "He was back in Seattle. Craig never did paperwork," says Desmond. And after all, he still had a cable business to run.

When he arrived at the offices of the FCC, Desmond witnessed the most chaotic scene he had ever seen. Dozens of men and women crowded the hallways, carrying boxes of paperwork on hand trucks. Some were on their hands and knees, hastily collating last-minute sheaves. Outside, taxicabs were pulling up, disgorging stressed-out lawyers toting more boxes. Some applicants had even sent backup copies of their paperwork by plane or train. No one wanted to miss this deadline.

Thirty-three-year-old Craig McCaw, nine years out of college and the owner of a collection of tiny cable TV companies, was poised with others at the start of a fabulous race for the gold. Many of his rivals had more experience, more financing, more reputation, more reasons to expect victory. Nearly any of them was a surer bet than dark horse Craig McCaw.

"The land rush begins today," *Broadcasting Magazine* reported. "Hordes of hungry competitors are battling for licenses to get rich quick."

That exaggerated the situation slightly, for the truly big crowds of speculators were still to come. But this morning's crush was hectic enough. Desmond had to step over secretaries, messengers, and $400-an-hour lawyers to get to the FCC counter, where he deposited Interstate Mobilephone's boxload of documents—five cubic feet of paper, counting the original and four copies. Unlike a paging application, which might run twenty pages, a cellular application required hundreds of pages. Some applications had cost hundreds of thousands of dollars to prepare. Interstate's marketing study alone filled an entire binder. AT&T's applications arrived by truck, totaling 57,600 pages. That day, 191 applications were filed for the thirty markets, an average of about six per city. The size of a city did not necessarily correlate with the number of applications. Chicago had only two, while Tampa, Florida, had eleven. Just finding room for the paper proved burdensome for the FCC.

With or without partners, Craig McCaw had also filed in San Francisco, San Jose, Denver, and Kansas City. There was no elaborate strategy behind his choices. He loved San Francisco, and you couldn't go for that city without also trying for San Jose; Denver and Kansas City had good demographics (a high percentage of mobile professionals) but weren't sexy enough to attract much competition. McCaw went for only six cities because that was all he thought he could handle. McCaw always thought big, but never beyond his grasp.

To show the FCC financial strength, he cobbled together different balance sheets from partners, lenders, and even Daniels & Associates, his broker for cable properties. It was an aggressive bid for McCaw's little company, though the idea of going for a national cellular presence came only much later. "We weren't *that* arrogant," says Wayne Perry.

As soon as the applications came in, everyone looked around to see who had filed and where. The results were astonishing. Wayne Perry was shocked that not one of the big technology companies, such as

Boeing, Hewlett-Packard, IBM, or EDS had applied. Neither had Disney, nor any television or radio network. He and McCaw thought cellular was going to be a huge business for commuters, yet no car companies had applied. If General Motors had installed a car phone in each of its cars, the unit costs would have plummeted and GM would have jump-started the industry. Perry later said that revenue from GM's cellular business could have exceeded its car revenue.

The filings revealed some guesswork and colossal errors, but also hard work and brilliance and dumb luck. Some applicants had over-strategized. Assuming that others would go for the large markets, many applied elsewhere, leaving only a few applications in some large markets and many in smaller markets. In Chicago and Boston, for example, only two applied, while in New York City, Philadelphia, Washington-Baltimore, and Los Angeles, four or five applied.

As his strategy for Metro Mobile CTS, George Lindemann simply applied where he expected the fewest competitors. He avoided New York City and filed for Tampa. He also applied for Miami, which drew thirteen applications, and for Phoenix, San Diego, Cleveland, Denver, Minneapolis, and Kansas City. He had been following no grand design, he said later. He simply submitted as many applications as he could prepare with his limited staff. The Washington Post Company, which was slow in deciding on cellular, applied for Washington-Baltimore, Detroit, and Miami.

Boston proved to be McCaw's lost opportunity. Only two had applied there, Graphic Scanning and Kluge's Metromedia. McCaw had wanted Affiliated—with its ownership of *The Boston Globe*, its cash, its political clout, and its great image—to join him in applying for Boston. But Affiliated did not share McCaw's enthusiasm for cellular. In fact, it worried that its cable partner was being distracted by cellular. "Poor Affiliated didn't get the opportunity," says McCaw.

Affiliated had another reason to avoid cellular: fear of another license battle. They had spent fifteen years in court battling the Choate family over a TV license in Boston. The Choates already owned the *Boston Herald*. Affiliated feared that if the Choates won, they would use the TV revenue to bolster the *Herald* and destroy the *Globe*. Affiliated had claimed that the TV license would give the Choates too much power in Boston, the very argument that could be turned against them in a cellular hearing. Affiliated preferred putting its extra cash into buying newspapers. "Despite what the analysts said, there still was uncertainty" in cellular, explains Dan Orr, Affiliated's vice president for acquisitions.

McCaw's impatience with Affiliated would lead him to other funders for his cellular dreams. Within ten years, that Boston cellular license would be worth $798 million.

Graphic Scanning, a large paging company, emerged as the infant industry's biggest player on the nonwireline side. It stunned everyone by arriving at the FCC with two semitrailers carrying paperwork for all thirty markets, including Seattle. Chief executive Barry Yampol promised quality service at low rates. While most applicants said they would charge $25 to $30 a month for basic service, with airtime at 15 to 30 cents per minute, Yampol said he would charge just $4.95 a month, plus 30 cents a minute for airtime. Many in the new industry regarded Yampol as a disreputable operator. At McCaw Communications, they called his company "Graphic Scamming." But Yampol wasn't interested in making friends and called his critics "fools or liars."

That proved to be the first shot in a war among the competing cellular applicants. In the competitive hearings held by the FCC, there would be no oral testimony. Instead, in lengthy filing documents, each applicant picked apart its rivals. The strategy involved finding a weak point such as shaky financing and loudly proclaiming it to the FCC. The attacked applicant would file a reply making its own attack. The papers piled higher. Someone compared the process to getting everyone to stand in a circle and shoot at one another.

Interstate and others took a hit of sorts even before anyone had time to read the applications. As a gag, the FCC staff had given out informal awards for the packaging of applications. Some had come dressed up in fancy binding. Others arrived as stacks of paper secured with rubber bands. The staff summarily tossed out a Chicago application that bore too much similarity to AT&T's trial system application. Deciding that the applicant had simply changed a few words in the AT&T paperwork, the staff issued the "Imitation Is the Highest Form of Flattery Award."

A useful, minutely detailed index by a law firm received the "Green Beret Award to Most Well-Organized Law Firm." The heftiest earned the "Georgia-Pacific Fallen Tree Award for Largest Single Application."

The applicant that literally tossed in the Philadelphia Yellow Pages won the "Richard M. Nixon Memorial Wretched Excess Award." The staff awarded an applicant who submitted a five-inch-thick binder the "Thundering Brontosaurus Award for Largest Single Binder." Ram Broadcasting's Artcom division, a Seattle applicant, took a hit for its cheap cover, winning the "Penny-Wise, Pound-Foolish Award for Worst-Quality Binders." And Interstate Mobilephone's appealing cover art, featuring a map of the Northwest with eleven planned cellular transmitters, won the "Brooke Shields Most Attractive Cover Award."

Sensing an advantage to Interstate Mobilephone, Ram Broadcasting formally protested the awards, according to Charlie Desmond. Ram asked the FCC to throw out Interstate's elegant binder and replace it with a plain manila cover. "That's the shit we got into," says Desmond.

But Interstate Mobilephone played the game, too. In Seattle, Interstate faced off against Graphic Scanning and Ram's Artcom division. In Portland, it faced MCI, Ram, and a partnership representing a family who owned lumberyards. To defeat these rivals, they looked for flaws in the opposing applications. Was there an error in an engineering report? A gap in a market study? Desmond checked the rivals' claims. If they identified a planned cell site, he visited its owners and asked whether they knew they had agreed to have a ninety-foot pole hung with metal tubes defacing their property. In some cases, the owners would sign a paper canceling their previous deal that Desmond filed with the FCC, forcing the rivals to hunt for new cell sites. Meanwhile, to solidify Interstate's own site agreements, Desmond fully briefed property owners and gave each a $200 down payment.

In June 1982 the FCC began the slow process of scheduling comparative hearings for the first thirty markets. Five months later, the FCC accepted applications for the next thirty markets, a process called Round Two. This time, about 350 applications came in for markets such as Akron, Sacramento, Albany-Schenectady, and Orlando. For the nonwireline side, the applications averaged out to about twelve per market. In March 1983 about 550 applications came in for Round Three markets such as Fresno, Tacoma, Omaha, and El Paso, averaging about seventeen per market. West Palm Beach, Florida, drew twenty-three applications.

The paperwork piled ever higher until the FCC simply ran out of storage space. At one FCC warehouse in Gettysburg, Pennsylvania, steel shelving collapsed from the weight.

For applicants in Round One, the hearing process became a game of chicken to see who would fold first as costs rose. Interstate Mobilephone's costs during the hearings hit $1 million, double what it had expected. The costs began to worry McCaw's partners, who admitted they lacked his nerve. The money owed to lenders kept rising, but that didn't seem to bother McCaw. "I can't go to bed owing somebody a billion dollars . . . but he could," says Gordon Kelley.

Charlie Desmond especially resented Ram Broadcasting's attorney, who gave the impression that his influence over the FCC meant others should concede the field. Desmond wondered whether they should accept a buyout offer from Ram. The hearings caused a serious drain on the small paging companies. But Interstate's lawyer in Washington, D.C., remained hopeful. "We're going to kill 'em," he kept saying.

Interstate was emboldened by the arrival of the Washington Post Company and its deep pockets. After a belated decision to get into cellular, the Post Company decided to join a Round One applicant with promising filings and offered $1 million for a one-sixth interest in Interstate Mobile's two applications. McCaw considered the offer too low— a vivid and early demonstration of his faith in cellular and his willingness to bear losses. "I don't want to muddy the deal, but you're selling too cheap," McCaw warned his partners. Still, he recognized the pressure they felt. "McCaw was more comfortable facing all these dollars than we were. He was accustomed to being in debt from cable," Desmond says. Offer accepted, the Post joined the partnership in October 1982.

Work began to accelerate. As hearings continued over the Round One applications, McCaw Communications had to place its bets for Rounds Two and Three. Each new bet meant higher legal and other costs. John Stanton, the Harvard MBA working as a consultant, urged in December 1982 that the company expand its horizons. McCaw had been planning to apply for five markets in Round Three, but Stanton argued that the FCC comparative hearings process would collapse. The agency would have to switch to another approach that would favor volume, he predicted. "We have to get our chits in," he said. Try for fifteen markets.

McCaw's response was unequivocal: He hired Stanton as a permanent employee and told him to go for it. It was classic Craig McCaw logic; the mere fact that McCaw Communications didn't have the money to build even one cellular system was no reason not to aim for many more.

Stanton was an amazing workhorse, but even he was staggered by how much work lay ahead. For the next three months, he worked sixteen-hour days without a single day off. He hired a team of people to visit the markets, to quickly scout for good transmitter sites, and to sign hastily drafted agreements with property holders. The company was in such a rush that when Ed Hopper met a bright clerk at a hotel, he offered her a job starting the next day. She became the site selection coordinator.

Another employee with experience in political campaigns hired college students to form a phone bank and call people in selected markets for demographic data. The students dialed every tenth number in the phone book, asking what people would pay for a cellular phone and how often they would use it. That approach cost far less than the $50,000 a professional surveyor would have charged. The reports were prepared by hand, in the era before personal computers, word processing programs, and automated spelling checkers. A secretary typing the reports got by on four hours of sleep. "Wichita" was misspelled on the cover of the application, a potentially devastating error caught and corrected just twenty-four hours before the deadline.

As the McCaw company's cellular ambitions grew, so did its appetite for cash. The nascent cellular division at this time employed about a dozen people and earned no profit. Each new application accelerated expenses, while winning licenses meant system construction costs and even bigger losses for years. How to fund those losses? Bankers refused to lend for cellular speculation. Why should they put their money at risk? skeptics asked. No one really knew what profits the cellular business could produce—if any. The projections were guesswork. The big telephone companies would dominate the business. Independents like Craig McCaw would do no better than the independent paging companies had.

Finally, with the help of Tim David of Daniels & Associates, Hopper found a potential money source. E. W. Scripps, a family-controlled newspaper company, wanted to put some money into cellular as a purely speculative investment. But how much? Craig McCaw controlled 55 percent of his company, but he would never give up control, so what could he offer Scripps?

One day in September 1983, John Stanton, Wayne Perry, Ed Hopper, and Craig McCaw sat brainstorming in McCaw's Bellevue office. It was a typical McCaw session. McCaw had already mastered the art of analyzing others' motivations. Did Scripps want to be operators of a cellular system? To compete with a Bell company? No—it wanted only to make a good return on its investment.

Stanton had a brilliant idea, suggested by a case he had studied at the Harvard Business School, in which British Petroleum had merged with Sohio, an American oil company. The deal required that a value be set on the oil rights BP owned in Alaska's North Slope, yet neither party knew how much the oil there was worth. So the two companies agreed to a minimum and a maximum value. Stanton proposed a similar strategy. He suggested offering Scripps 40 percent ownership of the cellular division, a generous offer based on McCaw's current value. But if McCaw's company grew, Scripps's ownership would shrink in stages to 15 percent. In either scenario, Scripps would be guaranteed a handsome return on its investment.

McCaw liked the idea because it provided him with both another motivation to grow the company and a path to maintaining control. But how much money would Scripps offer for this package? Hopper said he wanted $12 million. The McCaw executives laughed. A conservative company like Scripps would never put up that much. But why not ask for that figure, outrageous as it seemed? "You might as well shoot for the moon," McCaw said.

Having once been a banker, Hopper knew how to talk to conservative people. He knew how they did reports, how they looked at their own businesses. He understood their style and language. He knew their motivations.

At the meeting with Scripps, Hopper explained the radio spectrum. He told them about POPs, a new way of presenting cellular's potential. The term came from the cable business, where a system's value was partly measured by how many members of a given population, or POPs, could be served by the coaxial cable—a measure of potential customers who lived along the path of the cable. Hopper said the same sort of analysis should be used in cellular: not the number of actual customers but the total within the transmission radius.

Hopper explained how POPs gave McCaw a reasonable estimate of the cellular division's expected value. Assuming McCaw would win licenses, he discussed projections of company growth based on different scenarios. He argued that Scripps should expect an arrangement where it got neither too much nor too little from McCaw. In the end, he convinced it to focus on a financial result—say, 25 percent compounded return—rather than on the percentage of equity it would receive.

To Hopper's surprise, Scripps agreed. Everyone at McCaw was amazed by Hopper's talents. Hopper himself chuckled at the deal, later calling it "one of the most unlikely stories ever to occur in finance." The deal not only provided $12 million of badly needed cash, but it also preserved McCaw's flexibility. Scripps assumed that all the money would go to build systems, but the terms allowed McCaw some precious flexibility, including the option of spending the whole $12 million on even more licenses.

The McCaw team worked hard to make sure that Scripps did well with its investment, but felt they had outsmarted the newspaper company, which didn't see cellular's huge potential. "If I were them, I never would have agreed to it," Stanton said. Of course, he always believed cellular licenses would eventually reach enormous values.

Meanwhile, as everyone else looked for money and hoped for licenses, AT&T kept rolling.

Loaded with cash, prestige, and hubris, AT&T and GTE began moving to get permits to build their systems. As part of its forced divestiture effective January 1984, AT&T retained its cellular hardware division and released its cellular service group to the now independent operating companies—the Baby Bells. This largesse was not given much thought at AT&T; cellular was still viewed as merely a niche business. But the wrongheadedness of that decision became evident over the next decade. The cellular giveaway was one of AT&T's rashest acts, and the giant would pay dearly to undo that mistake.

US West, the Baby Bell newly formed to serve fourteen western states, placed its Advanced Mobile Phone Service (AMPS) regional headquarters, coincidentally, in Seattle—Craig McCaw's backyard.

Dubbed US West NewVector, the fledgling company announced it would spend $14 million in the Seattle area to build a thirteen-cell system. The company wanted to begin service by July 1984, but McCaw Communications and other applicants for Seattle complained that the early start gave NewVector an unfair advantage. They asked for a delay of NewVector's launch until the second group's system was ready.

The FCC decided on a compromise, requiring US West to set aside some capacity for a reseller and its customers. US West would assign certain cellular numbers to the reseller, which would use them on its own system once it was operational. After a round of hearings that went well for the McCaw alliance, Interstate Mobilephone won the Seattle license, and in September 1983 it received a permit to begin construction.

McCaw had expected this victory. "There wasn't a scintilla of doubt in my mind," he says. "We were a winner from the day we had filed, even though our application wasn't that good. We were going to win because we were the presettled local guys. [The FCC] *couldn't* give it to anybody else."

At last McCaw and his partners held one of the precious licenses. Then they won Portland, too. But they faced a powerful Baby Bell, a monopoly power with huge revenue, and a direct, entrenched relationship to customers—a competitive situation powerful companies had regarded as hopeless. But McCaw anticipated the challenge. "People are driven by some adversity to want to do greater things," he says. "If life is too easy, you take the easy part of it. You have to be driven by competitiveness, which is usually driven by adversity."

Nothing energized him more than a situation others saw as hopeless.

CHAPTER

10

"Like Negotiating with the Russians"

Financing Comes from an Unlikely Ally—AT&T

In October 1984 a Seattle-area newspaper printed a photo of a man in his car holding a new sort of telephone. Doug Hauff, the recently installed president of Interstate Mobilephone, grinned at the camera and held aloft the gizmo as if it were a powerful wand, a talisman of a new era—which of course it was.

The article described thirty-one-year-old Hauff as a "high achiever" working eighteen hours a day to prepare his tiny company for competition with the cellular subsidiary of US West, a telecommunications giant. Hauff looked both tough and confident as he sat in his Mercedes. The garrulous salesman had a way of convincing listeners that he had won the contest even before it started. The reader might have overlooked a fact underplayed in the article: Hauff's phone was a mere prop. It didn't work.

But the cellular revolution was finally coming to American consumers, including Craig McCaw's friends and neighbors. McCaw had won the right—what the less confident might call the burden—to compete with US West's NewVector Communications, the wireline cellular service. Along with his partners in Interstate, McCaw had seen the future, spread the vision, found the money, and done the deal. Now it was up to others to handle the details such as hiring employees, building a system, and launching the service.

Hired in 1984, Hauff worked for McCaw for three months before even meeting him. Hauff was expected to be creative and get the job done. For McCaw, this approach to business serves both the company and the individual . . . at least his sort of person. "Autonomy is really a central part of my life," McCaw says:

I believe that it drives the kind of behavior in individuals that we want. And it really made a major impact on my life and how I respond to others. And my belief is that if you can pass autonomy as far down in any grouping of people as you can, you will get extraordinary results if you ask for a lot.

McCaw did ask for a lot. Essentially left to himself, Hauff had to build a company from scratch, a huge job made more onerous by having to explain to people—over and over again—what "cellular" was. (It had nothing to do with biology.) And McCaw's ultradelegated management approach wasn't always successful or entirely pleasant. Underlings might flourish or fail with their independence and often felt that their boss knew nothing about their hard work and the myriad activities that brought success or failure.

Some resented McCaw's seeming detachment; these people would soon depart. Others simply accepted that they worked for an unusual boss. McCaw is "a very smart, visionary individual," says Doug Hauff. "For us normal human beings, he is very difficult to understand. He has a tendency to talk in riddles."

After several promotions, Hauff reported directly to McCaw for eight months. Yet Hauff always felt bewildered:

> Craig would call me up nearly on a daily basis and propose some questions. There were days [when], if I understood the question and answered correctly, I was in good shape. There were days [when], if I didn't understand and didn't answer correctly, I was not in good shape. One of the challenges for all of us was understanding where he was going, what he was saying, and what he wanted. It was very, very difficult.

McCaw understands that his style sometimes puts a strain on employees:

> I'm not the perfect employee of the company. I'm impatient at times . . . and [I'm] certain people have trouble understanding what I'm saying. The more literally they listen to me, the more trouble they have understanding. I'm a conceptual thinker. I speak in conceptual rather than literal terms. Figuratively rather than literally, if you'll take that. Therefore, a very literal person has a

tough time understanding what I'm saying, but after a while, I can be impatient. I have a lot of flaws even within my own goals, you know, within the values that I would want to live by. I'm as hypocritical as the next person. But I do my best.

McCaw's peculiar management style has sometimes led to peculiar hiring practices. Though he is often extraordinarily deliberative in picking people, other times he has put people on the payroll impulsively. If he met an interesting person he thought would add value to the organization, he would sometimes hire him on the spot and let him find his own place in the organization.

Brian McCauley is a case in point. In 1985 McCaw hired McCauley, a talented former aide to Washington governor John Spellman, and assigned him to handle a complex transfer of cable franchises. Later, McCaw gave McCauley various other tasks, such as evaluating radio and TV stations in Alaska. McCauley would present a broadcasting deal in Alaska only to have McCaw point out that his money would grow faster in cellular. But when McCauley offered to help Hauff and Stanton with their cellular work, both men declined.

McCauley left within two years, a bit baffled by his experience with McCaw but grateful for the opportunity. "I had some learning to do [about business] after being in politics," McCauley says. "Craig wasn't a screamer. To this day, I appreciate how Craig worked with me. He had issues clear and wanted to solve things." McCauley eventually became publisher of *The Christian Science Monitor*.

It is remarkable how frequently McCaw subordinates made company history without his presence. Many of the company's more significant deals were done without McCaw's direct involvement, some before he even knew about them. A top aide might buy a collection of cellular licenses and inform McCaw afterward. So long as the deal took the company a step closer to its broad goals, McCaw preferred to ignore the details. Unlike Microsoft, for example, where CEO Bill Gates injects himself into every major event, personally closing the deals and giving the speeches, the McCaw story is often one of action without the chief executive. McCaw is felt but not there. He may visualize the outcome, but he lets others find the way.

In the early days, Doug Hauff enjoyed the freedom and the challenge of working for McCaw. He had previously run Executone, a company that sold telephone services to hospitals and businesses, including mobile phones and paging services. Thus, Hauff knew a lot about mobile communications in the Seattle market. He held firm to two key convictions: Cellular phones had a great future, and competition with US West would be easier than it seemed. Like many in the McCaw organization, Hauff regarded US West as a giant, but a lumbering one that knew little about marketing and, distracted by the lingering complications of the AT&T divestiture, thought little about cellular and its future.

McCaw himself once described US West as "one of the dumber companies in America—ever." Based on how US West handled cellular in its early years, it would be hard to argue with this harsh assessment. Rather than aggressively accumulating licenses and investing in systems and marketing, US West's bureaucracy treated cellular as a mere niche, which became a self-fulfilling prophecy.

Richard Callahan, president of NewVector, says he shared Craig McCaw's vision of cellular as a broadly used consumer product, but could never get the backing he wanted from headquarters to buy licenses and expand into new territories. Corporate financial executives blocked his moves to buy licenses in Detroit and Ohio, warning that licenses would never outgrow certain modest values, though of course prices for licenses doubled and tripled and still kept growing. They just didn't see what Callahan saw—that a duopoly in a growing industry couldn't miss.

So at US West, cellular was an entrepreneur's business trapped inside a stodgy organization. "As late as 1986, people were telling me cellular would go nowhere," says Callahan. To the old "Bell heads," says Callahan, NewVector "was always a stepchild." It was a frustrating situation for Callahan, but a brilliant opportunity for Doug Hauff.

To Hauff, the very name US West chose to market its cellular service was a clunker, music only to a tin ear. "What's a NewVector?" Hauff asks with a derisive laugh. (The vector name actually derived from Latin and meant "new carrier.") US West eventually conceded the point and dropped the name. By contrast, Interstate Mobilephone had licensed a more understandable brand name, Cellular One, from a Washington, D.C., carrier. That brand would soon mean something to the public, Hauff believed. Service hadn't started, but he already tasted victory.

Hauff set up his headquarters in an unfinished building that faced Seattle's Elliott Bay, where oceangoing container ships and sailboats cruised against a backdrop of mountains that glowed pink at sunset. The spectacular view compensated for the absence of certain minor business necessities—such as a telephone and a desk. Fortunately, while Interstate's office was being completed, the building owner let Hauff use a conference room.

Technically, Hauff reported to the representatives of each of the six Interstate partners, though he most often dealt with John Stanton or Ed Hopper of McCaw Communications, and with Bill Ford, the Washington Post Company's representative. Rival US West led a Seattle partnership that included GTE Mobilenet, Whidbey (Island) Telephone Company, Telephone Utilities of Washington, Yelm Telephone Company, and Mashell Telephone Company. Taking advantage of its head start in securing a license, US West went on the air with cellular service on July 12, 1984, with Washington governor John Spellman making the first call. But under the terms of the FCC compromise, Interstate was allowed to purchase airtime on US West's system and resell it to Cellular One customers, using phone numbers starting with 972. Interstate launched its reseller service on July 20 with a call placed by U.S. senator Slade Gorton.

Craig McCaw's cellular company was on the air. But a familiar problem loomed: finding money.

Hopper and Stanton were already trying to find cash to build the Portland and Seattle cellular systems. The best potential source was an unlikely one: AT&T. To prove its business independence postdivestiture, US West NewVector had abruptly decided to cancel an order with AT&T for a multimillion-dollar switching system for Seattle. Ed Hopper was told that Richard Callahan had framed that unsent check to AT&T and hung it on the wall, a symbol of his independence and a new era. An astonished AT&T didn't know how to react to this humiliation at the hands of its former corporate child. "There was a lot of animosity and a lot of hurt," Hopper said later. And AT&T was left with a load of expensive hardware sitting in a warehouse near Seattle.

When Hopper approached AT&T offering to buy the system, the telecommunications giant stalled. Everyone was confused by divestiture, especially AT&T, which wasn't sure it could sell the warehoused system to an independent company. "Just think of the mentality," Hopper says:

They didn't know what all this breakup stuff was going to mean, and in walks this guy from McCaw—who the hell is he?—and says, "I want to buy your switch. I know you got one in the Seattle warehouse." And these guys are smarting from the fact that [NewVector] shined 'em off.

Interstate lacked cash but not moxie. Hopper decided to ask AT&T not only to finance the sale, but to put up another chunk of money for operating capital until Interstate's system began making profits.

Stanton, Hopper, and later Hauff worked hard on persuading AT&T to do the deal. But negotiating with so many layers of managers, reexplaining the details of the deal, and otherwise navigating the culture of such a massive organization was torture. Hopper managed to persuade one senior executive to accept the financing idea, a giant step that delighted and astonished Stanton. But then a new AT&T manager arrived to declare that AT&T did not do financing.

Stanton handled most of the meetings as the designated "battering ram," constantly pressing for closure. "It was like negotiating with the Russians in the good old days," Stanton said later. When Stanton got stuck, Hopper came in as the gray eminence to detail previous discussions. In all, Hopper made at least eight trips to AT&T headquarters in Basking Ridge, New Jersey.

McCaw gave Hopper extraordinary freedom to design and close the deal. Hopper loved the independence, but sometimes when he wanted to confer with McCaw, he couldn't find him: McCaw would be kayaking or flying somewhere or busy with the cable division. The idea that this might inconvenience his executives would have astonished McCaw, who felt he was giving them a gift by not being around. "If somebody's got the ball, it is theirs to run," says McCaw. "If I hang around and act important and give orders, I'm going to wreck the whole thing." So he kept his hands off the AT&T negotiations. "I don't think McCaw met an AT&T executive until years after," Hopper says.

Despite the foot-dragging, some at AT&T wanted to see the deal with Interstate completed. Like NewVector, AT&T had something to prove. As potentially the largest seller of cellular equipment in a billion-dollar market, AT&T wanted to show it could deal with the nonwireline companies. On the equipment side, it faced several competitors, including Motorola, Ericsson of Sweden, and Northern Telecom of Canada, which had won a NewVector contract for Seattle. So Craig McCaw's negotiators pushed for a good deal.

At 2 A.M. during one marathon session in New York, as Stanton and Hauff kept pressing for concessions, the treasurer of AT&T finally stood up and roared: "I have given and given and given. I'm not going to give anymore!" He walked out, leaving Stanton and Hauff to wonder whether they had negotiated their way out of the deal they needed so badly.

In the end, though, AT&T did agree to an amazingly generous loan. It gave the multimillion-dollar cellular switching system, plus several million more as working capital, to a start-up cellular company with grand ambitions but no profits, and no hope of any for years to come. From a traditional business perspective, Interstate Mobilephone hardly looked creditworthy. So why did AT&T make the deal?

Perhaps it was anxious to unload a switch or give US West a little payback for the insult. But the significance for the cellular industry was enormous. As Hopper explains, the AT&T deal was a crucial sign that cellular had a future. The loan was secured only by the FCC cellular license. Thus, the world's biggest communications company was saying, in effect, that a license in this unknown industry had real value, even on the nonwireline side. Cellular had a big enough future to sustain two providers in a single market. And AT&T was demonstrating its willingness to bet against its former affiliates.

"If there ever was a time when people did understand the value of spectrum, it was there," says Hopper. The deal "broke the whole race open."

John Stanton would later say that Hopper's 150 percent financing was one of the most critical proposals in the company's history. Without AT&T's loan, the McCaw company would have had to use Scripps money for its share of building the Seattle systems. That would have kept McCaw from bidding for other licenses and would have assured Scripps a large share of ownership in McCaw Cellular.

Instead, there was now enough cash to build a system for Interstate Mobilephone. Hauff was in a hurry to catch up with NewVector. He needed to have at least twelve transmission sites selected, designed, and built. Every site involved finding a spot from which a particular service area could be covered, locating and persuading the property owner to allow the building of a tower of up to 150 feet, and getting city building permits.

Often Hauff's biggest challenge was simply explaining the concept of cellular service. At one public hearing, a former navy man stood up and warned neighbors about the dangers of high-energy radio waves. During slow times, the navy man said, his shipmates would focus radar on a bird and fry it in midflight. Hauff scrambled to the podium to calm a frightened audience. He told them about cellular's different use of the spectrum, its relatively low power, and its safety record, and managed to avert a public relations debacle.

In dealing with government regulatory agencies, it helped that NewVector had already paved the way in building its own towers. Yet there were still frustrating delays. When Hauff got close to identifying all the tower locations, he found that the King County government objected to his using a water tower as a base for his transmitter. A bureaucrat claimed that it violated regulations, even though the county itself hung an antenna there. Hauff visited a King County councilman who picked up the phone and—poof!—made the objection disappear.

In time, Hauff lined up all his cell sites, and Interstate's system went on the air in the fall of 1985.

Soon cellular began to click in consumers' minds. It was easy to see the fun and convenience of making a phone call from anywhere, anytime. But there were obstacles in selling the equipment. A telephone priced at $2,000 stopped hearts. NewVector and Interstate tried to ease the sticker shock by folding the sale price into monthly plans and crediting some of the cost if the customer signed on for a year's service. This strategy made a difference, but not enough.

Hauff wanted to kill at birth the notion that a wireless telephone was only a rich person's toy. Instead, the cell phone was positioned as a business tool, a "freedom machine," as Hopper called it. So the early newspaper stories about cellular carried interviews that promoted the simple logic: Everyone gets stuck in traffic. Why not use that time to keep in touch with customers, to check in with the office, to turn an hour of commuting into an hour of productive work? Lawyers, real estate agents, physicians, and anyone in sales could use a cellular phone.

Hauff repeatedly claimed that the cellular phone would soon

become as vital and familiar as the typewriter (this was before personal computers got big). "I see everybody buying cellular phones," he told reporters.

Still, there was no denying the costs were steep. Service in Seattle started at a monthly rate of $19.95 and 60 cents a minute for peak-time calls. Heavy users were offered seven hours of free airtime at $199.95 per month. Once they tried the service, customers loved it—in many cases, too much. Some used their new phones heavily, then deluged the company with complaints over the shock of the first huge bill. Hauff stressed the business tool argument. Just use it wisely, he said, and your cell phone will be a smart investment.

By 1985 McCaw Cellular had emerged as a major victor in the competition for licenses. In the FCC hearings for the thirty largest cities, McCaw had applied for and gotten six. Now, as Hauff labored to serve just two markets, Craig McCaw wanted more licenses, even for tiny towns hardly anyone wanted. Craig worried about growing, not about the fact that he lacked the staff or money to handle more licenses. The shark had to be fed.

11

"What Do You Want for a Sacramento?"

A License Lottery Creates a Trading Frenzy

I n July 1983 the FCC stunned the young cellular industry by announcing its intention to drop comparative hearings for licenses. Having received 353 applications for the second round of thirty cities and another 567 for the third round, the FCC realized it would take forever to hold hearings for each application and to sort through each applicant's claims and counterclaims. There was simply too much paper to review. A single city—Austin, Texas—attracted thirty-four mammoth applications. Plus, there was the storage problem.

Despite protests by Craig McCaw and others who favored the hearings, the FCC chose a process that would be the fastest route for delivering cellular service to the public: a simple lottery. Every qualified application would receive a single chit in a drawing. If fifteen applications came in for a city, then each would have a one-in-fifteen chance of winning a hugely valuable license.

It was simple and easy to explain. Whether it made sense or was fair was another matter.

The announcement dramatically shifted the ground in the industry. Previously, cellular had been a game for a relatively small group of investors who were quick to see a business opportunity and bet some money on it. Now cellular was becoming a speculator's game. Rather than spending big for careful engineering studies, the speculators mass-produced applications. They didn't bother to nail down transmission sites or even to meet the FCC's published criteria. "You looked through [the speculators' paperwork], and it was all bullshit," John Stanton says.

McCaw unsuccessfully tried to get the FCC to continue the hearings at least through the second round. The company was confident of outclassing the speculators, but now, in a lottery, a speculator had as good a chance of winning a Round Two application as a prestige company like the Washington Post or Cox Communications. Having won a share or control of Denver, Kansas City, Portland, San Francisco, San Jose, and Seattle in the first round, McCaw had gone for five Round Two licenses, betting on winning in a comparative hearing through the quality of his application. But the lottery favored anyone who filed in volume.

It was a rare miscalculation by McCaw. Stanton later figured that the change in process cost the company three or four million potential customers. In ten years, that group would have been worth $500 million.

It was a significant test of McCaw's leadership. His company needed to change tactics, fast. The next several months would display his management team's determination to stay in the game even when events threatened to marginalize them. Rather than giving up, they just worked harder.

The lottery announcement triggered a host of deals and consolidations. Some companies rushed to find partners, while others, seeing their chances diminish, chose to get out. The departures sparked a flurry of articles wondering whether cellular had cooled. *Forbes* magazine noted that the Indianapolis Telephone Company had signed up only 350 cellular subscribers in its first six months, far fewer than expected for its $7 million system. The magazine quoted an expert who said that some cities would show big demand for cellular, but many would see slow growth. "There will be few, if any, fast payoffs even though new systems eventually may become profitable," *Forbes* said. "Cellular radio, like cable television, may be a growth industry whose time will be very slow to come."

Knight Ridder, owner of a chain of newspapers, became one of the first major players to lose heart. At a meeting in Bellevue, McCaw and his lieutenants discussed approaching Knight Ridder, which had tentative approval for several licenses. McCaw realized that the arrival of speculators would make it more costly to buy licenses, so he wanted to quickly buy as many as he could—a strategy the company employed for the next few years. But how could they buy what Knight Ridder did not yet formally own? The FCC's past decisions in radio and television had blocked sales of licenses in application. To McCaw's lieutenants, the agency's policy seemed clear: no sales.

That didn't stop Craig McCaw. "I don't care," he said. "Get the rule changed." Elroy McCaw's presence was being felt. Elroy had always been the last to bend a knee before rules, and now his son was following suit. John Stanton and Wayne Perry met with the Knight Ridder people in Washington, D.C., during the Fourth of July week. (Knight Ridder was based in Miami, but assigned its cellular team to Washington.) On a sweltering day, the McCaw men walked past a Beach Boys concert on the Capitol lawn and entered a building without air-conditioning for the meeting with Knight Ridder. Sweating and exhausted, the two teams designed a complex deal and cut one of the first cellular sales at what some thought was an outrageously high price—$2.50 a POP.

Perry knew it was a steal. "They didn't know what they had," Perry said later. And McCaw had been right about the FCC. After a bit of lobbying, the commission let the deal go through. In effect, the FCC said, We don't allow this, so don't do it again.

Meanwhile, the effort to consolidate continued. George Lindemann of Metro Mobile, John Kluge of Metromedia, Donald Pels of LIN Broadcasting, and others met in New York. All had some licenses and pending applications. Lindemann saw no point in everyone's carving one another. Why not form an alliance, combine licenses, and apply for other East Coast licenses as a group? It was an intriguing idea, but there may have been too much ego or suspicion in the room. As some recalled it later, the idea died when Pels, with a large share of New York City, declined to participate.

But the meeting had some value, for it led to a later group that gathered in New York to try to negotiate agreements for their second-round applications. Nearly all of the major players, which now included MCI and Western Union, attended that meeting at the New York Friars Club, where Lindemann was a member. The group represented at least 50 percent of the applicants for each Round Three market.

Normally, Hopper would have gone to such a meeting, but because of a schedule conflict, Stanton went instead, without much briefing. It was a moment when the larger players were attempting to seize markets and shut out the little guys. Craig McCaw understood the situation and the high stakes, but he stayed home. "I wasn't that worried," McCaw now says. "There's so much ebb and flow of things." He characterizes the meeting as an example of "the technical things" that didn't require his presence. He figured Stanton could try to win some concessions for the McCaw forces, but if he lost, they could fight the battle on a different front.

McCaw's blasé attitude was based, in part, on his reading of the FCC, which, he figured, would not allow small companies like his to be completely cut out. If large companies like Kluge's began to overwhelm the smaller players, the FCC would put a finger on the scale. "The little guys never got completely smashed. Government doesn't do that. It's not bad being a little guy," McCaw says.

When Stanton walked in, he was astonished at the size of the gathering. Nearly every key player in the cellular industry was there—hence the group's informal nickname, the "Grand Alliance." Dwarfing McCaw's twenty filings in the three rounds, the group included truly big players such as Lindemann with his fifty-five applications, George Perrin of PageNet with fifty applications, Peter Erb of Millicom with fifty-three applications, and others. Stanton's mission was to delay or derail the alliance, hoping that somehow the FCC would decide to hold comparative hearings after all. It was a tall order for a small player like McCaw.

As the meeting unfolded, the members of the Grand Alliance came up with a plan to pool everyone's interests by merging applications. If ten members of the Alliance each had an application for Austin, for example, each would be given 10 percent of a single merged application for the Austin lottery.

Stanton disliked that the proposed partnership agreement favored "paper filers," the people whose many applications showed little understanding of the cities they sought to serve. He began raising questions and objections to the point of annoying the other attendees, especially the meeting cochairman, communications lawyer Barry Adelman. Adelman had never met Stanton, who looked at least a decade younger than everyone else in the room. At one point, Adelman yelled, "Who the hell are you?"

"I'm John Stanton from McCaw," Stanton replied. That didn't help. Few had heard of the private Northwest cable TV company that served about 250,000 customers.

"Thank you for enlightening me," Adelman sarcastically replied. "Who's McCaw?"

As the meeting progressed, Stanton kept raising intelligent objections, gradually earning Adelman's respect but winning no converts. "We were ostracized," Stanton said later. The Grand Alliance was formalized in February 1984. When the FCC finalized the switch to the lottery, the alliance's twelve members controlled 55 percent of the applications for Round Two, giving the Grand Alliance tremendous bargaining power over the rest of the industry. McCaw Communications was left exposed.

Some of Craig McCaw's great successes have been based on smart strategy, cunning analysis, or hard work. Others have been sheer luck. McCaw Communication's recovery from the Grand Alliance setback began when Stanton went to a meeting in Washington, D.C., with a number of small companies that had applied for the Salt Lake City license. The meeting was to attempt an alliance or agreement for that market, but it soon became clear that the attendees all had something else in common: They were *not* members of the Grand Alliance.

Richard Sherwin, representing Graphic Scanning, which held sixty applications in Rounds Two and Three, suggested an interesting step: Why discuss only one city when we could discuss many cities at once? If enough applicants came together and negotiated deals for each market, the FCC would have no need to hold a lottery. The industry itself would work through who got what. But would the FCC agree to this process? And how could the 100 or so companies that had not joined the Alliance organize themselves into a coherent association?

Stanton could see just how difficult it would be. Many of the remaining applicants were small firms, such as paging companies, applying for a single market. For example, one person had applied only for Fresno, another only for West Palm Beach. Other applicants were industry pariahs with a history of FCC troubles. Still others were regarded as flakes. Furthermore, these smaller players were scattered all over the country. It would be a huge job to track them all down, brief them on the plan, and get them to agree. And many of them would have to agree in order to gain any leverage over the Grand Alliance.

With Stanton in the lead, the new group solicited members and easily got more than half of the 100 to join. But that left thirty to forty applicants who had not yet joined for various reasons. Stanton decided he had to visit them personally. So from April to July, Stanton traveled seven days a week trying to sign up every last one. By August, miraculously, he had signed nearly everyone, just as the FCC announced that the lotteries would be held on October 2.

Now McCaw was part of a group that would join with the Grand Alliance and find a way to negotiate agreements. If all of the applicants could agree on some sort of settlement, then there would be no need for an FCC lottery. The group sent a representative to the FCC to informally determine whether the commission would relax its past lottery rule against having more than one chit per market. It would also have to drop its historic ban on trading in "unbuilt licenses"—that is, franchises in cities where a license had been awarded but the system had not yet been built.

In an informal conversation, one FCC representative—whom Wayne Perry refuses to name—gave the green light, assuring the negotiators that the commission would accept any trades for licenses that the group could agree on. Since the FCC wanted to hasten the process of establishing cellular service and minimize lawsuits, it had good reason to allow the settlements. "Was this good public policy?" Perry asks rhetorically. "You bet. This shortened up [the process of launching] cellular, getting to the next tier of cities—markets thirty-one through ninety—by years. This was public policy at its best." Following the FCC's lead, the IRS also made a key concession, agreeing to treat license transactions as tax-free.

As Perry had wanted, the government was quietly revamping a policy it had spent years developing. The action certainly accelerated the process of getting cellular to consumers, but critics like Millicom's Peter Erb considered it proof that the FCC's initial plans had been ill conceived. In any case, there is no doubt that, without asking for a penny, the FCC permitted the Grand Alliance to grab a huge portion of the public airwaves. Years later, critics would fault the FCC for giving away public assets, but at the time few were certain that cellular would ever be profitable. The policy settled upon was arguably the best the FCC could do under the circumstances.

In September 1984 representatives of nearly all of the Rounds Two and Three applicants gathered at the New York law offices of Rubin Baum Levin Constant & Friedman on Fifth Avenue. They had just a few days in which to swap chits representing license applications for sixty cities as big as Columbus, Ohio, and as small as Charleston, South Carolina, markets that in total served scores of millions of people. Thousands of trades would have to be done before October 2, or the lottery would go forward.

The bizarre events that followed were technically illegal, because the FCC had yet to formally allow such transactions. Even at the time, one participant joked that what they were doing could land them all in jail had it not been legitimized by the presence of so many lawyers. Strangest of all, although the license-trading session determined the future course of the cellular industry, eventually made multimillionaires out of many people, and quickened the development of a new industry, only a few insiders knew of its significance. What proved to be one of the decade's biggest events in the communications business got no mention in any major newspaper.

The rules for trading were laid out. Chits would be traded based on the number of people represented by a license application. If a person held one of ten applications for a city of 100,000, then that chit represented 10,000 POPs, or potential persons served. Everyone knew that certain cities would be more profitable than others, but it would have been nearly impossible to get everyone to agree on a demographic value for each city. In the interests of simplicity and speed, a POP in New York City would be deemed equivalent to one in Seattle or Tulsa. By mutual agreement, no one could pull out if he didn't like how the trades went.

John Stanton arrived in New York armed with a strategy. Having already bought out Knight Ridder and some other applicants, McCaw Communications wanted to solidify its base in the Northwest and build from there. At that point, even ambitious McCaw had no dreams of building a cellular empire east of the Mississippi River. Perhaps no one had that lofty a vision.

Another goal was to dilute Scripps's ownership share of McCaw. Under the terms of the Scripps loan, the lender's shares would decrease if McCaw gained licenses in certain markets with attractive demographics. If McCaw could get Austin, Texas, for example, Scripps would lose. A state capital, Austin was also a college town with high incomes and lots of professionals—a cellular promised land. So Austin became Stanton's first target, followed by Oklahoma City, Albuquerque, and Wichita.

Encouraged by the FCC to move quickly, the traders worked for two weeks. About eighteen people traded from 10 A.M. till as late as 2 A.M. Chinese food or pizza arrived by 8 P.M. Cigarette and cigar smoke filled the room. The traders provided an interesting slice of the cellular industry. Some were lawyers representing as many as four different companies. Others controlled big companies. Some were pudgy middle-aged men who had made big money elsewhere; others were lean and hungry newcomers. "It was crazy and a great deal of fun," says Lindemann, who compared the experience to a faster, real-life version of Monopoly in which people shouted across the room as they traded cities.

Working with Barry Adelman, a computer technician struggled to record the trades, dozens of them each hour, as participants tried to keep track by scribbling notes to themselves. A couple of nights, Adelman slept on a cot in his office and got up to find records of trades slipped under his door. Everyone was working furiously. "It was like the Wild West," Stanton recalls.

As the players maneuvered to gain control of certain markets, calls went to holdouts with a single chit, enticing them with money or a percentage of a license. Traders bluffed, cajoled, begged, and lobbied one another. When traders noticed others going for the same market, some began offering cash for POPs, first $1.50 a POP, then up to $7 or higher. One deal hit $40. McCaw bought out people at around $6, a very high price considering that no one had ever made a profit in cellular. At times, desire outstripped logic. "You didn't know what was going to be a hit," says Lindemann. "It was all seat-of-the-pants. There were no scientific studies, no established patterns [of cellular usage]. It was all guesswork." Many of the traders offering cash had no idea where the money would come from.

Nonetheless, the exhausting process proceeded smoothly until trading started for Sacramento. All twelve applicants were represented in the room. The two groups that most wanted the city, MCI and Graphics Scanning, had obtained all but one application, which was held by cigar smoker Lindemann, who Stanton believes might have been taken off his game by a long lunch that day.

As Stanton tells the story, MCI vice president Herman "Whitey" Bluestein approached Lindemann and traded Albuquerque for Sacramento. But a few minutes later, Lindemann traded Sacramento again, this time to Graphic Scanning.

"A dozen people were standing around the room, mouths agape," recalls Stanton:

> We'd been working at this thing for a day and a half, built on a year's worth of work, and here's this guy who's going to destroy the process because he's going to trade things he doesn't own. Someone finally explains this to George . . . and he goes, "I'm short. I'm short. Who's long Sacramento? Who's long Sacramento? I've got some Flints here. I'll trade you some Flints. What do you want for a Sacramento?" He's yelling like he's in Chicago in the options market. He's shouting for twenty minutes!

The mix-up threatened to undo more than 1,000 trades and destroy the entire settlement effort. One suspect trade would foul others, since people were retrading interests that had gone through fifteen or sixteen owners.

Finally, the mess was straightened out. The first trade stood, the second was canceled, and according to several participants, Lindemann wasn't allowed to do any more trades without his lawyer to initial the deal.

Lindemann offers a different view of that night. Lindemann says that far from acting disorganized, as some saw him, he was pursuing a strategy of disguising his intentions, which were to gain 100 percent control of markets that adjoined one another. He looked for cellular licenses where he already ran cable companies, such as the Carolinas and Arizona, plus whatever markets seemed overlooked, such as Connecticut. Later, he would be amused that so much attention had been focused on Florida while hardly anyone wanted the New York–Philadelphia corridor, which became very lucrative. Not many traders were thinking about driving patterns, he says.

Lindemann deliberately kept some of his trades to himself. As he describes what happened, the Sacramento mix-up began when Richard Sherwin of Graphic Scanning offered to buy Lindemann's interest in

Sacramento. Not really intending to sell it to Sherwin, Lindemann thought he was just waving him off, not signaling agreement. After that, Lindemann thought he had a legitimate deal with Bluestein, one of 250 trades done by Lindemann or his aide, Jack Brennan.

Lindemann does think he made a mistake by inadvertently trading Wichita. Later, he told people that others had made similar mistakes. Millicom and Metromedia both traded cities twice, he says.

Stanton had been up all night before the last day of trading, trying to locate some holdouts in the middle of the night and persuade them to sign deals. By morning, it looked as if all but three markets were settled. Lotteries would be held for Salt Lake City, Fresno, and the northeast Pennsylvania market.

Stanton had worked hard, even by his legendary standards. While many executives had to consult with the home office on deals, Stanton, typical for a Craig McCaw manager, operated with almost total autonomy.

McCaw had no desire to be there. "Why would I want to do that? To me, those are the kinds of places where you make too many mistakes," he says. "You're too close to it. I never want to do stuff like that. I never want to lose." In other words, McCaw feared wanting a deal so much that he would pay too high a price—the risk of being emotionally involved.

McCaw, who would regret being swayed by his emotions in a later New York deal, has always tried to make a business virtue out of his inherent detachment from groups. "More than that, I'm not a negotiator. I want to tell people exactly what I want the outcome to be; I don't want to worry about how to get there. Other people are much better negotiators than me," he says.

McCaw was not troubled by having delegated so much power over his company's future to a twenty-nine-year-old, especially John Stanton:

I had no fear whatsoever. First of all, I trusted him. And he had a wonderful command of details. He was interfacing with Wayne and Ed and me, and I felt perfectly fine about it. But then I'm the kind of person where Wayne will go out and make a [cellular acquisition] deal like he did in Miami [and then tell me], "By the way, I did a deal today: fifty-six million." [At the time] we didn't

have a million in the bank. I said, "Fine. Let's go find the money."
That's the kind of company we were. You knew who to trust. In all
the people we had, there were only a couple who made dumb
mistakes.

So Stanton, who loved independence, had his freedom. Working
without a bureaucracy, Stanton could work faster and more efficiently
than the lawyers who, as big-company representatives, had to check
back with their clients. Stanton also worked harder than most people.
During the trading frenzy, he slept little and never even cleaned or
removed his contact lenses. The contacts became so clogged with smoke
that they dried painfully onto his eyeballs. His eyes turned bright red,
and he was in such awful pain that an attorney's wife rushed him to the
hospital. Soon afterward, he insisted on returning to work with patches
over both eyes. In a fevered environment, the craziness had become a
little crazier.

But Stanton was pleased with the business outcome. McCaw had
collected twenty or thirty lottery positions on cities it wanted, and the
FCC gave its approval to the traded applications. The company wound
up with a controlling interest in its number one objective, Austin, plus
Oklahoma City, Wichita, Kansas, and Tacoma.

In late December the commission staff called Barry Adelman, the
lawyer who had helped host the trading, and requested a report of the
results of the trades within a few weeks. So Adelman and another
lawyer, Larry Movshin, began the tedious process of tracking each chit
through its trades. Some trades, inevitably, had not been recorded.
Where they found a problem, they called the affected traders with questions, sometimes in the middle of the night: What did you do with
Wichita? How did you get West Palm Beach before you traded it?
Where did it go?

In the last week of work, as the deadline approached, the lawyers
worked with little sleep. Adelman insists he stayed awake for five days
straight, scared that a single undocumented trade would blow up the
entire settlement. But when they presented the FCC with a perfect
record of all the documented settlements, they ended the competition
for all but a few of the sixty markets.

The settlements represented a huge amount of business—franchises with a projected $2.5 billion to $3.7 billion each year in sales within the next three to five years, according to a projection by John Bain of Shearson Lehman/American Express. Customers were expected to total 1.4 million to 2.1 million.

In October 1984 *The Wall Street Journal* reported that the FCC had called off the cellular lotteries. "The lottery would have begun a litigation process, of companies fighting the use of the lottery and its results, that could have lasted for months," Stanton told the *Journal*. A spokesman for the FCC said it made sense for the marketplace, rather than a government-run lottery, to work out a way to distribute the licenses.

Not everyone was pleased, however. Steven Titch, editor of *Cellular Business* magazine, complained that the industry was attracting "fast-food applicants." That was certainly true. The marvels of cellular were no longer a secret. Speculators now flocked to the cellular land rush. The next thirty licenses attracted an astonishing 5,200 applicants. What had been a game for insiders was now a free-for-all.

CHAPTER

12

"You Went to Veterinarians
When You Needed Brain Surgery"

An Audience with Michael Milken, the King of Junk

The explosion of new players in cellular and the dizzying array of alliances displeased MCI Communications. Before anyone had a sizable base of customers, MCI had had the hubris to call itself a nationwide cellular company. It saw cellular as a nice fit with its core long-distance business and considered itself the cellular industry's class act. "Our applications are not trading chits in a game," sniffed Gerald Taylor, an MCI official.

But in the competition for smaller markets, the game was changing. MCI was forced to join the Grand Alliance and trade with McCaw and other companies in what one anonymous MCI official called "a mating dance of monarch butterflies." The deal making ultimately gave MCI a strong stake in several markets and control of several western cities. MCI ended up with an interest in eleven cellular licenses—good, but far from the dominant position it had expected.

By 1985 MCI's cellular dream had begun to fade, creating what became both Craig McCaw's greatest strategic opportunity and the greatest test of his nerve. Early that year, MCI lost the competition for the Los Angeles license, a critical blow to the company's national goal. Meanwhile, cellular was not yet catching on with customers as the industry had hoped. The forecast of several million cellular customers by 1990 was cut to less than 2 million. *The Wall Street Journal* took note of the gloom forming over the industry with a story headlined CELLULAR PHONE COMPANIES CALL BUSINESS A TOUGH ONE, WITH PROFITS YEARS AWAY.

Even cellular enthusiasts had to admit that profits seemed further away than previously expected. GTE's Indianapolis system had expected 1,400 customers when it launched in 1984; instead, it attracted 350. The

Arthur D. Little research company estimated that sales costs to attract one cellular subscriber were as high as $2,000. The cellular stampede, commentators were saying, had slowed to a crawl.

Furthermore, MCI had been slow to build in its licensed markets. It held majority interests in Denver, Minneapolis, Pittsburgh, Sacramento, Salt Lake City, and Fresno, plus minority stakes in San Antonio, Oxnard (California), Canton (Ohio), Akron, and Oklahoma City. But MCI had built a system in only one market, Minneapolis, at a cost of $9.6 million. The projected cost of building its national cellular system was a shocker: a cool $1 billion.

Profits on an investment that size would take years to materialize. This was gloomy news, especially arriving just as the company was reporting depressed earnings because of increased local-access charges for its long-distance customers. MCI decided to sell both its paging and cellular operations, which were united under the company's Airsignal division.

Craig McCaw had been watching MCI carefully for months. He knew of the company's money concerns and believed that its paging division, serving fifty cities, was losing money. When word got out that MCI wanted to sell, McCaw, Ed Hopper, John Stanton, and Wayne Perry met to discuss whether McCaw Communications should make an offer.

Years later, there is some disagreement over what was said. Perry recalls that he and Stanton were both against the deal because of its cost and the burden it would have put on the company's management. The MCI licenses would more than double McCaw's cellular stake, making it overnight one of the nation's largest cellular players—second among the non-Bell companies. The deal would also give McCaw a second-place market share at 12 percent, compared with Metromedia's 15 percent. Such a deal would move McCaw way up on everyone's radar, triggering both press attention, which Craig McCaw hated, and sharper scrutiny from competitors. Till this point, McCaw had been perceived mainly as an obscure Northwest cable company that dabbled in cellular, though the reality was more impressive: McCaw owned a majority cellular stake in seven cities and a minority stake in several other cities, while serving 70,000 subscribers in paging, compared to MCI's 135,000.

As Perry remembers the MCI discussion, Hopper pressed for the deal at almost any price. But McCaw listened to Perry and decided it was too big. That apparently ended the meeting. Everyone got up and left. But Hopper turned around and went back in to lobby McCaw some more. Within a few minutes, McCaw emerged and told Perry: "We're going to do the MCI deal."

MCI received three offers. It quickly dismissed an offer from NYNEX, the New York telephone company, in part because MCI did not want to help a regional Bell enter the cellular business. The other two offers, from McCaw and American Cellular Communications Corporation, were roughly equal at around $120 million. MCI regarded American Cellular as the more qualified buyer, given its Prudential-Bache Securities financing. McCaw's financing seemed shaky.

MCI picked American Cellular, but the deal collapsed on the very day in July 1985 that it was disclosed. MCI discovered that ACCC was heavily bankrolled by BellSouth, a Baby Bell—a deal breaker as far as MCI was concerned. MCI's pullout triggered a court battle. U.S. District Court judge Robert Vining later declared that ACCC was at fault for withholding information about its BellSouth connections, but he also criticized MCI for not examining ACCC's partnership, saying that officials "went to sleep on the job and got themselves into trouble." Nonetheless, Vining ultimately allowed MCI to find a new buyer.

That new buyer was McCaw, which happily found itself back in the game when the ACCC deal collapsed. Hopper got the call: Are you willing to pay $120 million? The answer was yes. He and Stanton flew to Washington, D.C., and negotiated the deal, which was disclosed in August 1995. The announcement triggered another round of speculation about Craig McCaw's ambitions—and, in some quarters, about his sanity. How could McCaw be buying licenses when the cost of building systems was so prohibitive? And where was this guy getting $120 million? The word filtered back to McCaw headquarters that no one thought the company could get the money.

McCaw was already looking. It wasn't the sort of thing he could stop at a bank for. "We had no operating profits. We didn't have anything," says Steve Hooper, the company treasurer. Construction and other costs were devouring profits. At that point, McCaw had only a consuming conviction—that cellular had a future—and a track record in cable of skillfully managing debt and keeping lenders satisfied even as he continually expanded.

To pay for MCI and some other deals, McCaw needed a bankroll of $225 million. McCaw had several options, which included finding a new partner or getting more money from Affiliated Publications.

McCaw's goal, as always, was to preserve his independence, flexibility, and control. Although he had qualified for the MCI deal on the basis of Affiliated's balance sheet, McCaw ultimately decided to go with a different form of financing, perhaps to show a measure of independence from his Boston associates. He went with junk bonds, a relatively new form of corporate IOUs at high interest rates, recently popularized by an already legendary trader at Drexel Burnham Lambert named Michael Milken.

Working from a Los Angeles office, Milken had created a $125 billion pool of capital that had helped tiny companies swallow giants and permitted obscure executives to gain control of world-famous businesses. So effective was his operation that a mere statement that Milken believed he could raise a financial war chest in pursuit of a particular corporate quarry—a so-called "highly confident" letter—could cause panic at the company targeted for takeover. Secretive, feared by competitors, and closely monitored by securities regulators, Milken already played an enormous role in the communications industry. During his time at Drexel, he channeled some $26 billion into MCI, McCaw, Metromedia, Viacom, TCI, Time Warner, Turner, Cablevision Systems, News Corporation, and other cable, telecom, wireless, publishing, and entertainment companies.

Milken dominated the junk bond market, but other investment banks' desire to get a piece of this newly lucrative business gave McCaw alternatives. The newer entrants were offering generous terms to attract clients. The only question was whether they could raise the huge dollars that Milken had proved he could. McCaw invited representatives of different investment banks to come to the company and pitch their services, in what the McCaw people jokingly called a beauty contest.

Salomon Brothers was especially aggressive. "Salomon was adamant that they could get this done," says Perry. So McCaw Communications picked a group led by Salomon Brothers and PaineWebber and

launched a road show, visiting possible bond buyers throughout the
United States to tout McCaw as a brilliant investment opportunity. The
McCaw executives traveled in a company jet, the bond people in
another plane. Perry, Stanton, Hooper, and others represented McCaw.
Rufus Lumry stayed home with his wife, who was overdue to have a
baby. McCaw stayed home as well.

The trips were exhausting, going on for months and hitting as many
as thirteen cities in five days. At each stop, lunch always seemed to be
another turkey sandwich. John Stanton developed a cheeseburger crav-
ing. But his bigger worry was the feeble financial results of the trip. As
the weeks wore on, Stanton was losing faith in Salomon.

Near the end of the trip, one of Salomon's investment bankers, a
young man who barely reached five feet nine, approached the McCaw
people, most of whom stood six feet two or more. The Salomon banker
grinned as he described the investors they were about to meet. "We've
got some real size players," he bragged. How big? he was asked. These
people, he responded, are ready to invest $25,000. Hooper prayed that
his ears were deceiving him, but they weren't: The amount wasn't $25
million but just $25,000. "My heart dropped," Hooper recalls.

At that point, the total fund Salomon Brothers had raised stood at
about $4.5 million—a long, long way from the $225 million they
needed. Salomon had been the wrong choice.

In Houston, one of the last stops on the road show, the discouraged
McCaw team couldn't bear the thought of traveling home after yet
another turkey sandwich. As they headed through one of Houston's
poorer neighborhoods, they directed the driver of their limousine to
visit a McDonald's drive-through, where they ordered bagfuls of fries,
Quarter Pounders, and soft drinks. Their arms loaded, they boarded
their plane and began to argue over the in-cabin music. Stanton insisted
on Motown, while Perry wanted country-western.

Stanton must have gotten his way. As the plane hit cruising altitude,
the stereo was blaring Marvin Gaye's mournful heartbreak anthem "I
Heard It Through the Grapevine." The McCaw team started singing
along. Stanton wondered how long it would take for Salomon to hear
through the Wall Street grapevine that it was being dumped in favor of
the king of junk, Michael Milken.

Salomon "failed for two reasons," Perry says. "They didn't understand the market very well. [And] they confused enthusiasm with competence."

So in the summer of 1986 Wayne Perry, Rufus Lumry, and John Stanton flew down to meet Mike Milken at his Beverly Hills office. As usual, McCaw stayed detached—in part so he could kill the deal if he didn't like it.

Milken had several offices where he kept clients waiting, much as a doctor keeps several patients in examining rooms. The McCaw executives who later described the scene sat and waited, wondering if all along Milken had steered things so that McCaw had no choice but to turn to him. Was Milken so powerful that he could put out the word that investment money was to dry up until clients came to him? That seemed far-fetched even for the legendary Milken.

Suddenly, a bowl of popcorn was brought in, and Milken made his entrance. Tossing kernels into his mouth, he got right to the point. "You've got to show strength" was his first comment. "How much you looking for?"

"Two-twenty-five."

"Then we'll have to show strength. We'll go for two-twenty-five," Milken said.

Lumry was incredulous. "How in the world can you get this done when no one else can—when Salomon and PaineWebber can't get this done?"

Milken smiled. "Your problem is, you went to veterinarians when you wanted brain surgery."

Financing from Milken vastly accelerated McCaw's buying. Within a few months, the company used Drexel-managed junk bonds to buy MCI's cellular and paging operations for $120 million. Soon after the MCI deal closed, McCaw bought a large number of POPs in the southern United States, nicknamed the "Dixie POPs," from Maxwell Telecom Plus (a $70 million deal) and from Charisma Communications (an $85 million package). These deals gave McCaw control of Nashville, Knoxville, Chattanooga, Memphis, and Johnson City, Tennessee; West Palm Beach, Orlando, and Tampa, Florida; and Birmingham, Alabama.

McCaw moved quickly to add value to the MCI assets. Even before it had formal title to the Pittsburgh license, McCaw began building the system, racing to meet the FCC's rule that systems be built within three years of licensing. Only nine months remained on the MCI license, but McCaw built the system in six months when such a system normally would have taken a year to build.

The deal with MCI drew snorts of disapproval from skeptics, but in time, it was recognized as a masterstroke.

On the financing side, going to Milken proved to be enormously helpful to the company, compared to any alternatives. An equity deal would have relied on an assessment of McCaw based on a conservative valuation of POPs. Stanton made a rough calculation that McCaw would have had to give up 60 percent of its equity to raise $225 million in such a deal. When the company ultimately went public a year later, that same 60 percent would have been worth $1.2 billion. The difference—nearly a billion dollars—is what Milken saved McCaw in that one 1986 deal. "In my mind, it's probably the most significant financial transaction that we made," Stanton says.

Over three years, Milken raised almost $2 billion for the company, a service for which Drexel received about $45 million. Milken came under investigation by federal authorities during this period, but the McCaw people say he always treated them well.

Even after Milken went to prison for violations of securities and tax laws, nobody at McCaw would speak ill of him. "He helped us, he believed in us, he cared about us," McCaw says. "As a customer of his, he did for us as much as any human being could." Perry adds, "[Drexel Burnham] made money, but so did we."

Milken was proud of his connection to the McCaw company. McCaw executives became featured speakers at Milken's annual Drexel High Yield Bond Conference, better known as the Predators' Ball. Attended by some 1,000 businesspeople, the gatherings became famous for their elaborate presentations, their clever videos (such as a dubbed clip of Sean Connery as Agent 007 introducing himself as "Bond, Junk Bond"), the entertainment by stars such as Frank Sinatra, and, some say, the prostitutes paid for out of Drexel's coffers.

The McCaw people, however, insist that they were there only to work. Perry says the gatherings were an enormously important opportunity to brief investors. He says they did notice men accompanied by women who weren't their wives, but they took the women to be girlfriends, not prostitutes. The McCaw people generally skipped the parties, he says.

"Drexel never involved us in any of this stuff. They knew you absolutely could not bribe McCaw," Perry says. "McCaw set that tone for the company. The joke in the investment community was that the corporate drink at McCaw was Perrier." (McCaw himself later switched to Evian.)

For all the controversy surrounding Milken's business tactics and his role in the boom-and-bust Wall Street of the 1980s, his contribution to McCaw Communications was important. Money raised by Milken allowed Craig McCaw to buy MCI Airsignal, easily the cellular deal of the decade, and transformed McCaw Cellular from an obscure regional player into a national presence, forever changing Craig McCaw's life. "Forget all that bullshit about what they had in the Pacific Northwest," says Tim Donahue, an Airsignal executive who later joined McCaw. "That acquisition *made* Craig McCaw."

Shortly after formally gaining title to the Airsignal assets, McCaw sold MCI's paging operations for $75 million. Counting a few other transactions, the cost to McCaw of buying MCI's cellular properties worked out to $46 million. Within seven years, those same cellular properties would be valued at more than $1 billion. Perry couldn't believe their luck—they'd gotten a deal that worked out to a bargain-basement $1 a POP.

Later, the McCaw people had to restrain themselves from gloating over what they regarded as MCI's goof. "They made this terrible blunder," Hopper says. "They were so focused on the long-distance market that they forgot the future."

MCI would later try to get back in by offering to buy or invest in cellular companies. It settled on a strategy of reselling other companies' cellular services. By 1995 MCI was calling cellular a low-profit commodity, a reseller's business, not a provider's. That claim made Perry laugh. "If you've got no air force and everyone else is trying to figure which jet to deploy, all you can say is that the next war will be fought with tanks," Perry says.

Hopper, for one, had favored financing the MCI purchase with Affiliated, which wanted to support the deal and, in Hopper's view, was owed some loyalty. "We jilted Affiliated for Milken," Hopper says. While he can't argue with the success of McCaw's approach, Hopper saw a problem in the changing nature of his relationship with McCaw.

McCaw had delegated so much power that Hopper felt almost

completely independent—the chief executive of a start-up company that kept hitting home runs. Cable remained a growing concern, but cellular was growing at a much faster pace, and the values of cellular licenses were accelerating. Hopper found that McCaw was around more, asking more questions, and showing more interest in details.

One day, McCaw remarked, "Hopper, you're having more fun than I am." It was a joke—but a pointed one. Hopper marks that day in 1986 as the day he really lost control of the cellular company. "I remember walking away feeling very discouraged because I knew that McCaw had jumped over on my side of the fence," Hopper now says.

He adds, ruefully, that McCaw's "move over to cellular was absolutely inevitable, because there was too much executive talent and time being devoted to [the] cable company [while] giant home runs were being hit over on the cellular side in terms of just plain old value." Hopper stayed on with McCaw another two years, but he began to spend more of his time at home in Portland and to pursue separate interests in satellite transmissions. Hopper had discovered the limits of McCaw's autonomous subordinate policy.

For a time, there was an awkward division of authority. McCaw was not technically in charge, having gone on extended medical leave because of a chronic throat ailment—caused by an allergy, rumor had it. Typically, McCaw kept the details private even from Lyn Pawley, the assistant he worked with daily. "It was clear he didn't want to talk about it. He certainly didn't want it made known to people who were calling in," Pawley says. "He thought that it might be viewed as a vulnerable moment in the organization."

McCaw named Wayne Perry acting chief executive of McCaw Communications and stayed in touch from the Caribbean via fax and occasional phone calls. He was gone for six months during 1986. When he resurfaced, he announced that he had decided to split the expanded cellular company, leaving Hopper to take charge of the MCI units in Portland and Stanton to run the old McCaw Communications properties in Seattle.

Everyone except McCaw thought it was a bad idea. It made much more sense to coordinate all of the properties from one office. Stanton was characteristically blunt. "Both Wayne and I thought it was an unbelievably stupid idea," Stanton says, laughing. "There was some chaff that went with that wheat with Craig. Wayne waited a somewhat respectful period of time and then tanked the whole idea." Stanton was later given operational control over all the cellular properties.

Perry chuckles at the suggestion that Craig McCaw, the celebrated business genius, had *one* bad idea. That was false; McCaw had *many* bad ideas, Perry says.

"Craig will come up with ten ideas," says Perry, and

a few of them, no one in the world would have thought of them. They will make you unbelievably successful if you follow them. Two of the ideas are average or okay. A bunch of the ideas, you don't have a clue what he's talking about. [And] a bunch of the ideas will make you so broke so fast. The trick with Craig is to differentiate out of that set.

"My ego is based not on what they think, but on what the world thinks," McCaw himself says. "If I feel good because somebody doesn't give me the feedback I need, what did I prove? There were times when I had an idea and if it wasn't a particularly good one and it didn't get done, I didn't care."

That was only partly true. Sometimes McCaw really did have no ego invested in his ideas, so his aides were free to consider and ignore them. Other times, they misread his determination to do something, and he would be displeased. Reading McCaw may be the toughest thing about working for him. "Craig can get enamored of things," says Scot Jarvis. "[But] the ardor can fade. The trick is to predict what will fade."

The one constant was McCaw's intense ambition and his focus on the future.

After the Airsignal sale, Tim Donahue quit MCI and joined the McCaw company because he loved the spirit and intensity of the people he met there. Only later did he meet McCaw, to whom he reported while running the paging division.

"His approach was always the same," Donahue says:

He never wanted to talk about what was happening that day, week, or month. He always wanted to know how we could make this a world-class organization, how to make it first-class for the customer. He'd say, "Tell me how much money you need to do that, and I will get the money if you can build me a long-term franchise." He was always thinking about the long term.

When providing good service required buying some costly equipment, McCaw hated to hear the fact stated as if it were a negative. As Donahue puts it, "He would get upset with us. He'd say, 'If you built it the right way, and you're taking care of customers, we'll make it back tenfold. Don't worry about capital. I'll worry about that.' "

There was McCaw's faith again, denying uncertainty. The message was always the same: Build it right; keep customers happy; quality wins. That mantra was a crucial element of McCaw's success, though far from the whole story.

13

"It's Getting Awful Lonely"

McCaw Consolidates His Empire as Independents Fall

For McCaw Communications, the MCI deal dominated 1986. The company grew at a furious pace, and though employment on the cellular side remained smaller than the cable TV division's, the escalating value of the cellular licenses would soon overtake the cable systems' worth.

Shortly before McCaw took his medical leave, the company moved from its modest wood building in Bellevue to an elegant, modern glass-and-steel structure in nearby Kirkland, on a site facing Lake Washington and Seattle. McCaw took an office in the back of the building, close to the staircase. Always wary of unsolicited contact with people, he wanted to be able to come and go without anyone's knowledge. "Management by walking around was never his style," says Brian McCauley, a former company vice president.

Much as Craig McCaw enjoyed his solitude, to call him simply a loner would distort his personality. He enjoyed seeing close friends, whom he took boating, kayaking, and traveling. When he turned forty in 1989, his wife threw a huge party at the Seattle Golf Club, where friends from all over the country found rooms custom-decorated with antiques, fancy draperies, and other exotic finery, and where the best chefs and pastry cooks were on hand to feed the assembled revelers.

So McCaw clearly had a social side. At the same time, he cultivated a sense of himself as apart from the crowd, apart even from many of the people who worked for him. Above all, he did not want to become captive of other people's thinking or of their judgment of him.

In an interview with the American Academy of Achievement, McCaw spoke about his philosophy toward the press and outsider criticism. In comments that reveal much about his personality, he says he makes a practice of never reading what people say about him:

because if you read what they say and you care, then they won. . . . It's necessary that you insulate yourself from what others think. The greatest ideas you will ever have are the ones that other people don't understand. And if you're in that position, and you care too much what they think, you will not do the right thing. And therefore, I purposefully have long ago decided that if I live by the moral code that I want to live by, then what people think of me is not so important, because I'm doing what I believe is right and I'm not trying to hurt other people. So long as my success, such as it is, does not come at the expense of other people, then I'm happy, and I don't mind if they don't agree with me. In fact, it's a lot of fun when they don't, because life is a long time, and the more they criticize you, the more they compliment you later if you're right. And sometimes, by the way, you're wrong, and you have to be prepared for that.

In 1986 a lot of people said that Craig McCaw was wrong. The future of cellular had apparently dimmed. It was time, many observers claimed, for the independent cellular companies to make way for an inevitable industry consolidation. Independents like McCaw Cellular had had their fun. Now they would be bought up by the Baby Bells.

McCaw was determined to stay independent—to prove the observers wrong.

Pacific Telesis, the Baby Bell for California, announced a deal in mid-1985 to spend $435 million on Communications Industries, one of several partners with McCaw in the nonwireline license for San Francisco. (GTE owned the local wireline license.) Then PacTel announced a deal to buy another partner, giving it more than 50 percent of the Bay Area license.

McCaw asked the FCC to block the deal, arguing that half the nonwireline licenses—the "A Block" of frequency—had been deliberately withheld from the Bell companies to promote competition. McCaw argued that the FCC wanted two carriers with different histories and approaches to vie in the marketplace. PacTel's first loyalty, McCaw said, was to its wireline business. This could only lead it to hobble the Bay Area Cellular Network, which was trying to bypass

PacTel's switching system. How could PacTel support a company that wanted to take away its local access revenue?

So went the argument. But some analysts noted that McCaw himself had contributed to this problem by supporting the settlements negotiated by Stanton in New York—settlements that had yoked many sets of unlikely partners to a single license. Under the circumstances, conflicts of interest were inevitable.

As the first time that a wireline company had tried to buy into a nonwireline license, the PacTel case was enormously significant for the industry. If PacTel won in San Francisco, what would stop any other Baby Bell from buying other nonwireline licenses? This was one of Craig McCaw's nightmares—that the promise of cellular would be smothered in the embrace of the telephone giants, who had no strategic reason to innovate. McCaw figured if the Bells could buy, the price of POPs would skyrocket, the independents would stop buying, and the fast growth of the cellular industry would stall.

The McCaw company won many arguments before the FCC, but not this one. The FCC ruled that the set-asides of the A Block for nonwireline companies had applied only to the initial licensing, not for all time: The "fence" was not a permanent one. McCaw later tried—and failed—to block the deal in the courts.

PacTel's victory brought a fundamental change in the cellular industry's strategic landscape. But that victory wasn't complete. It faced a shotgun held by Craig McCaw.

When the San Francisco cellular partnership was formed, McCaw had insisted on the right to force his partners to set a sale price for their half of the license. The trick was that, if they set too high a price, McCaw could force them to buy his half at that same price. The purpose of this shotgun provision was to force the partners to set an honest price for the license. And McCaw had sole discretion to decide whether he wanted to buy or sell at the price the partners set. This one-way condition gave him leverage over PacTel or anyone who was interested in taking PacTel's place in the partnership.

PacTel developed a new appreciation for the deal-making savvy of Craig McCaw. Uneasily, the two sides stayed partners.

Meanwhile, a new executive was pushing US West NewVector outside its boundaries. John DeFeo had succeeded Dick Callahan at

NewVector in 1983, having worked on the development of two-way radios for General Electric. A trim, self-controlled engineer, DeFeo had graduated from the New Jersey Military Academy. And he believed in cellular.

Headquartered just a few miles south of Craig McCaw, DeFeo drew inevitable comparisons with the "reckless" McCaw. Inside US West, jaws dropped at the McCaw deals, and analysts predicted McCaw's failure, saying that the more prudent DeFeo would eventually take his pick from the ruins of McCaw Cellular. But DeFeo himself admitted his respect for Craig McCaw and his management of debt. And like McCaw, DeFeo thought the Bells were oblivious to the big future of cellular; in fact, he made a point of hiring people from outside the Bells.

DeFeo wanted to buy a license in San Diego, but his bosses at US West headquarters in Denver were unenthusiastic. They saw cellular as a niche business, as wireless had been for twenty-five years. US West had other spending plans: expanding the Yellow Pages business, building entire systems for larger customers, even buying real estate. But after some prodding, it agreed to support DeFeo's San Diego plan. In the 1985 deal, DeFeo paid a record $25 per POP.

DeFeo saw himself as a Bell company maverick, but Zane Barnes, chairman of St. Louis–based Southwestern Bell, would outdo him in zeal for cellular. In his forty-five-year telephone career, Barnes had worked his way up from a job as a lineman—a "wire twister," as he put it. In June 1986 Barnes stunned the telecommunications world by agreeing to spend $1.65 billion for John Kluge's Metromedia cellular and paging assets. The deal sent a signal that the fat-wallet Bells intended to dominate cellular—niche business or no.

The deal set another record at an estimated $35 to $55 per POP, and it gave Southwestern 100 percent of Chicago; 50 percent of Boston; 55 percent of Baltimore-Washington; 66 percent of Worcester, Massachusetts; 45 percent of New York City; 49 percent of Philadelphia; and 16 percent of Dallas. In all, Southwestern acquired properties in markets with a total population of 21.9 million, bringing the company's overall total to 45 million people.

Litigation between Metromedia and LIN Broadcasting, its partner in New York and Philadelphia, ultimately fouled the deal. Southwestern later got 100 percent of three cities—Baltimore-Washington, Chicago, and Boston—plus Metromedia's paging division, for the smaller price of

$1.2 billion. Even this lesser deal demonstrated Barnes's nerve. He was moving to compete head-on with another Bell in its own market, and in doing so was buying an operation years away from its first projected profit. "It is risky," he told *The Wall Street Journal*, "but it's a reasonable risk."

Although Southwestern had to borrow to finance the deal, Barnes said the company would continue paying its $1.60-a-share quarterly dividend (nearly sacred to Bell investors). But shareholders still thought poorly of the deal, and the company's stock fell $7 to $102.50.

McCaw Communications protested this deal, too. For openers, it created a problem for the Cellular One brand, which McCaw was using under an arrangement with its owner, the Washington-Baltimore system. Cellular One had been a popular brand for nonwireline companies, but now it was falling under the control of Southwestern Bell, which could either block McCaw from using the brand or use it in markets adjacent to McCaw's, disrupting McCaw's marketing.

But it was becoming clear that the FCC and the courts would not block the Metromedia sale. Judge Harold Greene, who had presided over the Bell system breakup, had already signaled his attitude. In approving PacTel's purchase of Communications Industries, Greene wrote, "The entry of regional companies into cellular communications may actually accelerate the development of the cellular technology and enhance competition in the local telephone market."

Yet these putative benefits came at a price. Facing the high costs of building their systems, the independents were selling—not to one another, but to others with larger checkbooks. In 1986 BellSouth of Atlanta sought federal approval to buy 50 percent of Mobile Communications Corporation of America's cellular subsidiary for $107.5 million. MCCA held licenses for 10.3 million potential customers. Industry consolidation was happening more quickly than anyone had anticipated. "It's a major change going on; the [non-Bell] companies are cashing in . . . and getting out," said Dick Callahan, who later became a group vice president at US West. "We're looking at a whole bunch." *Financial World* magazine called the Bells "virtually the only companies that can afford to spend whatever is required to compete for the long haul." Craig McCaw and his diminishing fraternity could not.

The independents were feeling the pressure. "You won't see many of us left in five years," Jack Brennan of George Lindemann's Metro

Mobile CTS told the *Washington Post*. "I can't afford to buy South-western Bell out." John Stanton made a similar point in *Forbes*: "We're moving toward an industry dominated by the telephone companies. What am I supposed to do, tender for PacTel?" He added, "We intend to stay but it's getting awful lonely." *Communications Week* speculated that McCaw, too, would have to sell eventually.

The MCI deal left McCaw Communications as the largest independent cellular company, with 25.6 million potential customers compared to LIN Broadcasting's 16.2 million. But big McCaw was puny compared to the Bells. For 1985 McCaw counted just 14,800 cellular customers, who paid the company $297,000—no financial competition for the Bells, who as a group earned $7.5 billion on $63.3 billion of revenue in 1985.

Stanton acknowledged that McCaw had considered but then blinked at the price of Metromedia's cellular properties. Craig McCaw feared the Bells' buying power. He knew it would be difficult to outbid them. Equally important, he feared what they would do to the industry. He believed the Bells would not innovate, would not push, would not recognize cellular as central to their future. Keepers of the copper lines, they would not see the cellular telephone for what it could be—a "freedom machine."

McCaw's team worried that the Bells's deepest motivation was simply to buy out a potential threat to their landline business. "The telephone business—and the new technology shaping it—is cellular," Ed Hopper said later. "Cellular is directly substitutable for landline-based telephones."

Reed Royalty, PacTel's vice president for external affairs, ridiculed that thought. The FCC, he pointed out, did not allow the same Bell to own both the wireline and nonwireline cellular business in the same market. Nor could a cellular system handle the volume of any region's regular telephone traffic. In Los Angeles, PacTel's cellular system struggled to handle 60,000 customers; how could it ever serve the region's 13 million people? The Hopper argument, said Royalty, "doesn't pass the sanity test."

But Craig McCaw was looking further down the road. He believed that the Bells saw cellular as skimming off profitable customers. Also important, the Bells' buying up of nonwire licenses created obstacles to the creation of a future national cellular system. As a result of the

Metromedia sale, two critical markets, Chicago and Boston, now belonged to a Bell. The patchwork of licenses held by competing interests would keep cellular from reaching its fullest potential.

McCaw felt an emotional reaction as well. He was a businessman, but he was almost childlike in his affection for gadgets and the fun they could provide. He loathed the thought of cellular's being locked up forever by what many independents saw as the unimaginative drones who ran the Bells. Big phone companies were about monopolies and about winning rate increases from state utilities, not about freeing people. It was difficult to see how entrenched bureaucracies built around old copper wires and mainframe systems could develop the agility to serve the roaming worker. How could a bureaucracy understand the free individual? In this sense, McCaw's war against the Bells took on a philosophical—almost a religious—quality.

But there was a positive side. The failure of the lawsuit to keep PacTel out of the nonwireline side in San Francisco opened the A Block to all potential buyers, including the Bells. No longer was that block limited to buyers whom Wall Street viewed as financially overmatched. This meant that the A Block licenses were suddenly much more valuable. As a result, the value of McCaw Communications soared, and the new, higher value allowed McCaw to borrow more and buy more. Talk about irony: "The only way we could have succeeded the way we did was because we lost a lawsuit," says Hopper.

McCaw's tactical defeat became a strategic victory. But the ironies didn't stop there. The McCaw junk bonds were now backed by licenses that the Bells could buy in a second. So McCaw could promise potential investors that the security behind their bonds was rock-solid. In fact, the best thing for bond buyers, McCaw would say, would be for the company to default, forcing "CCC" McCaw to sell to an "AAA" Bell. "If we screw up, [the licenses] go to an RBOC and you get your money back," Perry told them. Because any cellular company was now a potential acquisition for a Bell, in a sense the independents' credit was backed by the Bells.

By now, cellular had established a toehold with the public, but only that. In 1986 the industry counted about 462,000 customers in eighty-three markets, far less than the 300 markets once forecast for that date. Some of the operating markets still lacked a nonwireline provider. Spending on cellular by customers in all markets totaled just $650 million a year, according to an estimate by Herschel Shosteck Associates, a Maryland consulting firm.

Furthermore, cellular was still an expensive way to talk. Each phone and peripheral equipment cost about $1,350, and the typical user bought 250 minutes of airtime for $93 to $158 a month. Shosteck estimated that the service price would have to drop to about $50 a month to penetrate the residential market, and that wasn't expected till the turn of the century.

The industry was expensive for consumers, but fabulously so for service providers. The constant hemorrhaging of cash caused by the high cost of system building tested the nerves of cellular executives. Virtually none of the forty or so providers was making a profit, except in a handful of lucrative markets such as Los Angeles and Dallas.

LIN Broadcasting reported a $6.8 million loss on its cellular business amid overall net income of $36 million on total revenue of $196 million. Brennan of Lindemann's Metro Mobile said his company at that point had spent $40 million on cellular. In Phoenix alone, Lindemann was losing $200,000 to $300,000 a month. "For every dollar the customer was spending, we were spending another dollar," he told *Forbes*. The business press saw gloom. "The promised payoff for all of these companies seems to have receded steadily and may now be as far off as 1990," declared *Financial World*.

As a private company, McCaw Communications did not break out its cellular numbers from its $78 million in overall revenues, but it, too, was losing money on cellular. Subsequent reports showed cellular losses of $12.8 million in 1985 and $38.5 million in 1986, when the number of McCaw's wireless customers reached 53,800. Not only were construction costs devouring profit, but so were marketing expenses. McCaw paid dealers $500 for each new customer.

But the numbers didn't worry Craig McCaw and his team. Cellular licenses were trading at all-time highs, unimaginable two years earlier, and McCaw wasn't selling. He was buying. He had not wavered from his belief that cellular was the best investment in America.

Rising prices had one positive benefit: They induced people McCaw had been courting to finally sell. "Whatever you can get, buy it," he told his people, and he was rarely satisfied that they had bought enough, fast enough.

CHAPTER

14

"Where Do I Sell My License?"

Speculation Reaches a Climax in an FCC Free-for-all

By 1986 cellular was no longer a secret. Thousands of investors were flooding the FCC with quickie applications for the license giveaways. The filings for Round Five totaled 8,109. The FCC figured that by 1988, the last year of lotteries, the applications for all markets would total 300,000.

Craig McCaw watched how the FCC lotteries gained momentum and awarded licenses to people he had never heard of. The speculators wanted quick sales; each had to be hunted down, courted, and persuaded to sign a sales agreement before others did the deal. So McCaw brought in a new collection of talent—young people with brains, endurance, and charm who were willing to spend months on planes. Inspired by his success at wooing owners of cable franchises to sell, McCaw sent these lieutenants out with authority to do deals. They were given a range within which McCaw Communications would buy and told to improvise on the details, so long as the deal got done—quickly.

One of McCaw's young deal makers was Robert Ratliffe, hired away from Seafirst Bank by John McCaw. The very day Ratliffe arrived, he was told to get on a plane for Washington, D.C. He traveled constantly. "Cost a marriage," says Ratliffe, who noted he wasn't alone in that respect: "There were a lot of fatalities in the marriage department." Ratliffe had been at the company a little more than a month when, charging up the office staircase, he noticed someone unfamiliar jogging his way. "I don't believe we've met," said Ratliffe, sticking out his hand. His boss, Craig McCaw, shook it.

The McCaw buyers vacuumed up the nation's cellular licenses. They bought from countless small-time prospectors on the cellular frontier: a beauty salon owner; an ambulance driver; a deep-sea diver; and a squadron of speculating suburban dentists. McCaw's people paid $700,000 to a guy nicknamed "the Fat Man" who played porno movies in his office; they paid $3 million to an Oregon man who lived deep in the woods in a mobile home. Some of the sellers drove hard bargains; others were softies. One guy was maneuvered into knocking $300,000 off the price by the promise of a free cell phone, says Ratliffe. One wealthy Nashville resident agreed to sell for McCaw stock, but not for cash. "I need cash likes a hog needs a Sunday shirt," he said.

Another seller of a minority share of the Sacramento license declared stoutly that he couldn't sell for less than $24 a POP. The seller happened to be a duck hunter who owned a hunting cabin. Ratliffe and several other McCaw people also hunted birds. Since Ratliffe had been authorized to pay $34 a POP, the asking price was no problem, but Ratliffe wanted the guy to feel like a winner. So Ratliffe, acting reluctant, said he had to call headquarters to check—purely a gambit, since Ratliffe went into every negotiation knowing McCaw's exact limit. After a decent interval, Ratliffe came back and said that McCaw Communications would consider the deal, but only if the seller threw in a trip to his hunting cabin.

One couple in Arkansas collected $48,000 from the sale of their piece of a partnership in a cellular license, just five years after they had bought it for only $2,000. They happened to be the state's governor, Bill Clinton, and his wife, Hillary Rodham Clinton. No one from McCaw's top management team dealt directly with the Clintons, who were just two of several partners. But McCaw figured it wouldn't hurt to have the young governor's favor if business problems ever arose in Arkansas. The Clintons' $46,000 profit represented the couple's second most successful financial transaction, after Hillary's notorious cattle-futures deal.

A couple who operated a beauty school in Santa Rosa, California, saw an infomercial, invested $15,000, and won the license for Yakima, Washington (population: 60,000). They sold to McCaw for $1 million.

The team from Kirkland did deals fast. They flew directly to owners of cellular licenses, presented a one-page sale agreement, and asked, "What will it take to get you to sign right now?" The papers would be signed, the seller gleeful at getting more than expected, and the McCaw official would fly home while competitors were still writing memos to headquarters about their purchase plans. "We had competent people.

We knew exactly what we wanted to do," says Perry. The simple formula worked.

In one deal, Cellular Communications Inc. had had a difficult time dealing with a certain New Yorker and his partners who owned the franchise for Santa Rosa, California. Finally, they agreed on $100 a POP. "We had a deal," recalls George Blumenthal, CCI's secretary-treasurer. "It comes time to sign the paper, and we get a call from them saying, 'We're selling to McCaw. They just wired one million into our bank account.' John Stanton's work. Whatever we bid, they topped it."

Perry loved those stories. Sometimes a rival bidder would see the announcement of a deal and call McCaw to demand the truth. "We're sorry, but what can we say?" Perry would reply with a grin. Not only were McCaw's people fast, but Blumenthal found their nerve breathtaking. CCI had wanted a contract with the Santa Rosa sellers, whom Blumenthal considered "loony." CCI wasn't about to give them $1 million without a formal agreement. The McCaw company did the deal with almost no paperwork. "McCaw was very aggressive," says Blumenthal.

But they also weren't fools, as Perry would point out. They could tie up an acquisition without a book-length contract. From their background in cable, they knew the essence of a fast deal. Besides, buying a license was not a complex transaction. The sale agreement, Perry says, could be reduced to a single page without risking a thing.

The furious bidding for licenses spawned a business never imagined by the FCC: brokers serving licensees who never intended to operate a cellular business. To save people the bother of preparing a fifty-page application, including the required engineering study, these promoters would hire an engineer and then charge dozens of applicants between $500 to $600 to use the same study.

Some applicants saw buying cellular lottery tickets as a reasonable investment risk like any other. A Washington, D.C., cellular telephone consultant named William Moorhead told *The Wall Street Journal* that he had spent $40,000 to apply for franchises in 140 small cities, even though his chance of being awarded the license in any one of them was only about one in 500. "I'm trusting the gods and calling psychics," he said.

The *Journal* followed Moorhead as he went to a crowded FCC meeting room in downtown Washington and watched a clerk pulling numbered Ping-Pong balls from a hopper, indicating the license winners for Mayaguez, Puerto Rico, Biloxi, Mississippi, and thirteen other areas. Moorhead watched eight drawings, lost all eight, and left. "I have the feeling that somewhere, someplace I'll hit one," he said.

Like Moorhead, most of the speculators showed no interest in actually building a cellular system. "Where do I sell my license?" one winner immediately asked an FCC clerk.

In Los Angeles, American National Cellular Inc. hired television crooner Mike Douglas to make videotapes and advertisements extolling cellular as "the investment of the decade . . . possibly of the century." The company signed up 1,000 agents to push applications for $5,000 apiece. The shady practices of American National sparked dozens of complaints, including one from a widow with two children who invested $10,000 in two applications. She said an American National agent had assured her that she would win a piece of licenses in Modesto and Visalia, California. After losing the lottery, she doubted she had the money left to pay for her children's education.

An executive recruiter in Charlotte, North Carolina, swapped a $53,000 condominium for applications in thirty cities. He said an American National agent told him his investment would quickly triple in value. He won something, but only tiny pieces of franchises of dubious value. Eventually, the state of Arizona sued American National for fraud and misrepresentation and won a $3.4 million default judgment. Finally, the Federal Trade Commission persuaded a federal judge to shut down the company altogether, after an American National spokesman acknowledged to the *Journal* that its representatives had painted a picture of lottery chances as a "little more rosy" than warranted.

But there were other schemes, some clever, some marginally legal or worse. Lottery losers howled that attorneys who specialized in license applications had simply rounded up people with no real interest in communications, formed a group, and then had each of them file solely to boost their chances of winning in each drawing. Sometimes, the get-rich schemes actually worked. One Maryland housewife and her switchboard-repairman husband won a drawing; a disabled truck driver won part of the license for Nashua, New Hampshire, along with an octogenarian, a highway engineer, and three Californians who had never seen Nashua.

"It's the great American dream," said the truck driver, Robert Pelissier. "It's like going to Reno and hitting the jackpot." With winners turning around and selling their franchises for as much as $5 million, it was actually better than hitting any jackpot.

Perhaps the most successful broker of cellular licenses was Mark Warner, who as a twenty-seven-year-old attorney became a middleman for investors in 1982. A Harvard Law School graduate and former Democratic Party fund-raiser, Warner worked out of a Washington, D.C., office and put together applications in exchange for a 5 percent ownership in the venture if the application won. Since most winners wanted to sell their licenses, Warner also offered to serve as broker for the sale.

It was all perfectly legal. The stock sale and commissions made Warner a fortune estimated at $100 million. "He was quite entrepreneurial, quite a deal-maker, a rainmaker for the industry," Bernard Gray, who worked deals with Warner in the 1980s, told *The Washington Post*. "He created an awful lot of wealth for a lot of people, including himself."

But the FCC had begun to rue its decision to give away licenses. "The scandal is we're giving away [franchises] for nothing," said Peter Pirsch, the FCC's chief planner. Today many agree. Some feel that the cellular speculators fattened themselves at the public trough. "The whole process was fundamentally flawed," says John McMillan, an economist at the University of California at San Diego. "It was just a massive giveaway from the public to the big corporations."

"These people screwed their fellow Americans and walked away with fortunes by doing nothing except using the system," says Don Ritter, who as a Republican member of Congress from Pennsylvania fought to revamp the licensing procedures in the early 1990s. The new rules required license holders to operate a system at least a year before selling their license. Ultimately ending the license giveaways, the FCC in 1994 switched to an auction system and collected hundreds of millions of dollars from license buyers.

For his part, the millionaire broker Mark Warner says he worked within the rules, but he acknowledges that later changes were appropriate. "It's kind of Monday-afternoon quarterbacking, looking back on it now," he told the *Post*. "Should there have been [rule] changes? Yes. You were in an industry that was growing by leaps and bounds, one that some people didn't believe would ever get off the ground." Besides, he says, radio and television licenses were also given away free in the early days of those industries. "Except that it happened at a much faster rate, how is [cellular] any different than the broadcasting industry?" he asked.

Warner used some of his cellular wealth to enter politics. In 1996 he ran for the U.S. Senate from Virginia against incumbent John Warner (no relation). He lost.

* * *

Much as the frenzy they fed may have contributed to price increases, Warner and others created a huge opportunity for anyone trying to assemble licenses. Unlike television and radio, where licenses have always traded at a measured pace, cellular opened up a large number of markets very quickly, creating tons of supply for anyone who wanted it.

McCaw did, but there was never enough cash to buy all that he wanted. He was always wooing lenders or others with deep pockets. McCaw often had to start by imparting his vision of cellular: it was not a toy but a revolution. He would take people away from New York, where cellular service was awful because of inadequate systems, to another city, where it worked. McCaw would invite bankers to briefings on cellular long before approaching them for a loan. He wanted to work "the puppy effect": put a cellular phone in their hands and watch them call home from a car. They'll fall in love, like kids in the pet shop.

McCaw also knew that playtime moves minds. To build relationships with lenders, McCaw would invite them on river-rafting trips in Oregon. Chief Financial Officer Rufus Lumry helped with the planning for these outings, fussing over each participant's preferences. If someone preferred Evian to Perrier, Evian it was. The spectacular Rogue River provided the entertainment. After a few hours, friendly splashes turned into roaring water fights under the sun, and men with loan portfolios felt like boys again. Word got around about the ultimate squirt gun fight that was settled when McCaw's team called in a helicopter—equipped with a water cannon. The days would end with hamburgers around the campfire and a little business talk.

"Rufus knew if he treated people well, they would lend him

money," says Tim David, the broker with Daniels & Associates. Of course, it was all a little more complicated than that, but undoubtedly a pleasant weekend left a friendly glow that lubricated many a deal. "You built a relationship with people," says Steve Hooper, the controller who worked with Rufus Lumry. After just one rafting trip, the lenders "would beg" to come back, says Patti Cannon, who helped prepare the meals.

In the summer of 1986 Craig McCaw flew down to Los Angeles to meet his most important source of money—Michael Milken. McCaw was impressed and amused by the sight of Milken shuttling from room to room, suggesting strategic directions for clients. It reminded McCaw of a master surgeon gliding from one operating room to another. "He would have been a great doctor," McCaw said later. The junk bond king had played a huge and largely unrecognized role in building the cable TV and cellular industries. Before bankers would touch either, he was raising billions of dollars for both.

Now McCaw told Milken that McCaw Communications wanted help to buy more cellular licenses. But Milken saw a new threat to Craig McCaw. "You're exposed," Milken said. McCaw was trying to grow two capital-intensive businesses at once while facing deeper-pocketed competitors on both fronts. He couldn't grow in both cable and cellular for long. Milken warned McCaw that his company was too deeply in debt. There was an irony—the foremost apostle of debt telling Craig McCaw that his financial strategy was too risky. According to Perry, McCaw didn't show much reaction. He just took it in thoughtfully and said merely, "Hmm. Okay."

But Milken was right. The Southwestern buyout of Metromedia's cellular business showed how the bigger boys were prepared to snatch licenses that McCaw needed. Previously, McCaw had been annoyed by industry talk that his company was spread thin. To his face, the chairman of PacTel had called his company a "house of cards." "I was tired of hearing about how much leverage we should take," McCaw says. Hearing the same message from Milken gave it a new urgency; it "hit McCaw right between the eyes," Stanton said later. McCaw had to focus his company on one business or the other.

But which direction to choose?

McCaw had an emotional attachment to his cable business, which by then ranked as one of the nation's largest systems with more than 425,000 subscribers in thirty-seven markets. Once the delivery system was built, cable was a wonderfully steady, predictable, and profitable business. And McCaw Cable had grown at a fabulous pace. Between 1980 and 1986 revenues had grown from $4 million to $107 million and subscribers from 28,000 to 434,000.

But cable was a changing industry. In 1984 deregulation had begun to lift controls on rates. This eliminated one of the cable industry's biggest headaches, dealing with local governments. But that had been a competitive strength for McCaw, and now it was gone. "We didn't need deregulation. We worked in partnership with the cities to give the people what they wanted. We got better rates and better returns than anybody else by being nice to people," McCaw says:

> Our people delivered the goods, and we did it with a minimum amount of money, simply and efficiently, and we were really terrific at it. Well, when they passed deregulation, everything we did was thrown out the window, and, hey, our time was past. Marketing and scale and things like that became important. We were too small.

Cable remained a great business. But compared with cellular's Saturn-rocket growth, it was a maturing industry; a dollar invested in cellular had a vastly superior rate of return (based on POPs sales alone, because operating profits were years away). More important, while the McCaw company was only a midsize player in cable, in cellular it had the opportunity to become the leader of an industry of limitless potential. As a business, cellular was a high-speed, high-stakes chess game, a contest among deal makers and visionaries, all having an exciting time—the kind of field that would have attracted Elroy McCaw. Put simply, cellular was just more fun.

So the decision, however painful, seemed inevitable.

McCaw invited the top members of his team to join him on a rental yacht in the Bahamas. Afterward, some called it the "Iguana Meeting," after the lizards that scampered everywhere on the islands. Out at sea in the main salon of the sixty-one-foot boat, McCaw gathered Wayne Perry, John Stanton, Rufus Lumry, John McCaw, and others to hash it out. Should they stay in both cable and cellular? If not, which of the two should they hold on to?

What followed was a forceful, even emotional, debate. Stanton and John McCaw led the argument, with Stanton pushing for cellular, while John McCaw, who had spent his entire career on the cable side, argued for cable. Cable, he insisted, was a steady business, and now, with easing government regulation of rates, profits were certain to rise. But John McCaw couldn't argue against the greater opportunities in cellular. Gradually, he came around as the ground shifted and everyone agreed that more company resources should go to cellular. The members of the group began to talk about moving money and employees out of cable, with John himself suggesting some of those changes.

Finally, John McCaw realized that by agreeing to move his staff to cellular, he had effectively talked himself out of a job. "Hey, what a minute. What about me?" he blurted. Although everyone laughed, Craig McCaw took pride in how his brother had conducted himself. "He'd just painted himself out of a job," McCaw says. "It was one of the most poetic moments of my life, I have to say, and not at his expense, because he'd supported [the decision favoring cellular] and had placed the company above himself." McCaw compared it to someone's giving away so much of his food that none was left for himself.

Craig told John not to worry—he'd be taken care of. (He wound up as executive vice president for acquisitions in the cellular company, where he stayed until 1991.)

Word filtered back to company headquarters that more emphasis would be given to cellular. But within a few months, the company shift evolved into an outright decision to sell the cable division. However logical, the decision stunned even some of McCaw's more senior managers.

Steve Hooper, Rufus Lumry's aide, had only recently been named to run the cable division. Hooper remembers how he got the news: a call from Perry, who said, "Steve, I need to talk to you. I have some unfortunate news. We've given it a lot of thought, and it's nothing to do with you, but Craig has decided to sell the cable operations." Hooper went on to success in the cellular division, but at that point he felt the floor had dropped out of his career.

Within a few months, the cable system was on the public auction block. Company longtimers who had known the McCaws as teenagers were distraught, fearful of working for anyone else. Senior managers realized that their jobs would soon be at the whim of different owners. Hooper, who bore much of the burden of answering people's questions, says, "It was painful. It was traumatic."

It pained Craig McCaw, too, but for the observer it provided a lesson in how he did business. He wasn't sentimental about making a change, even if it involved selling the little Centralia company left to him by his father. He wouldn't cling to something if it didn't make strategic sense.

Those who watched Craig McCaw detected another personal factor: that McCaw would get bored with any business once it settled into a predictable routine. To get his juices going, he wanted to face risk and uncertainty. He liked picking a path where others saw chaos.

Many cable industry observers thought McCaw was crazy to sell his cash cow. An offer came quickly from Jack Kent Cooke, owner of the Washington Redskins football team. The dapper Cooke, who suffered from claustrophobia, hated to fly. But he was so eager to get to McCaw first that he flew from the East in his personal jet in short hops, stopping periodically so he could escape the confines of the cabin. Prepped in advance by a numbers man who had examined McCaw's books, Cooke reached Seattle, asked about the cable systems' cash flow and some other topics, "and we had a deal with him in about ten minutes," as McCaw says with only slight exaggeration. (Perry says it took closer to sixty minutes.) Price: $755 million.

The deal was marked by typical McCaw creativity. McCaw's goal was to get the money and put it quickly into cellular. Since federal and municipal regulators could tie up any sale involving scores of cable franchises, McCaw proposed that Cooke pay the money, while McCaw's team would continue to manage the systems during the franchise transfer process. (The sale of southern Oregon's systems also needed permission from Affiliated Publications, which owned control of those systems as well as 45 percent of McCaw Communications.) If any franchises didn't go through, a price adjustment would be triggered and that system would be sold to a third party. This clever structure meant not only that McCaw would get his money, but also that Cooke could not be extorted by cities that demanded concessions as they held hostage a franchise in transition. And since Cooke was already getting his cash flows, he could afford to be patient.

The now ever present Milken was naturally involved. Cooke had tried raising money for the purchase elsewhere, but he soon came to Milken, who raised the cash in three weeks. It was just a small piece of the $18 billion Milken raised at Drexel for deals in cable, cellular, and entertainment. Cooke was very pleased with the price he paid, low by the standard of what cable properties were then selling for.

"He thought he was taking advantage of us and he was, probably," McCaw said later, "but we had better things to do with the money."

McCaw was in a hurry.

15

"The Mad Scientist"

His Company Goes Public, McCaw Stays Private

To Craig McCaw, going public in 1987 did not mean *he* had to go public. The plan was to raise $2.3 billion from a stock offering, plus another $400 million from bonds sold to investors—giant gulps of gas to help the McCaw organization move faster, pay off some debt, and grab still more cellular territories. It would have helped for McCaw to wave the company flag in public at such a crucial time. But he chose not to make the traditional appearances before analysts and other Wall Street groups, claiming he wasn't good at orchestrated events.

Instead, Wayne Perry led the McCaw team on the road show to London, Boston, New York, and elsewhere. What might have seemed a liability—a chief executive seemingly missing in action—ultimately proved an advantage. McCaw in person was certainly a business visionary. But McCaw as the mysterious figure whose absence embodied his unusual style, whose thinking was so lofty that doing a road show would be a needless distraction . . . now, that was a *real* visionary.

The McCaw company was trying to be different by playing an old game in a new way. McCaw, now thirty-seven, came across through the stories told by his subordinates as shy, often inarticulate, and decidedly different: eccentric, mysterious, perhaps even weird. More than a clever businessman, a familiar breed on Wall Street, he was a genius, a seer, even "the mad scientist," in Perry's words.

If there were doubts among the crowds of potential investors about the invisible man at the top, those feelings were quickly dispelled by the apparent analytical brilliance, cunning, and pure energy of Perry, John Stanton, Rufus Lumry, and the others. At one standing-room-only event after another, they sold the company's numbers and strategy, but they also sold Craig McCaw. Where had a great idea or strategic maneuver come from? Always their answer was Craig McCaw.

McCaw did appear at one Wall Street meeting hosted by analyst Dennis Leibowitz of Donaldson, Lufkin & Jenrette, an early champion of cellular. As Perry tells the story, McCaw decided he didn't want to give a standard presentation of financial numbers, so he put together his own slide show on what he saw as the industry's future. McCaw stood up and started clicking through his slides abstractedly, murmuring, "No, I don't want that" and "No, I'll skip that," as Rufus Lumry, a fanatic for preparation, became increasingly nervous.

Finally, McCaw tossed aside his prepared remarks and started improvising as a feeling of doom settled over Lumry. But when the speech was over, Dennis Leibowitz came up to Lumry and said, in tones of admiration, "This guy really is a genius!" McCaw had pulled it off.

McCaw Cellular Communications was one of Wall Street's hottest initial public offerings in 1987. Demand for shares was so strong that the offering was increased from 10.5 million to 13 million shares. "I'll be lucky to get 50 shares," one envious broker told *The New York Times*. The $2.39 billion IPO was the largest ever by a northwestern company— the Microsoft offering a year earlier had raised just $59 million.

Of course, McCaw was personally enriched by the move. The complex web of family ownership made it difficult to be completely certain, but it appeared that the sale put a value of $156 million on McCaw's shares. For any other businessman, it would have been an enormous triumph. But McCaw called it "the worst day in the history of our company." Going public had been a traumatic event for the secretive McCaw. He had spent years quietly buying cellular licenses before others discovered the incredible bargains available. Now anyone with a McCaw prospectus could learn the company's goals, see its overall financial structure, and try to guess its next steps. No longer could the McCaw company pursue what Perry called its "run silent, run deep" strategy.

McCaw didn't welcome the attention directed at him and his company. Now Wall Street analysts would constantly push for earnings data and continual profit growth. Some would challenge the company's long-term strategy of buying more licenses with profits still years away. There would be new pressures on the company.

McCaw also fretted over the personal distractions. In the go-go 1980s, many chief executives craved attention, loved posing for photographs of themselves at black-tie galas or zooming to meetings in corporate helicopters. McCaw, who as a real pilot could appreciate fine aircraft, found such displays distasteful. So the first jolt of attention he received in his new high-profile role was an unpleasant surprise. *Business Week* put McCaw on its cover in December 1988 with a story bannered THE HIGH-RISK EMPIRE OF CRAIG MCCAW. "He could become the modern equivalent of Theodore Vail, the legendary telegrapher who at the turn of the century assembled AT&T by buying up dozens of small phone companies," the magazine declared.

The submarine had surfaced, and its surprising size made quite a splash. Analysts and journalists were stunned by McCaw Cellular Communications' incredible nationwide collection of cellular licenses— enough to cover 37 million people in ninety-four markets, twice as many as the nearest competitor. The company, now with 750 employees, had long since bought out its original cellular partners in Seattle and Portland. In just the past year, the McCaw company had more than doubled its assets to $1.3 billion and increased its revenues sevenfold to $150 million.

Despite this big money, there was still not a dime of profit. In the same year, losses had skyrocketed to $120 million, a sixfold jump. And the company offered no hope of profits for years. Its immediate goals were to develop regional clusters, build high-quality customer service, manage money carefully, and generate cash flow. Profit was a more distant objective.

The company also offered no hope of outside shareholders' controlling the company. The McCaws and Affiliated retained the Class B stock, which maintained overwhelming voting control of the company. The public was offered only Class A stock.

In just eight months, the company would issue its first annual report, devoid of color or photographs. "You may find this to be a somewhat unusual annual report," McCaw wrote to his new shareholders. Rather than running photos of himself or other traditional scenes, he instead offered a tutorial on cellular and his company's commitment to its future, stressing its defiance of conventional wisdom. "We believe that cellular technology will help to gradually transform the way we and future generations will think about communications as well as the way in which we work and live," wrote McCaw:

> Those of us who use the service quickly learn that the opportunity to communicate in places and at times not previously possible is an important part of our freedom of choice. As we (both individually and collectively as a society) avail ourselves more and more of the flexibility of mobile communications, we may begin to associate a telephone number more with a person than with a place. We will no longer have one number in our home, another in our office and another in our car. We will have one number where we can be reached at nearly any time.

McCaw saw a future where we "define how and where we will work." He promised diligence and few flashy mailings to shareholders or expensive events for the news media. "We intend to be a relatively quiet company focused on the growth and value of our assets," he wrote.

About this time McCaw felt it necessary to organize his thoughts in a series of messages to employees in the company newsletter, *Comline*. No one doubted that he personally wrote these messages. They were singularly McCaw: simple, blunt, at times surprising and original. Run next to a photo showing his crooked smile, his first message boiled his philosophy down to a simple message titled "What We Stand For":

Keep it Simple: Simple solutions solve complex problems. Complex solutions rarely accomplish anything.

Be Humble: If you think you're great, you're probably not.

Pursue Excellence: The pursuit of excellence is what gives real meaning to life.

Stay Close To The Customer: Otherwise, when we're gone, nobody will notice (or care).

Employ Good Judgment: It's one of the few things man does better than machines.

Consider The Future: Short-term gratification is just that; SHORT-TERM.

Hire Great People: If you don't surround yourself with great people, you're a turkey.

If you follow the above, you'll have fun and enjoy more spare time.

Craig McCaw

Over the next several months, McCaw tried to amplify his views to the employees of his growing concern, now spread across the country. Many would never meet him, but *Comline* gave them a clear sense that they weren't working for a standard-issue chief executive. This was a deep thinker—maybe not a classic MBA or the world's most elegant writer, but someone who thought about the nature of organizations, the ego, human motivation, and what it all meant for his business.

McCaw's essay on teamwork was probably his best. It analyzed business in almost moral terms, as a struggle against the venal to achieve a larger good. Since McCaw has rarely written anything of length, it's worth quoting in detail:

Great accomplishments are usually the work of a small, highly focused team with a clear goal in mind. A team is a group of people who have agreed to channel themselves together in a common direction toward a goal with a dedication that transcends their personal wishes. Any student of human behavior knows that we are all different, have conflicting needs, and with proximity, find it difficult not to notice offending traits in our fellow man.

Why is it so hard to get a real team? Why does a team, when successful, so often degenerate into bickering, clawing for credit and selfish behavior? It is, unfortunately, our own insecurity that prevents us from bringing the best out in each other. Great teams are built by great people who are secure enough with themselves to join with other great people, and to share the opportunity for success in the most humble manner. Therefore, the first and most important step in building a team is to agree upon certain principles of behavior which will prevail. The second step is to agree upon common objectives. We <u>must</u> acknowledge that we wish to submerge our personal whims for the good of the team in accomplishing its goal. Unless and until a team has been forged through the channeling of energy into a common cause (through submission of our fragile egos), there can be no team; merely a crowd.

Teamwork fades fast when one of the team members decides that he or she deserves the lion's share of the credit; his or her pandering for glory soon makes others insecure, turning the team into a selfish rabble. This behavior must be avoided at all costs; (we are all vulnerable to the dark side of our psyche). The true test of leadership is the ability to keep these forces within us at bay. The true test of a team member is his or her ability to draw personal success from the team's success. We *all* learn soon enough that in a good team, any one member is expendable if the team has been properly built by its leaders. The real test of management is to build teams that are deep, not shallow—shallow teams build the "messiah complex" in their best person or people. The cruelest fate for any of us is to have those around us be worshiped not [as] peers, for they mislead us that we are greater than our own abilities. Awareness of our own shortcomings should come gradually, everyday, not all at once in a big jolt.

No endeavor is as pointless as the attempt to accomplish meaningful work with people whose selfish goals constantly transcend those of the would-be team. In this context, lots of rules will be created, but they cannot take the place of the need for an overriding set of common goals. We all crave the sense of common purpose, the camaraderie and the pride that accompanies a cohesive effort. You can feel an extraordinary power when people focus together on getting something done. It is far too common, however, that the leaders feel the power of directing others with the false pride that accompanies shallow power over other people. Please remember what teamwork is, a group pulling together, focused on a common direction, working at the peak of their ability for the good of the whole. Sure it's hard, but when a team clicks, it's something to behold!

This was the real Craig McCaw, or at least as much of him as he felt comfortable revealing to his employees. Management is a topic McCaw is willing to discuss openly. Going public, however, drew uncomfortable attention to one of his unbreachable zones of privacy: his family.

Till now, the McCaws had labored in relative obscurity. Only friends and close business associates knew them and their status, which suited the family just fine. Like Elroy, they loathed public attention, seeing it as a risk without benefits. Shortly before the company went public, McCaw even tried to drop "McCaw" from the company's name, but that would have delayed the public offering. (He liked "Cellular One," but Southwestern Bell wouldn't release the brand name.) So when the company went public, the family's cherished anonymity vanished. Seattle suddenly discovered it had another billion-dollar family, including four men all under forty, each worth more than $300 million, joining Microsoft cofounders Paul Allen and Bill Gates on *Forbes* magazine's list of the superrich.

McCaw's hometown hungered for details. Who was Craig McCaw, this prophet of the new telephone? Through the company's publicity, the public learned some details which, ironically, seemed to make him seem less rather than more familiar. He was a young billionaire, like Bill Gates, but he didn't eat pizza or slurp cola till 4 A.M. like the other high-tech geniuses profiled in the business press. McCaw didn't seem to fit into the new category created by Microsoft, or into any of the old ones.

People considered Gates fascinating; they felt the same about McCaw. But the king of cellular was a riddle whose answers came from silence. He sat in a corner office in Carillon Point, often alone, facing west—a symbol, he would say, of his focus on the future. Late in the day, the sun would sink over the Olympic Mountains, and light would retreat from the office. The expansive glass and marble floors made the office seem Spartan, temporary, lonely, and cold except on the warmest days. The objects in the room, such as an antique telephone and a telescope for viewing watercraft, seemed to say nothing about McCaw—at least nothing truly personal.

In cold months, McCaw might switch on a few lamps, but the place remained dim, a couple of portable electric heaters fighting the chill from drafty windows. When a guest is present, McCaw speaks softly and sips from a bottle of Evian water. The place feels less like a CEO's office than a monk's cell or a scholar's study.

The typical executive does a lot of talking. McCaw cultivates silence. When he meets people, he might be sociable, moody, or preoccupied. When he is nervous or letting a question turn in his mind, his eyes dart from side to side. He stares for the longest time into the eyes of a visitor . . . then his own eyes begin darting again.

When he speaks, he isn't always clear. Sometimes he selects the wrong word and has to start over to clarify his meaning. For example, he has called himself "fixated" when he meant "focused."

"He is not a great communicator," says James Barksdale, who became McCaw company president and COO in 1992:

> It takes me a while to understand what he means. He's the first to apologize for that. He says a lot of times [that] he sometimes speaks in allegories and parables and in tangential ways, and you've got to really pay attention to know what he's talking about. He understands that he has a problem with that.

McCaw might meet with an important customer, make a commitment, and mention it casually to a senior executive, who then had to wonder, "Oh, does that mean we've got to do something? I guess it does."

At times McCaw deliberately has tried to disrupt people's straight-line thinking as a means of prompting deeper thought. He once gathered a few company executives and posed a question: "What business are we in?"

The episode captured Craig McCaw in action: the alert look to his face, nostrils flared as if sniffing for danger, but also his control and calm—head tilted back, soft voice, measured words, gentle hands in slow movement.

The executives looked at one another, dumbstruck. At a place called McCaw Cellular Communications, wasn't the answer obvious? McCaw wouldn't say. He started calling in more executives until twelve or four-teen people were wrestling with the question. A lawyer present felt as if he were back in law school. *Just tell us the answer,* one company lawyer thought.

The meeting ended with no specific outcome.

Months later, the executives were still talking about that meeting. Of course, that may have been the idea. McCaw wanted them to keep thinking about it. "I don't think we know," says Tom Alberg, then a senior vice president. "It's the communications business of some kind.

Obviously, it's not the whole world, but it's more than the cellular business."

McCaw's actions are often difficult to explain. In this instance, there was a point to his behavior. He didn't want his company getting too comfortable. In that sense, it was the same ethic that Bill Gates brought to Microsoft: Be adaptive. Run scared. Never assume a franchise is permanent.

McCaw is scrupulous about those he selects for his senior management group. He subjects potential hires to a series of interviews with top managers, plus a meandering, soul-searching, character-exploring encounter with him. While McCaw was traveling once, he asked a candidate for a high-level finance position to meet him at the Denver airport for what was supposed to be a one-hour meeting. McCaw swooped down from the clouds in his private plane and left his wife and others to wait as he probed the candidate's childhood, life experiences, ideas, and values. The session expanded to fill six hours. Finally, McCaw said the candidate had his blessing, and if Wayne Perry didn't offer enough stock options, he would give some of his personal holdings.

According to Senior Vice President of Finance Peter Currie, the boss wants independent thinkers, not toadies:

A lot of entrepreneurs follow the Idi Amin Organizational Structure: There's one guy at the top and a whole bunch of mediocre people underneath doing exactly what the chief may insist that you do. "Do it this way. I'm smarter than you. I talk louder than you and I'm right, get it done." They say, "Yessir, boss," and off they go. McCaw isn't like that. If his employees reacted to him like that, he wouldn't fire them. He'd just ignore them. He'd turn them into nonpeople, because he wants to get feedback. He wants to raise controversy. He doesn't want to raise contention, but he wants issues to be circulated and dealt with in a very real way.

At one company meeting, McCaw told the gathering that he wanted to hire "invigorating, dangerous, and interesting people who are not all the same and who cause trouble, because that's how you get things done." He said he believed in "the principle that one person makes a huge difference. That if you empower people and give them a lot of responsibility, you get a disproportionate benefit, even though you may make mistakes."

Gardiner Davis has known McCaw for decades. Davis was one of McCaw's unusual hires: McCaw thought his old English teacher from Lakeside might be handy around the office as a writing coach. Davis is willing to field questions about McCaw, but he doesn't claim to have solved the brain twister of who Craig McCaw really is. "I'd sort of like to meet the real person and find out what he really thinks," says Davis.

Once McCaw is comfortable with a person, he'll open up, says Cal Cannon, a longtime employee. "A lot of people don't understand him. They say, 'Cal, how do I get to him?' " Relax and be sincere, Cannon would reply. McCaw was always quick to spot a phony. That meant it was generally futile to try to disguise yourself around McCaw . . . despite the fact that McCaw always maintained an opaque layer between himself and others. Shyness served as a self-protective mechanism. It wasn't that he disliked people, but that he wanted to minimize random contacts as a means of focusing on what mattered to him.

McCaw fiercely regulates the information that reaches his desk for fear it will clutter his mind. He will sometimes interrupt his mother to say he doesn't need to know that much detail, and she understands. He wants only essentials and just enough detail to allow him to analyze a situation from a fresh perspective, a lesson he has taught subordinates.

Another executive says McCaw brings a different dimension to business analysis. While others crunch numbers or parse legal niceties, McCaw studies the personalities involved, sizes up their motives and histories and the corporate cultures at work, and predicts how things will go on that basis.

Though courtly in personality, he despises hierarchies, formalities, neckties and formal clothing, and unnecessary meetings. He believes his company should promote good health: a staff "wellness person" has designed employee fitness and diet programs. Mental health is important, too. McCaw likes vigorous debate, but people must always show courtesy toward one another.

"You need to respect other people," McCaw says, "and one of the most destructive things in an organization is sarcasm and making fun of other people. If you want to send my blood pressure through the roof,

[try] making fun of people. Because that is pure destructive behavior. . . . Eventually, it turns people on each other behind one another's backs."

Yet for all of McCaw's seriousness about his role, he also has a playful, boyish side. He routinely skips the elevator, preferring to run the four flights to his office. It's "my favorite thing to do. I love to run up and down the stairs," he says. "Why walk? I'm enthusiastic to be here, and when I get here, I'm wound up."

The admired strategist generally comes to his office with few activities planned in advance. "You wait for life to give you a clue as to where to go that day. I hate the orchestration of life. Most executives die frustrated [because] they have been orchestrated into boxes." An aide once walked in to find the chief executive resting his chin on his hands as he stared at Lake Washington. The aide got the feeling McCaw had been staring for a long time—perhaps working through a strategy.

McCaw loves pranks and games. Sometimes he'll enliven a meeting by honking a horn. "He's a kid at heart," says Robert Ratliffe, who became McCaw's vice president for communications.

The prankster could take a joke as well. One time Ratliffe spotted McCaw's gym bag in a stairwell and couldn't resist tossing the bag high atop a water pipe. The chief executive later had to climb ten feet to retrieve his bag. Ratliffe kept his job.

McCaw hates routine and kept pilot Rick Hess on constant standby. When he got the urge, he would call: "What are you doing this afternoon?"

"Nothing," Hess would say.

"Let's go for a plane ride," McCaw would say. And off they'd go, usually with McCaw at the controls, to the Olympic Peninsula or British Columbia for the afternoon.

Overnight trips would follow a routine—a search for some remote spot where McCaw might paddle his kayak alone, letting Hess fly ahead four or five miles. They slept in tents or in cabins; the billionaire would complain about Hess's snoring. McCaw did some of the cooking and often brought the one possession that, for him, rivaled a cell phone—a squirt gun. He shaved every day, read little, and talked mainly about the scenery or airplanes. He took pride in knowing facts, such as the mean temperature 7,000 feet up a certain Canadian mountain.

He was finicky about leaving the campsite clean, says Hess. "Heaven forbid if you drop a piece of paper and leave it," says Hess. "He'll rip you for weeks. Not that he's nasty, but he's that way. If he's walking in downtown Seattle and sees paper [on the sidewalk], he'll pick it up."

Steve Countryman, McCaw's friend from Lakeside days, tried to keep his weekends clear in case McCaw wanted a getaway. They might fly to Canada or go south. On those trips, Countryman never asked McCaw about business, figuring his role was to help his friend relax. "McCaw does stuff with me to escape," says Countryman.

McCaw didn't rough it on every outdoor trip. Like the rest of the McCaws, he enjoys yachts. In the Puget Sound area, he keeps the seventy-seven-foot *Cellular One*. In the Mediterranean, he moored the *Calixe*, which stretched 205 feet, including the pad for McCaw's helicopter. One of the largest privately owned yachts in the world, the ultrasleek *Calixe* came from the famed De Vries shipyard in Holland and features spacious rooms for ten guests, various salons and dining areas, quarters for a crew of fourteen, and state-of-the-art electronics. The *Calixe* may have seemed cramped, however. In late 1999 *The Seattle Times* identified McCaw as the owner of a 344-foot-long yacht under construction at a German shipyard. The new boat had room for a crew of twenty-six, a forty-foot "picnic boat"—and two helicopters.

But nothing engages McCaw more than flying. At different times he has owned a Falcon 900, an intercontinental luxury jet that seats nineteen; a Citation jet; a top-of-the-line Gulfstream IV jet; and two small prop planes, a Super Cub and a durable Beaver Seaplane.

"Some of his happiest moments are when he's flying. He just loves to fly," says Mick Deal, a friend since high school. Rated for multi-engine, instrument flying, McCaw stands among the elite of civilian amateur pilots, which is especially remarkable because such skill requires countless hours of training, study, and certification. Few of America's CEOs know much about the corporate jets that take them places. McCaw does and is qualified to fly them.

Executive Vice President Mark Hamilton remembers the time he and others were riding into Washington, D.C.'s National Airport in a plane piloted by McCaw. As the plane made its approach, the control panel showed that the landing gear was not locked down. They flew past the tower, where controllers said the gear looked okay, but nobody was sure.

Most people on board were very nervous. One passenger started talking rapidly, asking questions, clearly agitated. Hamilton forced himself to stay quiet.

Emergency vehicles roared down to the runway. McCaw brought the plane down without trouble. Everybody was relieved but badly unnerved.

Hamilton left the plane but went back later to fetch his briefcase. There in the plane, by himself, was McCaw, calmly eating dinner. Hamilton was amazed that anyone could hold down food that soon after such a hair-raising experience.

"Aren't you nervous?" Hamilton recalls asking Craig McCaw. McCaw ate some more.

"A little bit," McCaw finally replied. "This will help me collect myself."

Since then, Hamilton has never felt fear with McCaw at the controls.

McCaw's penchant for secrecy shrouded his married life in the most profound darkness of all. The world knew almost nothing about Mrs. Craig McCaw, the former Wendy Petrak. Their waterfront home in Bellevue had once been owned by a shipping millionaire, Ned Skinner. They also owned property at Bliss Landing in Canada, a pristine region known for its stunning rugged vistas, privacy, and great salmon fishing. However, Wendy was said to dislike its remoteness and the mosquitoes; she preferred spending the weekends in another home they kept on the beach in Santa Barbara, where she loved to jog with their Great Dane, Sunny.

Wendy stayed out of the public eye, rarely allowing their Seattle home to be used for business gatherings or social events. Some of McCaw's top people spoke about her only in whispers. They felt vaguely unwelcome at the McCaw home and privately regarded Wendy as demanding. As the unofficial company decorator, she would show up at headquarters and decide if someone did or did not need a couch in his office. No one challenged her.

Wendy was also said to be passionate about animal rights and healthful eating, so there were only meatless barbecues at the McCaw home, although Craig himself might take a bite of meat when he was on the road. Wendy adopted stray animals, which were kept outside because of her husband's allergies.

McCaw became wary once when asked about his wife's opinions on animal rights. "She believes—and, I think, legitimately—that there's a lot of mindless, needless cruelty to animals, whether it's in farming or in medical research," he said, but quickly cut off further inquiries. "I don't want to get my wife into this," he concluded.

Rather than talk about himself or his family, McCaw prefers to sit in his office, gazing toward a point in the distance and speaking expansively about the freedom that comes from telecommunications. Perhaps unintentionally, his musings offer insights into his personality. He speaks of how the cellular phone can liberate people from the wire, "the leash that chokes us," in his words. "It means we stop running for the phone and let the phone come to us."

As he warms to the topic, he moves away from the specific topic of telephones and reveals his philosophy of how people should live and work. Business in the future will have "whole-person thinking," he says, sipping his bottled water. "The level of change in technology now exceeds the ability of humans to cope with it. The rhythms of the body must be accommodated." Such talk can baffle listeners, but it, too, is part of the McCaw business plan.

Clearly, the Craig McCaw who achieved business stardom in 1987 was a new kind of corporate executive—almost a philosopher-king of business. Yet no sooner had he emerged into the limelight with his now public company than he was forced to assume a very difficult and, for him, most painful role: that of corporate warrior.

16

"Take Tarawa"

A Hostile Takeover Creates a Truly National Service

Craig McCaw knew that his emerging cellular empire had a strategic weakness. He held licenses covering 50 million POPs—potential customers—as the nation's largest independent cellular company, 68 percent larger than Pacific Telesis Group. But McCaw Cellular still didn't provide truly national service. Though it controlled markets across the West, into the South, and along the eastern seaboard, McCaw Cellular could not provide a customer with the ability to roam from city to city without losing a call. The dream of a call "finding" a customer, no matter where he might be, was still far off. McCaw's nomad could not be truly served.

McCaw told his engineers to find a way to build a system for national roaming. The costs were high, the technical challenges were great, but all he said was "Do it."

The gaps in coverage were underscored by the painful fact that McCaw lacked the two biggest prizes in the cellular service sweepstakes: New York City and Los Angeles. McCaw's maneuvers to cure that problem were complex, bold, and brilliant, taking advantage of his most powerful opponent's only weakness.

New York–based LIN Broadcasting owned television stations and controlled cellular licenses in New York, Philadelphia, Dallas, and Houston. It also owned 35 percent of Los Angeles, for a total of 18 million POPs. McCaw knew that he had to somehow form an alliance with LIN or see its valuable licenses go, as seemed inevitable, to a Baby Bell, perhaps dooming his own chance of establishing a national cellular company.

McCaw had twice lost big deals to a Bell. First, in 1986, he had lost Metromedia's cellular assets to Southwestern Bell. Then, two years later,

BellSouth had outbid him for Mobile Communications Corporation's eleven-city operation, including Los Angeles, Milwaukee, and Houston. Now nearly all the Bells were on the prowl, sniffing for deals, expecting to outbid McCaw's company.

McCaw's astounding growth now exposed the company to the huge cost involved in building the systems he owned. Though Steve Hooper, the eventual CFO, says the company never borrowed too much, McCaw nonetheless labored under $1.8 billion worth of debt, with interest payments each year amounting to $200 million.

Despite all this, McCaw couldn't let LIN go. Beginning in 1988, he bought pieces of the company, eventually increasing his stake to nearly 10 percent. McCaw also began cultivating Donald Pels, LIN's pleasant, well-regarded chief executive. A Wharton alumnus, Pels had left his post as executive vice president of Capital Cities in 1969 to run LIN, a grab bag of TV and radio stations, a record label, a film company, a talent agency, and a chain of franchised art galleries. He sold all but the broadcasting properties and one other item, a radio paging unit serving New York that had revenues of $500,000.

Pels liked one thing about paging: its generous 40 percent operating margins. In the late 1970s, Pels expanded the beeper business into Houston and in 1983 and 1984 won cellular licenses. Compared with McCaw, Pels pinched pennies, investing over five years what McCaw might spend in a single year for new equipment. "Don believed in investing for a return now, not down the road," a Pels friend later told *Forbes* magazine.

The McCaw people suspected that Pels didn't quite know what to do with his cellular properties. He showed little enthusiasm for cellular, often skipping trade shows as though bored by the latest industry news. His minimal investments into New York's system resulted in such lousy customer relations and substandard service that cellular quickly developed a bad image on Wall Street.

While harried McCaw managers gobbled cheeseburgers in taxis, Pels preferred two-hour lunches and languid meetings. "Don looked like he had a pretty good, unrushed life," Wayne Perry said later. The more often McCaw met with Pels, the less likely an alliance seemed. While McCaw was ready to spend heavily on cellular's future, Pels, a generation older, moved cautiously. While McCaw was bidding furiously for rural licenses, Pels took a long time even to acknowledge that cellular might have a future in a big market like Houston. To hear the McCaw people describe it, Pels saw cellular growing at a stately, measured pace, while they saw an industry moving into warp drive.

The difference in attitudes meant everything. Pels would never spend aggressively, as McCaw would, to hasten the public's broad acceptance of cellular technology. Pels, like so many others, saw cellular merely as a nice niche business, while McCaw viewed it as the "freedom machine." Given the mismatch of cultures, it seemed ludicrous when Pels broached the idea of a new communications company formed out of Affiliated Publications, McCaw Cellular Communications, and LIN.

Another time, he suggested that McCaw and LIN join forces with McCaw as number two to Pels. Pels didn't realize that in every partnership, even with the old Boston money, McCaw had insisted on control. McCaw was too polite to tell him how wrong he was. "Interesting idea," was all McCaw said.

Pels had no idea that McCaw had been planning a takeover of LIN since 1986.

In 1989 McCaw found the money to buy more LIN shares by persuading London-based British Telecom to invest $1.5 billion in McCaw Cellular. BT paid $41.50 a share, a premium far above the recent trading price of $29. In return, BT got four of the nineteen seats on McCaw's board and 22 percent ownership of McCaw Cellular Communications.

Meanwhile, Affiliated announced that it would distribute its shares of McCaw to Affiliated shareholders. The move boosted Affiliated stock, which had long been burdened by carrying a portion of McCaw's losses. Affiliated's $12 million investment in 1981 was now worth $2.6 billion—a return that had astonished Affiliated's controlling shareholders, the Jordan and Taylor families of Boston.

McCaw did not publicly link the BT investment to a LIN bid, but the agreement specifically authorized McCaw to go for a LIN-size company. By now it was becoming obvious to Wall Street, and especially to Donald Pels, that McCaw was gearing up for a takeover—with LIN the likely target.

To avoid a hostile confrontation, John McCaw was brought into service again, in his familiar role as the company's "relationship guy." John was assigned to meet with Pels and discuss a structure under which a LIN-McCaw company could be formed, perhaps with Pels in charge at the start. Between late 1988 and early 1989 John met with Pels ten or fifteen times at Pels's homes on Manhattan and Long Island. They became friends.

Pels then shocked the McCaw company by publicly suggesting he might divide LIN's broadcast and cellular properties into separate units. It was a dramatic idea with profound consequences. Until that point, McCaw hadn't had to worry about a Bell's buying LIN; regulations prohibited them from owning radio or television broadcast properties. But the possible spin-off would eliminate that problem, and Pels's public suggestion was a signal to the Bells that their money might now be welcome.

The McCaw company had to act fast to get LIN, with or without Pels's consent. John McCaw flew on the Concorde to Paris to meet Pels, who was staying at the posh George V Hotel.

When Pels spotted John in the hotel lobby, a smile crossed his face. "There's John," John McCaw heard Pels say to his wife. Then Pels's face went white, as he suddenly sensed what was about to happen.

Pels loved his job, loved LIN, and was proud of his work. He had run the company since 1969, and, having raised its stock price from $3.375 in 1981 to over $100, he strongly believed he had done a good job for the shareholders. Yet if Craig McCaw had his way, Pels was going to lose his company.

A grueling, costly battle was about to begin. The soft-spoken Craig McCaw disliked confrontation, and he hated the thought of engaging in a hostile takeover. But he felt that he had no choice but to launch a corporate war on Pels. First, however, he felt Pels was owed the courtesy of formal notice and an explanation.

Tired from having been awake for two days straight, John McCaw handed Pels a letter from Craig that announced the McCaw company would seek to buy LIN in a hostile takeover. John explained that they had no other choice.

"Thank you very much. I think I better get on the phone," Pels replied.

John also raced to a phone to inform McCaw officials, who were waiting in New York to make public their intentions and unleash the lawyers, publicists, and investment bankers. "I've met with Don," John told them. "Go."

John booked the next flight home on the Concorde. As he boarded the flight, he spotted Pels and realized his own seat was across the aisle from Pels's.

"Don, I don't want to appear rude," McCaw told Pels. "[But] I think this flight might go a lot quicker for both of us if I could find another seat."

"That's probably a good idea," Pels replied.

On June 6, 1989, McCaw offered approximately $120 a share to LIN stockholders for control of the company. Pels and his board rejected the $5.85 billion cash offer. A six-month battle began.

The essence of a hostile takeover is simple: Go over the heads of management with an offer so generous that the shareholders can't refuse. If company X is trading at $50 a share, offer an attractive price with a realistic premium—say $60—but make sure you have the financing in place to write the check if the deal is accepted. And you can't get the financing without first doing an extraordinary amount of legal and financial analysis. Typically, the big money involved requires a consortium of lenders.

Management can try to attack the offer as financially shaky or throw up legal obstacles to the offer. Being insiders, they have more information about the company than the bidder does, which allows them to challenge the offer as ill informed. They can also try to raise doubts about the bidder as someone ill suited to successfully complete the transaction or manage the company. Management's third option is to offer shareholders an even sweeter deal, usually with the help of a "white knight" outsider.

A protracted takeover battle is emotionally and physically exhausting. As an analogy, consider this: Buying a house is not normally a complex or intensely emotional process, but it can be when bankers impose unrealistic conditions, inspectors want repairs done before the house is declared livable, the seller entertains counteroffers, and family members jump into the fray with advice and warnings. Now apply the same logic to a transaction involving billions of dollars, thousands of employees, complicated business assets with constantly changing values, a tangle of critical tax laws and regulations, investment-fund managers and journalists wanting answers—all of which need to be managed while still running the business you already own.

The battle for LIN was one of the major business stories of the year. Wayne Perry, Mark Hamilton, Peter Currie, and others spent months living at the Lowell Hotel in New York, working fourteen-hour days in the Sullivan & Cromwell law offices on Park Avenue. Night after night, dinner was steak at the Post House Restaurant or, for a break from looking at blue suits all day, Faces Restaurant, where the waitresses wore miniskirts. Perry and the others spent a lot of time on planes, flying to Boston to consult with Affiliated or to London by the Concorde to consult with British Telecom.

Not one but two platoons of investment bankers, lawyers, publicists, and other specialists helped the McCaw team, a surfeit of such biblical magnitude that the duplication was nicknamed "The Ark." After the initial round of maneuvers, McCaw had lost confidence in the first group he had selected. "The other guys showed us up, so we said, 'Oh, God, they're kicking our ass,' " he recalls. "If our guys were a seven, they were an eight." He didn't fire them, but effectively replaced them by hiring an entire second team.

To lead the replacements, he hired Wall Street's wise man, Felix Rohaytn of Lazard Freres & Company in New York, and his protégé Steve Rattner. Rohaytn provided critical advice, and his presence gave the relatively unknown Craig McCaw added credibility on Wall Street.

The McCaw offer put LIN into play, because management did not own enough of the company to unilaterally reject a buyout. Now anyone could top the McCaw offer. But the McCaw team had planned its moves carefully, having studied LIN's finances, its management, and its strategic position, as well as other potential bidders, such as Southwestern Bell, US West, and even the big-daddy long shot, AT&T. Perry called it "reverse engineering" any potential opposition, and it wasn't that hard to do. Because of McCaw's many partnerships and the availability of public documents filed with the FCC, positions were relatively easy to assess. "That was all in the mental database," says Perry. "If you have to hire people to come in and do that, it would have taken forever." As a result, "we knew more about LIN Broadcasting, the people who could buy LIN, the regulatory issues, the taxes, the [legal environment], the Harte-Scott-Rodino [antitrust] issues—we knew more about LIN Broadcasting when we launched that bid than LIN Broadcasting knew about itself."

Sensing the possibility of enormous fees as well as potentially huge trading profits, Wall Street wanted a bidding frenzy, and analysts immediately started talking up possible players. But McCaw was ready to trash its potential rivals.

AT&T? It had the money but not the will, the McCaw people said. It wouldn't want to bid for fear of stirring up a fight with the Baby Bells over the rules that kept their former parent out of local service.

Southwestern Bell? It had a problem in Dallas, where McCaw owned 10 percent of the local cellular license and could block a tax-free spin-off.

For its part, LIN dismissed McCaw as a "junk bond company." But in a move that made it certain that someone would buy LIN, Pels brought in BellSouth as a "white knight" with a buyout offer more to his liking—a complex arrangement that would spin off LIN's TV assets, merge cellular operations under Pels, and create a rival to McCaw as the largest cellular provider. BellSouth's plan, designed by Vice President Pierce J. "Jack" Roberts, artfully structured a huge acquisition without much effect on its bottom line. It was also a largely tax-free deal that promised a $20-per-share cash dividend worth $1.3 billion to LIN's shareholders.

"It was brilliant but brittle," Perry says of the Roberts plan. With a revenue base more than thirty times McCaw's $310 million, BellSouth could easily have won by simply raising its offering price until McCaw folded. But Craig McCaw knew BellSouth's weak point—its long tradition of growing its dividend. As then-*Newsday* columnist Allan Sloan said, keeping those reported earnings high was a Bell obsession. Thus, BellSouth's offer hinged on a complex accounting scheme that had little flexibility, says Perry.

In a straight-up fight, it would be no contest. "If it was good-old-boy, Corporate America, tee time at Augusta, we weren't going to win," says Perry. "We knew that. We knew we had to change the game. We had to be in a game where vision, strategy, other things were important." Like the Vietcong guerrilla forces, the McCaw team would try to force a more powerful adversary to play by unfamiliar rules, to make the game messy and embarrassing until it was forced to withdraw.

The McCaw strategy involved sending several different messages: to convince LIN shareholders that the better deal was with McCaw; to persuade others in the cellular industry that McCaw was the better steward of LIN's critical licenses; and to build pressure on BellSouth through political means and by convincing them they were in a fight with a ruthless opponent.

Normally eager to avoid reporters, McCaw started sending signals through the news media that he wanted LIN at practically any price. McCaw compared his company to anti-imperial Scottish warriors, the Islamic Jihad, and the anti-Soviet Afghan rebels. "We want them to think we're maniacs," he told *Forbes* magazine.

He sent John Stanton, Rufus Lumry, and other McCaw executives on a worldwide trip to raise money from bankers who were privately assured that McCaw would make no crazy offers. The group raised $5.5 billion—proof that Craig McCaw was not dependent on Michael Milken, who was about to have serious trouble with the law.

Meanwhile, on Wall Street, the McCaw team tried to raise doubts about BellSouth's offer by pointing out the Material Adverse Change (MAC) clause in the Baby Bell's offer. Routinely used by many companies in buyout offers, the MAC clause allowed the cautious BellSouth an out if problems erupted. The McCaw company had similar outs in its offer, but the team stressed how long Bells usually took to close deals compared to McCaw's history of rapid closures. A slow-as-molasses Baby Bell deal, they implied, stood a good chance of triggering the MAC clause and killing the whole arrangement.

Other McCaw aides tried to make political trouble for BellSouth, telling state regulators that the LIN deal would drive up local charges or violate agreements. Two U.S. senators from Washington State agreed to introduce a bill to block BellSouth.

Then came McCaw's flanking maneuver, what Perry calls "the beginning of the end" for BellSouth.

McCaw paid a visit to John Kluge's Metromedia office on East 67th Street in Manhattan, whose plain facade gave no hint of an interior suitable for a French nobleman. A private garage door opened, accepted a car, and then rotated it on a giant turntable. A guard showed visitors to a private elevator that whisked them to what looked like the private home of an art collector. Large vases held fresh-cut flowers. Fabulous oil paintings hung from dark, richly detailed paneling. Here, Kluge kept spacious living quarters for those nights he didn't stay at his enormous farm in Virginia.

McCaw deeply admired Kluge, a quiet, gracious man whose shrewd investments had made him one of the richest people in America. More than thirty years older than the young cellular entrepreneur, Kluge had the kind of manner McCaw sought in himself. Kluge rarely gave interviews and avoided attention, yet enjoyed influence in top business circles and in government. Perry thought McCaw overestimated that influence, but McCaw nonetheless valued his talks with Kluge and his former aide and now partner, Stuart Subotnick.

For his part, Kluge admired McCaw's nerve, but felt his business would remain incomplete until he landed a showcase market—a New York or Los Angeles franchise. "You've got to have an engine," he told McCaw. The fact that McCaw already knew that didn't make it any less true.

Now Kluge was enjoying watching McCaw bid for LIN because it achieved two happy purposes: He saw McCaw following his advice, plus he was giving trouble to Donald Pels, who had feuded with Kluge's own Metromedia. Metromedia and LIN each owned about half of New York's and Philadelphia's cellular markets in a partnership that gave the other the right of first refusal if either wanted to sell. The companies had been in litigation for years over the sale of Philadelphia. After years of court battles, Metromedia had won.

Stuart Subotnick recalls McCaw's visit to Kluge at the height of the LIN battle. He and Kluge were shocked at how tired McCaw looked. "He was really down," says Subotnick. "He was fighting an uphill battle."

McCaw told them the fight was not going well—that BellSouth was playing hardball, aided at every turn by Donald Pels.

Kluge and Subotnick admired what McCaw had done, to have come so far on nerve, creativity, and strategic brilliance. They wanted to help his company. To them, the solution was to take an even bigger risk.

"You're in a war, McCaw," Subotnick said. "They have more money. You're not going to win a war over money. You've got to do something unusual. You've got to do something they will never expect and cause them to rethink their commitment."

He and Kluge recommended a bold move that would rattle Bell-

South's board by making them worry about the fight's cost and effect on their earnings. Between them, they cut a very shrewd deal that put a higher price on BellSouth's ambitions. McCaw agreed to buy Kluge's 45 percent share of the New York cellular franchise for $1.9 billion. Once that was announced, LIN had to exercise its first-refusal right and buy out Kluge or allow McCaw to make the deal. If LIN did buy out Kluge, then LIN in turn would be a more costly acquisition for BellSouth. The alternative was for LIN not to buy Kluge, in which case BellSouth would ultimately wind up as Craig McCaw's partner in New York.

This strategy put BellSouth in a tight spot. It had to publicly encourage LIN to buy out Kluge. BellSouth was telling the world that cellular was a good investment, so it had to welcome a chance at controlling the nation's largest market. BellSouth's takeover offer set LIN POPs at $375; how could it say no to the Kluge POPs at $275? But McCaw and Kluge figured that BellSouth would be getting in deeper than it had ever wanted, putting tremendous pressure on a delicate financing structure built to avoid dilution of earnings. They figured that this flanking move would stun BellSouth.

"This was our Inchon landing," Perry said later. "The beauty of this [was that] there was no downside for us. If they turn it down, we wind up with cocontrol of the biggest market in the United States."

To fund the still-secret Kluge deal, McCaw decided to sell the company's licenses in the southern United States to Contel Cellular. Stanton flew to New York to meet with the Contel negotiators. Stanton had two people with him while Contel brought thirty, he said later.

The McCaw plan was to announce the sale to Contel and the proposed purchase from Kluge simultaneously. To get a good price from Contel, McCaw played what Stanton called the reluctant bride. That negotiating ploy would work only so long as Contel thought it had the sole deal in the works. Otherwise, it would offer less money, knowing that McCaw was eager for cash.

The Contel negotiations were going quickly. Then, at midnight, the Kluge deal hit a glitch. Wayne Perry, leading the Kluge negotiations, called Stanton, forty blocks away, and warned him, "I'm not ready. Stall."

Stanton, who already had been displeased with major errors in Contel's draft document listing their points of agreement, immediately announced that he was going to closely check every Contel document. "From now on," he announced, "I am reading every document word for word." That included one document 100 pages long. "I did some of my best dancing that night," Stanton said later. Hours passed. Stanton tried every additional stalling tactic he could think of, even a prolonged trip to the men's room.

Finally, at 6 A.M., Perry called. "We called him up and said, 'Go!'" Perry said later:

> And then he went and closed the deal with the Contel guys. Now the Contel guys are thinking they are going to be center stage and this is going to be page-one news—okay? So the deal gets signed. They hand out the press release on the Contel transaction. Stanton says, "Oh, one thing I should tell you. There's another press release here that's going to go out in five minutes." . . . And hands it to them, and they go . . . "Holy . . . !" Because [their deal] now becomes far lesser news. The Contel deal was huge—$1.4 billion. But the Kluge deal was even bigger.

Once the Kluge deal became public, McCaw had made it clear that he wouldn't give up in his battle for LIN. The jihad would continue until he won, no matter the cost. But BellSouth stayed in the fight, gamely announcing it would buy Kluge's share of New York and take the hit on its earnings.

Meanwhile, McCaw's bankers were beginning to get nervous. Federal banking regulators had recently tightened rules for highly leveraged transactions, ostensibly to end abuses in the real estate industry, but the effects were also being felt in communications deals. Jittery at the growing size of the deal, the bankers told McCaw they might not be able to lend much more, which apparently meant the McCaw company could not raise its offer.

As McCaw saw his position eroding, he came up with a brilliant maneuver. "Buy half," he told Perry. "He left the details of how to us," Perry said later:

> The genius of his management was that he knew we would do what he said. He would give these high-level commands. He would say

"Take Tarawa." He would not say, Attack from the south, attack beach number six at 0600 and then beach number nine. That was our job. But there was no question about who says "Take Tarawa" amongst all of the islands to take.

But how to take Tarawa? The banks refused to lend more, so where would the money come from? Perry, Rufus Lumry, and others brainstormed and came up with a clever idea: raise the per-share offer to $150 to gain 51 percent of LIN, and make a commitment for the other 49 percent that would not count as debt against McCaw's balance sheet. McCaw would then pledge to either buy the rest of LIN in five years, at a future price to be set by a group led by independent directors, or sell the 51 percent.

The McCaw company could not guarantee that it would buy the rest of LIN; otherwise that would count as more debt, which the banks wouldn't allow. Wayne Perry characterized the per-share offer as so generous, so oozing with good faith, that no one could challenge it. It would be, as he put it, "the Mother Teresa of offers."

The McCaw team went to the Ark, refined the details, then called a meeting of the people Perry nicknamed "the Cellular Mafia." The group included important Wall Street analysts such as Dennis Leibowitz of Donaldson, Lufkin & Jenrette, and Fred Moran of Moran & Associates Inc.; managers of mutual funds heavily invested in communications; and other opinion leaders of the cellular industry. Their support was key to maintaining McCaw Cellular's credibility, an intangible that was essential in a hostile takeover. An offer without credibility was worthless.

Craig McCaw stayed away; with rare exceptions, he avoided meetings with analysts, in part because he bristled at the complex rules and traditions that governed what a chief executive should say to Wall Street, in part because he sometimes proved to be too candid in public pronouncements. So Perry went with the plan literally in his jacket pocket. But he didn't simply present an outline to the Mafia. He wanted to maneuver the group into suggesting the ideas he had already adopted. So, pretending to be stumped about how to proceed against BellSouth, he began by asking the Mafia whether they liked one idea or another.

Piece by piece, the Mafia "suggested" the elements of the McCaw plan, including the idea of buying only half of LIN. It worked perfectly. When McCaw Cellular went public with its new offer, Perry and others called each of the Mafia members and whispered their thanks. "This was *your* plan," Perry told them. As a result, news articles about the deal carried praise from much of the investment community and key institutional investors. Had that group criticized the offer, McCaw's plan would have been DOA. "We would have been like a turd in a punch bowl," Perry says.

The value of the offer was $3.4 billion—$625 million more than McCaw's previous offer. McCaw told the world that he wouldn't lose this deal, saying he had lined up another $3 billion in financing from a group of twenty-two banks. "Funding has never been a problem for McCaw Cellular, although BellSouth has tried to make that an issue," he sniffed.

McCaw made it plain he would keep digging into that new pot of money. "This is the future of our business, a once-in-a-lifetime opportunity," he told *Business Week*. "You can't build a national network without access to New York, Los Angeles and other big cities."

BellSouth's Roberts showed his side was still in the game. "We've got more aces in the hole and more ways to do this deal than McCaw," he declared.

So what would BellSouth do? It had the money to outspend McCaw, and it had publicly declared it would fight to win. But by December McCaw had raised his offer again, to $154.11, and *The Wall Street Journal* carried a story speculating that BellSouth had "apparently lost its taste for the fight."

BellSouth still insisted otherwise. "We have lots of ammunition left," said Roberts. "It's just a matter of whether we use it."

In December, after the rival bidders had submitted final proposals at LIN's invitation, McCaw called his team together. The group sat around, wondering whether BellSouth had increased its offer. It had the money, but would it risk diluting its earnings? The McCaw strategy rested entirely on that long tradition of grandmothers holding utility stocks, always expecting regular dividends. The tension hung in the room. "It's like two gunfighters in the corral," McCaw said to Peter Currie and others. "We heard the shots. We just don't know who's going to stumble and fall first."

Exhausted after months of long hours and living in hotel rooms, some of the McCaw team flew home, while others awaited word. Finally, at about 11:30 P.M., the phone rang in McCaw's room. An emotionally wrung out Jack Roberts said his chairman had blocked another increase in BellSouth's offer. Though Roberts believed his rivals had reached the limit of their financing, McCaw had won.

McCaw politely told Roberts that it had been a good fight and nothing personal—though McCaw inwardly felt that Roberts had made it personal with some of his attacks on the McCaw company. But McCaw had a grudging admiration for Roberts, too. "If he hadn't been in the game, we would have gotten [LIN] much cheaper. He was a tough adversary," McCaw now says.

BellSouth would not counter the latest McCaw offer. Instead, it wanted to discuss what Wall Street called a "breakup fee," essentially a payment to the losing partner to help cover its fees for investment bankers, lawyers, and others. BellSouth had surrendered to a rival with a smaller checkbook.

"The U.S. could have won the war in Vietnam, but at what cost?" Perry later told *Forbes* magazine. In the end, BellSouth lost because it lacked the will to pay the final price.

But victory carried an enormous price of its own. First, McCaw owed its investment bankers $78 million for their work, an amount Wall Street regarded as generous but not excessive. More unusual, McCaw agreed to pay BellSouth $66.5 million and chip in another $26.5 million to a Los Angeles cellular system of which BellSouth owned 85 percent and McCaw the rest. Perry considered the deal too sweet, but it was McCaw's way of trying to make a friend of an adversary. This philosophy made sense in cellular, where everyone was always doing deals with one another. McCaw knew that BellSouth would always hunger for McCaw's licenses, which might someday prove useful if the McCaw air force ran out of gas.

Back in Kirkland, the rest of the deal team was still waiting to learn whether the months of hard work had paid off. The news came in comic fashion.

A riddle told by Perry had been circulating around the company: Every day, a certain neighborhood dog chases the same school bus. What would the dog do with the bus if he ever caught it? There's no answer to the riddle, because the dog has never thought beyond the chase.

Hamilton went out with his wife the night after returning from New York. While Hamilton was out, Perry got word of the LIN victory and called Hamilton's house. "A Mr. Perry called," the baby-sitter told Hamilton when they returned. "He said something about a dog catching a bus."

Whether from stress, relief, sheer exhilaration, or a combination of all three, Hamilton began to laugh uncontrollably. McCaw had his bus, all right.

* * *

The cost of LIN to McCaw Cellular Communications would terrify a financial conservative. The company's long-term debt was tripling to $5.2 billion, not counting the likelihood of having to buy the other half of LIN in five years. "We were up to our eyeballs in debt. We had to work our ass off to make it all pay," Perry says. *Business Week* quoted analysts who doubted that McCaw could boost business enough to service the debt. "The only victory in this battle may prove to be Pyrrhic," the magazine intoned.

That might have sobered some businessmen, but not McCaw. With 70 million potential customers, McCaw Cellular Communications was now the largest cellular company in the nation—more than twice the size of second-place PacTel. With this latest prize, Craig McCaw had evolved from the obscure entrepreneur who had paid $6 a POP in 1986 to a corporate raider on the front page of *The Wall Street Journal*—paying $320 a POP. The prices had changed, but not the overall perception that Craig McCaw was paying more than seemed sensible.

But McCaw had more big ideas. As Steve Rattner of Lazard Freres & Company in New York put it, his next move would be "the grand-daddy of all deals."

CHAPTER

17

"The Spirit Within Us Must Burn"

The Bill Comes Due for a Leveraged Giant

ummer in Seattle is a glorious season: the citizenry emerges from the long, wet spring to play in the sun, to sail, water-ski, or swim in the warm waters of Lake Washington, or to hike in the mountains that rise east and west of the city.

In the summer of 1990, Craig McCaw could look down from his company's new lakeshore headquarters in Kirkland, Washington, and see his seaplane or turn west toward Seattle and the Olympic Mountains beyond. On his days of deepest thinking, he could imagine the scenery beyond those mountains to the Pacific Ocean and, almost halfway around the world, the shores of Asia.

The gorgeous weather wasn't McCaw's only reason to feel good. There was also his recent capture of LIN Broadcasting, one of the few hostile takeovers of a communications company in U.S. history. Craig McCaw and his little "junk bond company" had outmaneuvered one of the proud Baby Bells. McCaw Communications was now the undisputed champion of cellular communication and the leader of the coming revolution in wireless telephones.

But McCaw wasn't feeling triumphant. He was worried. Across the industry, there were new doubts about the high prices of cellular acquisitions, especially McCaw's buyout of LIN. Since McCaw had set a record in the LIN deal, per-POP prices had fallen from $350 to $190. Even taking into account a reasonable premium for New York and Los Angeles, the drop reignited accusations that McCaw and others had overspent.

McCaw himself had his doubts. At the height of his battle with Donald Pels and BellSouth, he had watched the price of victory grow and worried about the costs. "Craig, in the end, wasn't sure he wanted to win," says Perry, who spent the summer of 1990 in Europe on a sabbatical. "He didn't know if the winner was the loser."

Pels, the loser, had been personally enriched by the battle. The takeover had driven up LIN's shares, including Pels's 3 percent of the company. He stood to gross up to $253 million, earning a spot on the *Forbes* magazine list of the 400 wealthiest Americans. McCaw, by contrast, came out of the fight worried about his company.

"It was the typical takeover deal. I was too emotionally involved," McCaw now says. It was a rare occasion in which he failed to stay detached. Years later, he still didn't know whether he had done the right thing. "I didn't have to throw in the last bit of money. We, of course, wouldn't have won if I hadn't been involved, but the shareholders could have made more money if we hadn't won. That's a very open question to this day. The [$154.11 per share] offer was too high. We paid too much money."

How much would have been the right amount? "Who's to know? We created a market hysteria and then had to buy against ourselves. [But] we probably paid twenty percent too much."

As the nation's largest cellular company, McCaw Communications was now the focus of any discussion about cellular. And that coincided with a dramatic change in the lending environment. Financing for highly leveraged buyouts was drying up; defaults on junk bonds were accelerating. A buyout of United Airlines collapsed; so did other leveraged deals. Nothing symbolized the radical change in the world of credit more clearly than the securities-fraud indictment in March 1989 of Michael Milken, the junk bond king who had played such a critical role in the growth of cable and cellular companies—the Drexel star who had supplied precious financial fuel for Craig McCaw's attack forces.

McCaw felt a personal loyalty to Milken, whom he regarded as an honorable partner and a trusted adviser despite whatever suspicions dogged the junk king's dealings elsewhere. Milken's indictment triggered events that ultimately destroyed Drexel itself, which paid $650 million in fines to settle its portion of the case and then filed for bankruptcy, a spectacular conclusion to a dizzying period of Wall Street history.

The combination of the weak lending environment with the perceived overpayment for licenses now precipitated a skid in cellular stocks. McCaw Cellular Communications shares fell from about $36 a share to

$11.50, a drop in market value from $6.5 billion to $2 billion. British Telecom saw the market value of its $1.5 billion investment in McCaw shrivel. A fund manager for IDS Financial Services announced that he had dumped his McCaw shares. *The Wall Street Journal*'s famously gossipy "Heard on the Street" column speculated that McCaw "might need to raise more equity by issuing shares to a big U.S. investor."

There was irony in all this. By becoming big, McCaw was perceived as weak. "It was a pretty ugly time," says John Stanton.

At the same time, another large independent, George Lindemann of Metro Mobile CTS, saw his company's market value drop from $1.5 billion to $540 million. Like others in cellular, Lindemann had spent years cobbling together his financing, never quite sure where the next dollar would come from. With guts and vision, he had built a company with 11.5 million POPs in eight states. But now he saw himself at the limit of his borrowing capacity, facing a recession that had depressed revenue and a projected company loss for the year of $80.1 million, Metro Mobile's biggest ever. Average monthly revenue from each of its 180,000 subscribers had fallen from a projected $85 to $60, and the company was in technical default on a big loan.

Within twelve months, Lindemann would sell his company to Bell Atlantic, leaving Craig McCaw as the last of the big cellular independents. To some, the slump made John Kluge a genius for having sold his cellular properties early. The only remaining buyers were the few still flush with cash—the big phone companies—and even they were now paying lower prices. *Forbes* magazine reported the cynic's view: "Cellular phone stocks have bombed. The bad news isn't over."

The FCC feared that scores of cellular licenses for rural service areas (RSAs) sold by lottery between 1988 and 1989 might be forfeited back to the government. The prospect of license holders abandoning swaths of frequency would further shake the industry. A giveback would diminish the value of licenses held by other RSAs and make it harder for the entire industry to get loans.

McCaw Cellular Communications had some unique problems. With recent twelve-month revenues of $890 million, the company carried $3.5 billion of long-term debt. Over the next two years, the company faced interest and construction costs of $500 million. Projected cash flow wouldn't cover interest payments for another three years, meaning that McCaw had to keep borrowing as the perceived value of cellular licenses fell and as lenders worried whether the recession would further slow cellular's revenue growth.

Principal payments on all this debt started coming due in 1994. By then McCaw would be facing huge new costs on bidding for new wireless frequencies to be auctioned by the FCC. Using a technology like cellular but operating at a higher-frequency band, the Personal Communications Services (PCS) licenses would likely go for high prices and bring in many new players. PCS offered an opportunity to fill gaps in the McCaw network, but the auction costs might be $1 billion or more.

Most analysts, however, were focused on McCaw Cellular's short-term money crunch. Martin Hyman, who watched cellular for Booz, Allen & Hamilton, said that McCaw Cellular faced a suspenseful future: "Anything that jiggles [McCaw's] growth, whether it's hard economic times, pressure on industry pricing or capacity congestion, could trigger a flash point."

To attack the cash problem, McCaw had convened a management meeting at a desert resort in La Quinta, California, near Palm Springs in early spring of 1990. Outside, golfers played their game on perfect greens fed by artesian wells. Inside, McCaw bluntly informed his aides that the company's survival depended on getting cash quickly. That meant selling some of the licenses that it had worked so hard to acquire. The McCaw company had sold in the past to trade up or to fund even better deals, as it had in the LIN transaction. But this time—for the first time—McCaw would be selling out of need.

"We're in trouble," McCaw said. "This is what we'd better do: Sell $500 million of assets now. I don't care what it takes. Do it."

He gave the assignment to his acquisition team, but it failed, in part because, McCaw says, the Baby Bells were hoping to force McCaw into a desperate situation. By not buying, they hoped McCaw's credit problems would force a fire sale.

The other problem was that his own people just didn't feel motivated to work hard for a sale. "They were used to buying. They hated selling," McCaw says. "It isn't any fun. Psychologically, you're always on the defensive with the other guy."

McCaw knew he had a crisis, but he didn't convey his fears to employees or to the Wall Street and banking communities. He worried about reports that people within the company were using panicky phrases in order to pressure employees to meet bank covenants. He suspected that people in Rufus Lumry's group were the source. "It was a distraction, because they scared the operating people too much," he said later. "It was a basic headquarters mentality that you have to scare 'em—you can't trust 'em. That's when we started to telegraph panic to the external markets, and we'd start to get the analysts on us."

In an interview with *Forbes* magazine, McCaw said his greatest worry was that his people would succumb to conventional thinking. "The worst thing that could happen to us," he said coolly, "is to be distracted by all the hysteria." Inside the company, McCaw used the *Comline* newsletter to dispel doubt—and to warn against hubris. "There are many who are expecting us to fail," he wrote.

He urged his McCaw employees to welcome their new partners from LIN and learn from them:

> We must be very careful not to raise ourselves up by putting other people down. The more successful you become, the more humble you must be, for people don't like those they perceive to be both successful and arrogant. . . . We stay ahead by keeping our eyes open and our minds flexible to new ideas. The spirit within us must burn with intensity, knowing that the further we come, the tougher it is to avoid losing our way.

Always the gambler, McCaw believed he might be able to work through his money problems. Starting with his LIN obligations, he could delay, redefine, or restructure (that is, shrink) his obligations. Since LIN had agreed during the takeover battle to buy half of New York from John Kluge, McCaw needed to rework that deal. In a complex tax-free transaction, he effectively assigned control of a Philadelphia license and one of LIN's TV stations to Kluge in return for a lower cost for New York.

On a second front, McCaw put his finance people on the road to persuade banks to ease the company's credit burden. The deal went well despite a taxi accident in Tokyo that left Rufus Lumry with a broken collarbone. Selling the Madison, Racine, and other Wisconsin licenses and making a few other transactions netted McCaw about $200 million. McCaw hated to give up spectrum, but he had no choice. He had depleted his cherished flexibility.

The moves brought relief, but not enough. McCaw still faced long-term vulnerabilities.

He had always spent considerable time thinking about competitors, potential competitors, and allies. Even while McCaw was talking to *Forbes* about distractions, he had already launched a secret effort to find a big-daddy partner. From the days of his cellular company's earliest expansion, he had known that it would be very difficult to maneuver his company into a position of strength to compete with the regional Bells. He could outhustle them, fool them, or scare them, but he could never outspend them. And as they had slowly come around to see the strategic value of wireless communications, they had begun to write ever bigger checks, both to buy licenses and to pay dealers who provided new customers.

The Bells, however, could never match his passion for what cellular could be. McCaw considered it almost a moral duty to give customers quality, especially in New York City, the center of the communications industry. Once he had control of New York, he would test the cellular system and report any problems to his resident manager. "Hello, Kemo Sabe," he'd say to Tim Donahue, the northeastern president. "It's me. I had two dropped calls. You might be having trouble with your handover parameters." Donahue, who was signing up 50,000 new customers a month, would promise to get right on it.

Nonetheless, by 1990 Craig McCaw had come further than anyone outside his company had thought possible. His company had established the beginnings of a national network, though it still lacked such key markets as Chicago, Boston, and Atlanta. For a long time McCaw had known that someday he would probably need a large partner to help him face down the Bells. It might be MCI or Sprint, but always the most logical partner was the biggest daddy of all—AT&T. If McCaw Cellular couldn't work its way out of its money problems, he would look to Ma Bell as his alternative path.

"AT&T was the back door because we knew [the Bells] wouldn't help us without demanding control," McCaw says. AT&T had the most money and the greatest need for cellular—though, in McCaw's view, it was slow to recognize its own best interests.

Just sixteen years earlier, AT&T, in settling an antitrust suit with the U.S. Department of Justice, had forever changed its future and the landscape of telecommunications. The original Ma Bell had divested itself of two thirds of its assets—twenty-two local Bell operating companies valued at $80 billion. At the same time, the company had abandoned a business it had thought too insignificant to keep—the cellular telephone. In the settlement approved by Judge Harold Greene, AT&T had cut itself out of the "local loop," the direct connection to customers.

In a later misstep, AT&T became a manufacturer of personal computers, blowing billions of dollars in a failed effort to compete in what quickly became a commodity business. In 1984 AT&T had projected U.S. cellular subscribers at 900,000 by 1995. Instead, subscriptions had blown past that figure in 1988 and were fast approaching 1.5 million in 1990. Yet as AT&T expanded its investments into credit cards and other new businesses, it showed no concern over cellular's growth.

Considering the entire record, McCaw executives saw AT&T as effectively paralyzed both by pride and by bureaucratic lethargy. They figured the company was too proud to admit its mistakes with cellular and too bound by tradition to change course dramatically. And for AT&T to return to cellular now would be to declare war on the Baby Bells, which would use their parent's return to the local loop as justification for them to enter the long-distance business, AT&T's mother lode of profits. Both parties would contest the other's plans before Judge Greene or various regulators—a war with unforeseeable consequences. So even if AT&T wanted to enter cellular, the barriers were formidable.

As the old Ma Bell, AT&T had been been on the McCaw family's horizon ever since Elroy McCaw had feuded with the company over long-distance charges for radio broadcasts and son Bruce had hidden the family's extra phones from company inspectors. Almost from the start of cellular, McCaw's strategic thinking had included AT&T as a player of some sort, whether partner or rival. It was a presence in every corner of telecommunications, from switching equipment to consumer relations. AT&T had even helped launch McCaw, lending him 150 percent of the cost of buying its cellular equipment, which had helped his company build systems in Seattle, Denver, Kansas City, San Antonio, and Austin. Now, in 1990, their paths seemed due to cross yet again.

In either 1986 or 1987 McCaw mentioned to Mike Senkowski, one of his FCC lawyers in Washington, D.C., that his dream was to someday acquire AT&T. Senkowski thought it unlikely, to put it mildly, that such a talented but small player in telecommunications could ever buy one of the world's largest corporations. "Well, it's good to have big dreams," Senkowski thought to himself.

(Told about this incident years later, Wayne Perry calls it an example of people not properly reading McCaw, the intermittent genius. "That was purely delusional," Perry says, meaning AT&T was too big for anyone to swallow, let alone McCaw. "Craig would talk about things. He's not always serious, but some people like Mike take Craig literally.")

However far-fetched, the idea of some kind of deal with AT&T soon got McCaw's closer study. In 1986 he commissioned a law firm to analyze the political and legal issues surrounding a possible AT&T purchase of McCaw Cellular Communications. Following his own dictum of analyzing all the potential moves, McCaw wanted to know whether AT&T's huge bankroll could ever help his business. If the high-flying McCaw company ever ran out of gas, AT&T would be the "biggest possible landing field," Perry says. The scenario presented problems, but in some ways it was simpler than the possibility of selling to a Baby Bell, whose licenses would frequently overlap with McCaw's, creating divestiture problems and serious tax issues.

The growing sense of McCaw's need for a powerful ally coincided with the arrival of Harold Eastman, who brought his smooth, casual approach to the role of McCaw company president in 1989. Unlike others in McCaw's senior management, Eastman had a long history of running several large companies, including a stint as a senior vice president of the Signal Companies (later Allied-Signal). McCaw had recruited Eastman with the goal of strengthening customer service and day-to-day operations.

But Eastman also brought McCaw a simple word of wisdom: The company needed more corporate friends. Having grown so rapidly and with management so intently focused on acquisition and construction, McCaw Cellular needed to raise its profile and dispel its image as a West Coast corporate raider. Few customers realized that McCaw had become a large provider of services. Nor had many considered how

McCaw could exploit its status as one of AT&T's largest long-distance buyers. Eastman took on the job of building personal relationships with executives at suppliers, customers, and other companies, spreading the vision of cellular and of the McCaw company.

This effort required Craig McCaw to get out and personally meet chief executives of some of America's largest companies, a task that he did not always welcome. He had other things to do and wasn't fond of meeting strangers. But he recognized how such contacts could benefit the company and its shareholders, so he went off to meet senior people at IBM, General Motors, and other companies.

"He was incredibly effective in those meetings," Eastman says. "He was disarming. His low-key style came across as very genuine. I was always pleased with how he handled himself."

Not all of the meetings were productive, however. Eastman recalls the lengthy processes with IBM and GM, which started with long agenda-setting discussions in advance. On the day of the GM visit, Eastman and McCaw went through three or four security checks and several different groups of handlers, meeting a new set for each floor as they got closer to the VIP offices. Finally, on the top floor, McCaw said, "Boy, customers will never find them here." That's about all he remembered of that visit.

Eastman's initial goal with AT&T was a $1 billion investment in McCaw Cellular. But there were some obstacles, both trivial and significant. Golf is one traditional means for executives to strengthen relations with AT&T, sponsor of the famed Pebble Beach Pro-Am tournament. But golf was hardly McCaw's strength. He wasn't merely bad, jokes Perry, but with his misdirected drives he was a veritable threat to humanity. McCaw didn't even dress like AT&T's golfers, some of whom wore lime green pants and white shoes (a loud style McCaw attributed to traditions found on old East Coast courses). Instead, like most Seattle golfers, McCaw dressed in more subdued hues. The contrast was a visible reminder of how out of place he felt in AT&T's old-style, inbred corporate culture. McCaw just couldn't play the role of hail-fellow-well-met, socializing on the course. "I didn't have a clue," he later confessed.

More significantly, McCaw came from a dynamic, entrepreneurial world of risk takers. The AT&T managers tended to join the company early and stay for decades, with clear and predictable career paths. These men had known no other life than Bell. McCaw couldn't comprehend such a rigid world, nor did he feel they could understand him. "The more they dealt with me, the less they understood me, because I couldn't relate to golf or cocktails." Feeling socially awkward in such stuffy surroundings, McCaw never did play in the Pebble Beach tournament. Nor did he ever play a round with Robert Allen, AT&T's chief executive.

Furthermore, the effort to warm relations between the two companies was hampered by Craig McCaw's past public criticism of AT&T's switching system for cellular. "They didn't pay much attention to their equipment in the early days," McCaw says. Annoyed, McCaw had pulled AT&T equipment out of Portland, Seattle, and Florida in the winter of 1988. In a letter to AT&T's then chief executive, James Olson, McCaw bluntly declared that AT&T's hardware products were lousy.

It was risky to rile the elephant, but McCaw felt that quiet measures had failed and that his customer service had suffered as a consequence. "Quality was always more important to us than anything else," McCaw says. But it was difficult to change AT&T's behavior. Over the decades, AT&T's employees, by then 250,000 in number, had created a Byzantine bureaucracy. It always took five to do the job of one. No one could make decisions, or so it seemed to the leaner 4,400-employee McCaw organization. (LIN employed another 1,900 people.)

Needless to say, McCaw's letter caused a tremendous stir within AT&T, especially with Olson, who cared about quality and service to one of his largest equipment customers. (Olson, at age sixty-two, died of colon cancer in 1988, just a few months after finally meeting McCaw. "He knew he was dying. You could see it in his face . . . wonderful man," McCaw says.)

Eventually, AT&T acknowledged it had a problem. In the fall of 1989 John Fisher, AT&T's vice president for wireless hardware sales, had dinner with John Stanton. How can we rebuild this relationship? Fisher asked. Have one of your people spend time with Craig McCaw, Stanton replied; but it has to be a senior executive from AT&T, not a lower-level sales representative. Look what Ericsson does, said Stanton. Its chairman flies out from Stockholm to ask McCaw for ideas. That helps.

Fisher agreed, and AT&T executives began working harder to strengthen relations, a process helped by McCaw's hosting AT&T vice chairman Randal Tobias and others from the telecommunications industry at the Seattle Goodwill Games in August 1990. Bob Allen did not attend the games, but AT&T executive vice presidents William Marx and Victor Pelson used the get-together to meet with Eastman at McCaw headquarters to begin discussing a marketing alliance and an equity investment by AT&T.

In November 1990 a McCaw delegation that included Eastman, Stanton, and Perry (who had returned from Europe) flew to Chicago for a second discussion. That meeting went well, and others followed.

McCaw attended almost none of these meetings, a tactic that preserved flexibility. He could always kill a deal he hadn't negotiated, sending Perry back to reexamine a point in the light of an objection raised by the "mad scientist" at headquarters.

Always sniffing for information of strategic value, McCaw tried to learn what he could about AT&T from how it handled the McCaw team, how it treated issues and disagreements. Looking ahead, he wanted to know how AT&T treated partners. McCaw "had an exceptional ability to ask the key strategic questions," says Eastman. "My joke about McCaw was that he had the ability to see around corners or over the curvature of the earth. He sees so far ahead of everybody else."

To McCaw, AT&T's need for his help was self-evident. Without a direct link to customers, AT&T was vulnerable as the Bells kept pressing regulators for authority to enter the long-distance market, which some figured produced 80 percent of the giant's profits. The McCaw company could provide the direct link AT&T desperately needed. But McCaw was no salesman. He left that to people like Perry, who had a way of making his suggestions seem both fun and sensible, and other views just dumb.

Perry knew that one of AT&T's great sources of pride was its fabled history, dating back to Theodore Vail. The trick was to move AT&T, an institution rooted in tradition, over to McCaw's vision of the future without offending the long-distance giant's belief in its received wisdom.

At one session with AT&T, Perry played to that sense of tradition. He whipped out a 1979 Bell Labs report about a then new technology called cellular telephony. The document laid out the cost of cellular systems, how they would be built, and who would use the phones. Except for underestimating the number of customers, the report was remarkably prescient. Perry made it sound as if AT&T's joining with McCaw was as inevitable as salmon returning home to spawn. The McCaw success was really AT&T's, or at least it could be. The past and the future were moving the companies together. Why fight it?

Perry held up the old report like a religious artifact recovered by the young McCaw team. "Folks, this is why we got into this business," he said. "We read your book. You guys are responsible for us."

The AT&T people loved it.

CHAPTER

18

"You're Marrying Off Your Daughter When She's Fourteen"

AT&T Makes an Offer That Can't Be Refused

Finally, Craig McCaw had AT&T's attention. To strengthen his own company, he had roused the giant, setting into motion forces he could not control. But as so often in his company's history, he needed to take risks to achieve gains. Failure could weaken Wall Street's confidence in McCaw Communications, damage the company's image of success, and raise doubts about his leadership.

"We weren't always sure whether [we] wanted the giant to know whether [cellular] was a great business or not," McCaw says:

> It's always a two-edged sword. If people know what you're trying to do and they recognize that it's a good idea, they may try to do it themselves. So that really put us in the course of doing one of two things: either being enemies [with AT&T] or friends, because once they launched on it and they realized that this was a good idea to be in the service side of the business as opposed to the manufacturing side, we really had a choice, which is we're going to meet them in the marketplace head-on or we're going to work together. Because we wanted them to be a great manufacturer, it was actually a fairly tough issue. So we went along and said: Well, where will this go?

The telecommunications giant had decided that helping McCaw would be helping itself. But talks between the companies were not going well. The two sides discussed a tantalizing deal for McCaw, an investment of $1 billion by AT&T in a joint marketing arrangement to which McCaw Cellular would contribute airtime and staff. But AT&T was understandably protective of its prestigious brand name and didn't want itself associated with substandard service, while cellular was still subject to frequent breakdowns. Despite the hundreds of millions of dollars that had been poured into systems, no cellular company yet had enough capacity to handle extreme surges in customer demand. Even McCaw couldn't promise near-perfect service, and that widened the gulf that separated the two parties, one primarily interested in protecting a great business, the other wanting to grow a new business.

It helped that McCaw had grown to trust Robert Allen, who, at fifty-three, had succeeded Olson as AT&T's chairman and chief executive. Fifteen years older than McCaw, Allen had spent his entire career working for the phone company, having joined Indiana Bell in 1957 immediately after his graduation from Wabash College. Bland in appearance, Allen nonetheless had managed to get himself noticed. He thrived in the Bell bureaucracies, winning a series of promotions, including the top job at what would later called Bell Atlantic.

None of this changed his personality. He spoke so quietly, his body still as a tombstone, that it was easy to lose track of what he was saying. Some jokingly compared him to Mr. Rogers, the affable children's TV personality. But as anyone who played golf with him knew, Allen had a fiercely competitive side. He didn't like losing. Nor did he intend to preside over any erosion of AT&T's market power. He saw the coming changes in telecommunications, and he knew AT&T needed to be bold.

"Bob is indeed deceptive in appearances," said David Nadler, chairman of Delta Consulting Group Inc. of New York, who had worked with Allen as a consultant since the early 1980s. "He doesn't fit your standard stereotype of a charismatic leader," Nadler told *The Washington Post*. "But he's a very good strategic thinker, and he has very strong feelings."

The overtures from McCaw Cellular came at a time when Allen was ready to look at new strategies. He had recently begun embracing the idea of integrated services to customers. Attracted to the notion of customers' using AT&T PCs to access data over the company's long-distance lines, Allen spent $7.5 billion in stock for computer maker NCR. (The NCR deal would prove to be a disaster.) Cellular fit with that ambition. "I always wanted to be in the wireless business, particularly as it began to accelerate," he said.

Though McCaw insiders joked about Allen's stuffy style and

ridiculed the many layers of management that separated Allen from customers, Craig McCaw offered no criticisms. Instead, he spoke of his personal regard for Allen:

> You watch how people treat other people, not what they say to you. First, he has a soft side and a kind side to him, I think. There is a softness of his character that you sense. I believe we share some characteristics; he is an introverted person with a strong series of beliefs, and will do what he believes is right as opposed to what's popular. Because I'm not used to being popular, all I know how to do is to do what's right, and so that was a factor [in our doing business together].

Craig McCaw stayed out of the ongoing discussions with AT&T for several reasons. As always, he did not want to be ensnared in the minutiae of negotiations. He also had to walk a delicate line as both the chief executive, representing all shareholders, and as the financial representative of the McCaw family. To avoid any appearance of steering the deal to favor himself, he delegated the work to a team that consisted of Wayne Perry, Executive Vice President Tom Alberg, Senior Vice President—Finance Peter Currie, and Senior Vice President—Law Andrew Quartner.

To the members of this McCaw team, the talks with AT&T seemed interminable. As soon as any item seemed to be understood and agreed on, AT&T would dispatch another vice president to start the process all over again.

Frustrated and a little skeptical about the seriousness of AT&T's intentions, the McCaw team secretly worked a "second horse," just in case the AT&T talks collapsed. It was McCaw's old adversary BellSouth. Thanks to some careful diplomacy following the LIN takeover (including a trip to the Kentucky Derby by Craig McCaw with BellSouth's chairman), McCaw had made peace with BellSouth, which still coveted McCaw's licenses. McCaw's staff now analyzed the issues surrounding a BellSouth investment in the company and concluded that, despite some complications, it could be done.

BellSouth, however, was looking for a bargain. So Craig McCaw's first choice was AT&T. Keep pressing the AT&T people, he said; eventually, the managers will realize how important cellular could be for their corporate future. "Keep ahead of them. Don't worry about what they're telling you they want," McCaw insisted. "Just do what's right for them and figure it out before they do. Don't worry about what they tell you, because it's just the fingers of the bureaucracy. It's not connected to the brain. They're connected to the elbow."

Knowing how difficult it was for a huge organization to change direction, McCaw figured that if his people kept talking up wireless communications, the idea of a deal with McCaw Cellular would gain momentum within AT&T—eventually. He wanted to "socialize the idea so pretty soon it starts to make sense. At the end of the day, if you get the chairman's ego involved, they always do the deal." It was a shrewd analysis of the inner workings of a vast bureaucracy, especially coming from a man who had never spent a day working for one.

At last McCaw figured the timing was right for a direct appeal to Allen. At a meeting in New Jersey away from AT&T's campus, McCaw and others made a presentation to Allen and several of his deputies that depicted cellular as a vital piece of the long-distance company's future. Without wireless, they said AT&T would soon face fundamental difficulties. McCaw Cellular was a marvelous fit for AT&T, they declared, and joining with McCaw would be a fitting return to the roots of cellular's history, a link between the inventor of cellular and its new champion.

It was an appeal to both Allen's head and his heart. Craig McCaw concluded by saying that all this was possible, but it would never happen at the current rate of negotiations. "This is going nowhere. It's just minutiae," he told Allen. He insisted that the talks had to become more substantive or be dropped: "We need a breakthrough."

Allen agreed to assign Alex Mandl, AT&T's chief financial officer, to the deal-making team. By age, temperament, and expertise, Mandl was the right choice for both AT&T and McCaw. Five years older than McCaw, the son of a literature professor who had brought his family to the United States in the late 1950s, the Austrian-born Mandl did not care for meetings, preferring direct communications that didn't waste time. He had acquired an appreciation of global communications and technology from his work as chief executive of Sea-Land Service, the world's largest ocean transportation company.

Another plus was that Mandl knew the Northwest, having been a student at Willamette University in Oregon, where he remained a trustee. Mandl had later gone to business school at the University of California at Berkeley and become a mergers-and-acquisitions specialist, joining CSX Corporation, which acquired Sea-Land. As head of Sea-Land, he had concentrated on cutting costs and streamlining management while pushing new technology and expansion into overseas markets. During his tenure, revenues jumped by 75 percent.

The McCaw team saw Mandl as a kind of positive virus within AT&T's body. He was also the perfect advocate for McCaw: Who better than the chief financial officer to bless the McCaw company's nontraditional balance sheet of staggering debt and no profits? Best of all, Allen respected Mandl, who was viewed as a possible future company chairman. The McCaw team knew that any deal Mandl cut would almost certainly pass muster with Allen.

But after months of further talks, one problem wouldn't go away. AT&T insisted on control of its brand name. The issue went to the very heart of how the partnership would be run. And there seemed to be no way AT&T could gain control of the partnership without also commanding McCaw Cellular. Though McCaw Communications had done well in many partnerships, including some with proud and powerful companies, Craig McCaw had never shared control. Yet as he watched the AT&T negotiations slowly unfold, he came to a painful realization: To get big money from AT&T and thereby move cellular and his company to the next level, he would have to offer AT&T the ultimate incentive—the possibility of control over his company.

That scenario, of course, meant that Craig McCaw would be out. He was incapable of working for anyone else. Except for the brief period of working for his father, he never had. No one could imagine McCaw surviving, much less thriving, in the Vatican-style circles of AT&T's top management.

McCaw now asked his top managers to discuss the control issue. Perry embraced the logic of the plan, but McCaw believed that Perry was at least partially influenced by the fatigue of having worked so hard for the company, and perhaps needed a long rest. McCaw thought Perry saw clinching an AT&T deal as a way of solving both his personal and his business problems. (Perry later claimed that all he'd really needed was one good hunting weekend.)

With McCaw watching, Perry led the debate, but the idea of ceding control drew fire from Alberg and General Counsel Roberta Katz, the McCaw company's highest-ranking woman, who had been helping in the AT&T negotiations. During an academic career, Katz had earned a Ph.D. in anthropology, which gave her an acute appreciation for the dynamic culture at McCaw and the excitement and independence she felt there. She saw AT&T as a lumbering giant, hidebound by bureaucracies and procedures and committed to fixed wires, while McCaw was as mobile in its culture as its phones were. The thought of AT&T's swallowing the McCaw company repelled her.

At a crucial moment in the debate, Katz turned to McCaw and pleaded with him to keep control. It was a mistake to sell just as the company had finally established a national footprint, she argued. "You're marrying off your daughter when she's fourteen," said Katz, the mother of a middle-school girl. AT&T, she said, was like a toothless old man—a repellent suitor for a fresh young beauty like McCaw.

"Roberta, you don't have a clue as to what the financial future of this company is," Perry retorted. "You don't understand the financial side of the company."

Blunt debate was common at McCaw, so no one was surprised at Perry's aggressive response to Katz. Exploiting Katz's weaknesses as someone who knew little about finance and who had joined the company just two years earlier, Perry dismissed her arguments as emotional and sentimental. Much as he, too, loved the company, Perry argued his case on the basis of cash flow, the company's debt, and its future capital needs. The choice was either to partner with AT&T or to face it as a competitor—sooner or later. "It's a matter of owning that brand or having it crammed up our tailpipe every day," he argued.

Finally, Perry turned to McCaw, saying he intended to go back to AT&T and keep pushing the deal.

"I'm going, Craig," he said. "[If] you tell me to stop, fine. Otherwise I'm going to keep going. It's the right thing."

"Well, we can look for a back door," McCaw replied. As always, he wanted flexibility, an opportunity to kill the deal even as Perry struggled to keep it alive.

* * *

In the summer of 1992 McCaw gave his negotiating team a new idea about how to break the logjam. Offer AT&T an option to buy the entire company, he said, but convince them it was *their* idea so they would embrace it enthusiastically. McCaw did not commit himself to doing such a deal; he would decide that as the details emerged. But he wanted to plant the idea and see how it would grow.

Selling control could take many forms. The McCaw team prepared by spending hundreds of hours analyzing how an option could be structured so that when AT&T "suggested" the idea, they would be ready.

Such a deal faced likely resistance from other phone companies, but the first obstacle loomed within McCaw's own boardroom. London-based British Telecommunications PLC held three seats on the McCaw board of directors and owned 17 percent of the company. BT believed it held veto rights over any sellout deal. But Perry had a "gotcha" ready if BT ever posed a problem. Deep within the voluminous agreement between McCaw and BT was a brief, obscure clause that gave McCaw tremendous power. In it, BT promised not to operate any business that competed in the United States with McCaw. Since the provision was not limited to cellular, McCaw had the right to enter any business it chose—integrated data networks, for example—and force BT to abandon it.

"I just don't think they understood," Perry said later. "It's not unusual to have incredibly complicated documents that have provisions that come back to bite people if they don't pay attention."

Repeating the tactic used earlier with the Cellular Mafia during the LIN buyout, the McCaw executives nudged AT&T's group toward their own idea of a takeover. Soon AT&T was conveniently raising the possibility of offering more money and establishing a "pathway to control." When that subject emerged, Perry called McCaw with the news. McCaw had the option of killing the idea; if he had, perhaps negotiations would have gone in some different, but still fruitful, direction. But McCaw spent no time agonizing over perhaps the biggest decision of his life. Seemingly at peace with himself and the future, Craig McCaw set in motion his own possible ouster from McCaw Cellular with a one-word command to his most trusted lieutenant: "Go."

Of course, there remained a host of details to talk about. Just how could AT&T get control? Would they pursue an outright buyout? A huge payment to the McCaw family? Stock swaps? At one point, AT&T talked about buying McCaw's stock for hundreds of millions of dollars above market price. As the controlling shareholder, Craig McCaw certainly could demand a premium. But he wanted the bulk of AT&T's money to go toward paying down the McCaw company's debt. He wanted to leave the old company in the strongest possible financial shape. Otherwise, AT&T would be less willing to spend big for new licenses or new systems.

In short, though exact numbers are elusive, McCaw was willing to give up millions of dollars to protect his legacy. Rather than making his vast pile of money even bigger, he wanted his "daughter" protected in her new marriage. McCaw "is not motivated by money," Wayne Perry said later. Perhaps choices like that explain how it's possible to describe one of the richest men in history in such terms.

After weeks of talks in Kirkland, Basking Ridge, Vail, Aspen, and elsewhere, the deal started to come together. Peter Currie recalls a moment that seemed to symbolize the shift in AT&T's attitude: Opening a meeting at buttoned-down Basking Ridge, Mandl greeted the McCaw team dressed in casual clothes. Seeing AT&T's chief financial officer tieless made Currie laugh. "It was great," says Currie.

The news broke in November 1992, just days after President George Bush's humiliating electoral defeat by Arkansas governor Bill Clinton. The voluminous political coverage pushed the announcement off page one of *The New York Times,* which reported on the front of its business section that AT&T was negotiating to buy one third of McCaw Cellular for $3.8 billion.

The money reportedly would buy British Telecom's 22 percent stake in McCaw and pay for newly issued McCaw stock, a transaction that would shrink McCaw's debt by $2 billion. The McCaw family and other insiders would receive $100 million from AT&T for a seven-year option to take control of the company. Exercising that option would cost an additional $600 million, plus interest of 7 percent a year, for a total payout to the McCaw family of nearly $1 billion.

The announcement showed that AT&T had at last embraced cellular as a key communications technology. "There's a revolution brewing in personal communications services and we're going to accelerate that revolution," Bob Allen told the *Times*. He said he wanted to put a cellular phone in everyone's pocket and provide customers with a seamless, national transmission network.

The *Times* gave a positive view of the news, which it called "a move that would increase the growth of both the established cellular telephone industry and the nascent personal-communications services technology." It described stock analysts as enthusiastic. "What the deal potentially does is lift McCaw one level above the rest of the industry," said Robert Morris of Goldman Sachs & Company. "For AT&T this lifts their frustration over not being able to have access, really, to the customers. Before now, they've had to pay pretty much 50 cents on the dollar to go through the local telephone companies."

The *Times*'s coverage reflected the spin that both companies wanted. Rather than have the deal perceived as a monopolistic move by AT&T, triggering antitrust scrutiny, the companies wanted to stress potential consumer benefits.

The Wall Street Journal emphasized the competitors' view of the deal. *Journal* reporter John J. Keller gave the cautionary view in his second paragraph: "The transaction would put AT&T in direct competition with the regional Bell companies for the first time since the 1984 breakup of the Bell system." Keller called it a "huge blow to AT&T's chief rival, MCI Communications Corp., since millions of new phone customers would gain direct access to AT&T's long-distance network via McCaw's service. That's an ironic twist for the usually savvy MCI, which sold its cellular and paging holdings in 1986 to McCaw."

One thing was clear: The pace of change in cellular was astonishing. On the very day of the McCaw-AT&T deal, another 9,000 customers in the United States signed up for service, bringing the total served to some 10 million people. That had been the forecast for eight years in the future. With the public embracing cellular far faster than expected, the idea of government barriers between local and long distance now seemed as absurd as the idea of a telephone's being tied to a fixed location. Increasingly, the public wanted go-anywhere, work-anywhere telephones; customer demand was emerging for McCaw's vision of a national wireless network. Craig McCaw, the self-styled "anthropologist," had guessed right.

But as old Ma Bell drove up in her flashy new sports car, demanding the right to travel as fast as she wanted, the government still retained the right to post speed limits. McCaw and AT&T had to get by the courts and the FCC to make their deal a reality by the planned closure date of summer 1993. Despite confident talk that the government scrutiny would pose no problem, the McCaw forces knew the Bells would mount a fierce counteroffensive, using every legal, economic, and political tactic they could devise. Inevitably, the Bells would demand permission to enter long-distance service if AT&T won entry into their markets.

A debate before regulators between AT&T and the Bells would present huge risks and opportunities for each side. After years of competition in a market still heavily regulated by government, each feared losing customers to the other. McCaw tried to signal to the Bells that he wanted to grow the business, not snatch away their share. With new, smaller, and more powerful wireless telephones on the horizon, he wanted to usher in a new form of communications business. "We're not going to take their gold; we're trying to mine platinum," he said at a press conference. "Why fight over low-margin, local exchange business; we're after the value-added, high-margin mobile services that will give people communications flexibility."

The outcome of the battle before the regulators would turn in part over who could define their arguments as best reflecting the public interest. The day the deal was announced, McCaw Executive Vice President Mark Hamilton, the company's head of government relations, unleashed a small army of lobbyists to brief state and federal officials about the cellular business as McCaw saw it—the gospel according to Craig. Hamilton had already practiced his own arguments repeatedly, including one 3 A.M. rehearsal with his newborn son, Sam, as his audience.

Hamilton and two staffers now visited the Washington, D.C., office of FCC Commissioner Ervin Duggan, an admirer of Craig McCaw's. They briefed Duggan, who nodded and seemed positive about the proposal. Hamilton left feeling optimistic about winning the support of a key regulator. Only later did Hamilton learn what had happened after they left. Duggan closed the door, turned to his aide with a puzzled look, and asked, "What does this mean?"

Duggan wasn't the only person with questions triggered by the McCaw-AT&T deal. Some wanted to know more about Craig McCaw himself. If AT&T now had a "pathway to control," didn't that mean the end of McCaw's career in the industry he had helped start? When *Forbes* magazine asked how McCaw could so easily give up his life's work, his reply revealed a decidedly different kind of chief executive— one still largely a boy at heart:

> I've never had more fun in my life than I'm having today. I get to work with wonderful people in a great cause and a fun business, at a time when the risks are huge and the opportunities are huge. But jeez, if somebody retired me today, I wouldn't mind. I'd go do something else. I'd take soybean oil and put it in diesels. It's environmentally smart, and we grow it right here in our own country. You could run the city buses in New York within 2 percent of the efficiency of diesel fuel. . . . There's so much to do.

"So much to do"? Of course. But which possibility would a suddenly unemployed Craig McCaw turn to next? Everyone was curious about his next big idea—including Craig McCaw himself.

CHAPTER
19

"Like Porcupines Making Love"

The Billionaire Leaves Home

Six days after announcing the AT&T deal, Craig McCaw attended a company employee forum where management gave briefings on news, policies, and awards, and answered questions. Typically, the forums were casual and full of good-natured banter.

On this day, however, the room at a hotel near McCaw headquarters pulsed with tension. For years the McCaw organization had seen itself as a renegade, the nimble outsider who consistently beat the slow-footed traditionalists. But this week's news had truly jolted the ranks: With its founder's blessing, McCaw Cellular Communications had allied itself with the ultimate symbol of corporate bureaucracy, AT&T, the company once so blind it had given away cellular.

The alliance was no match of equals. What did it mean that, under the proposed alliance, AT&T would get a "pathway to control"? Was giant Ma Bell about to swallow little McCaw?

Few people in the room understood the AT&T deal and its still-vague provisions. No one understood what the deal meant for Craig McCaw—not even McCaw himself. And that, to many, seemed the key to McCaw Cellular's future. He wasn't just the chief executive, but also the visionary whose unique management style pervaded the organization. The 200 people at the forum included some who had worked for McCaw during the cable days and some who had only recently joined the company, many lured by the appeal of working for a young, aggressive organization. They wondered why he had agreed to his own possible ouster.

It was a curious feeling. Their boss remained in charge, but only until AT&T chose to take him out. Was he already gone in spirit? Had they been abandoned? "Is McCaw jumping ship?" whispered one employee. It was the question everyone was asking.

Some of those at the forum had never met Craig McCaw before; some weren't even sure what he looked like. Within the firm, he was known largely through occasional corporate messages or an article passed around at the office. But there he was, sitting three rows from the front, dressed in slacks and a tieless dress shirt, a slight, rumpled figure with a lean face and an oversized mustache, someone who might easily be overlooked at a singles bar but whose decisions affected everyone in the room—and throughout the telecommunications industry.

McCaw stood to speak. The group strained to hear as he quietly gave a history of the relationship between McCaw and AT&T: how AT&T had invented cellular, financed McCaw's first purchase of a cellular switching system, and gradually came to recognize its need to join with McCaw. The relationship had had difficulties, McCaw admitted. The McCaw company had complained about AT&T's early cellular hardware and had had to tutor AT&T in the importance of cellular. "We've been training them for a long time," he said with a grin that brought laughter. "They've been learning about us. It hasn't been easy."

At the same time, he added, McCaw Cellular had matured, helped in part by its partnerships with larger companies, especially Affiliated Publications. McCaw surprised the group by saying that for a time he had wanted to get into newspapers and that his plan had been to take over Affiliated. "We could have bought them if we had wanted to. The fun part is, we didn't need to anymore, nor did we have a need for their business. That wasn't a degree of disrespect for them, but a recognition that we had gone on and had new ideas."

Over the years, the McCaw company had considered alliances or mergers with other companies, McCaw continued. MCI had asked for a deal more than once. Sprint had proposed merging "with us at least four times," he said. None of those proposals had worked. But eventually it became clear that the personal communications business would become so large that McCaw Cellular couldn't do it alone. No one company can get to that future alone, he said. "The key issue is how to do it together. How do we make it happen faster, better, more efficiently, so that we occupy the marketplace before someone else gets there?" The deal that could make it possible was with AT&T.

McCaw's dark eyes scanned faces in the room. He knew there were still doubts. He promised that the McCaw culture would not suffer but would thrive with AT&T as a partner. "We didn't do a deal so that you would be subject to old-fashioned business practices," McCaw said. "AT&T is trying to become like us. I only hope that we don't become like what they're trying to move away from."

He reminded them of the McCaw philosophy:

> . . . the principle that one person makes a huge difference. That if you empower people and give them a lot of responsibility, then you get a benefit from it, a disproportionate benefit, even though you may make mistakes. That you hire invigorating, dangerous, and interesting people who are not all the same, and who cause trouble, because that's how you get things done. If we all keep embodying that spirit, we don't have to be worrying about being swallowed by them or anyone else. . . . The way we manage is the [style] of the future, even though at times it frightens the outside world, and even us.

McCaw had yet to touch on himself and his future. He saved that for last. "You all know this deal includes the potential that they can fire me," he said. "They can't fire you, but they can fire me. We'll need to run the company so well, I won't get fired." He smiled. "Because I never want to be fired."

There was laughter, then applause. A measure of uneasiness remained, however. McCaw Cellular had always been independent. Now, as McCaw acknowledged, Ma Bell had a say in its future . . . and even in the personal future of its founder.

The next to speak was Jim Barksdale, the folksy executive McCaw had brought in just eleven months earlier to serve as company president and chief operating officer. Barksdale had been executive vice president and chief operating officer of Federal Express, where he had overseen rapid growth, expansion into overseas markets, and the maintenance of outstanding customer service. Four years older than McCaw, Barksdale had taken the slot left by Hal Eastman, who wanted out of day-to-day work and had taken the title of vice chairman. Barksdale had immediately become popular with the company's rank and file. He had southern charm and a way of summing up complex business problems in vivid, often witty phrases. A good salesman, he liked to say, "could talk dogs off a meat truck."

What few McCaw employees knew was that Barksdale had been aggressively wooed by McCaw—who had neglected to tell him about the ongoing talks with AT&T. Had Barksdale known, he would have thought twice about joining the company. He got the news about the takeover just fifteen days after his arrival. He kept his reaction secret from other employees, but made plain his annoyance to McCaw. "I was pissed," Barksdale said later.

McCaw had replied that Barksdale had no need to worry. If Barksdale thought the takeover was a bad idea, it wouldn't go forward.

Barksdale doubted that the AT&T deal was necessary; he didn't think McCaw's strategic problems were insurmountable. Yet he had gone along with the deal, despite the uncertainty it introduced. Now Barksdale, always the team motivator, was praising the deal to his troops. And his arguments had appeal: Thanks to the AT&T deal, the McCaw company's cash problems were eased, and it soon would have the right to use one of the most powerful brand names in the world. Furthermore, McCaw could enjoy tremendous synergies in using AT&T's assets: Bell Labs, the legendary research center; a global switching system; and a long tradition of strong customer relations, most recently seen in AT&T's hugely successful new credit card business. The best measure of the deal's strategic value was the fear it put into McCaw's competitors, he said.

Barksdale couldn't resist describing one immediate result of the McCaw-AT&T announcement. "This was a big story, coming right after the election. But we didn't know how big it was going to get. A story came over the wires saying one of the credit-rating services was going to put AT&T on credit watch. There we were, the people who had put the biggest company in the world on credit watch." The employees erupted with laughter, dispelling the remaining tension in the room. "It shows if you owe enough money you can bring *anybody* to their knees."

AT&T didn't know it yet, but that irreverence was typical of McCaw Cellular. When the McCaw company sent a team of executives to Florida to pound nails for Habitat for Humanity, *Forbes* magazine dispatched a reporter and photographer to chronicle the people who had wooed Bob Allen's AT&T. It seemed like a publicist's dream: Craig McCaw sleeping in a Boy Scout barracks after days spent building houses for the homeless. For the company, it served as a team-building exercise as well as a chance to do good in a market served by McCaw.

But it wasn't a cellular version of *This Old House* that *Forbes* put on its cover. Instead, its photographer caught Craig McCaw in a fun-loving moment: wearing sunglasses, a T-shirt, and a baseball cap, with a large snake draped around his neck. The snake was owned by a local boy who, as a gesture of gratitude for the executives' help, offered McCaw a chance to play with his pet. McCaw hated snakes, but he didn't want to reject the offer of kindness, so he allowed the teen to drape the snake on his shoulders. As the creature slithered around his neck, McCaw said, "Get the photographer. Wendy [Craig's wife] should see this." The photographer took a picture, and everyone chuckled, not realizing that *Forbes* had just captured a permanent image of Craig McCaw for hundreds of thousands of readers.

Following the Habitat work, the McCaw management group held a retreat at the Ocean Reef Club in Key Largo. *Forbes* described McCaw's reception at a dinner there. When he arrived at the podium, his subordinates pelted him with dinner rolls. "Thank you for that dose of respect," said the billionaire. The following night, AT&T's Robert Allen promised the McCaw managers that he would not interfere with their success or their renegade style. As if to prove his point, Allen completed his speech by pulling a dinner roll from his pocket and tossing it at Craig McCaw, who dodged it. It was certainly the first food fight in Robert Allen's managerial career. "This was not your standard dignified gathering of corporate brass," declared an amused *Forbes*.

In case its photo of McCaw and the snake didn't seem odd enough, the magazine slammed readers with a cover quote in large type: " 'I won't predict, *yet,* that we will do the acquiring of AT&T rather than them of us,' says billionaire vegetarian Craig McCaw."

* * *

Despite the high hopes with which the partnership between Allen and McCaw had begun, it was never a happy one. Back in Kirkland, Jim Barksdale had begun to work through the thousands of details involved in trying to finalize the alliance. But the central problem that had surfaced during the early negotiations over a licensing deal wouldn't go away. Who would control what? Barksdale, as the man in charge of daily operations, found himself forced into the conclusion that the alliance wasn't working. Each side was working too hard to protect itself. "Joint marketing with these entities is like porcupines making love," he said in a later interview.

What's more, he didn't really understand the terms of the proposed ninety-nine-year marketing agreement. (In truth, nobody did.) Barksdale said he'd need a lawyer with him every day to advise him on what he could and couldn't do. McCaw and AT&T had announced to the world that they were near agreement on the details of the alliance, but in fact the discussions soon broke down. Barksdale insisted that the rules governing the McCaw-AT&T relationship had to be understandable. "If you can't [put the deal] on one piece of paper, you can't execute," he said. That goal seemed to recede further with each day of discussions.

The negotiating delays began to stretch over weeks, then months. Meanwhile, McCaw worried that his company was essentially frozen in place. As the alliance discussions continued, he lost much of his beloved flexibility. He had less freedom to negotiate major new deals or to raise money through issuing debt or stock. In early 1993 McCaw told Perry, "Get some equity out of AT&T. I'm not going to talk to these guys another day [without it]." McCaw wasn't sure exactly how much equity he needed, Perry recalls, but the instructions were to commit AT&T to $400 million if the deal was not completed by a certain date.

After a long day of negotiation at a Colorado resort town, Perry and Alex Mandl stepped outside for a walk. Perry had in mind a very long walk. Both were in good shape, Mandl from his regular jogging and Perry from his fifty-mile hikes as a scout leader in Washington's Cascade Mountains. They took the uphill path that Mandl had used on his morning jog.

"Alex, we've been in this process for a long time," Perry said as the two began to gain altitude. "No matter what our ultimate relationship is, you want us to be a success." Perry went on to make the case for McCaw Cellular's keeping current on its interest payments as well as making necessary acquisitions. "Alex," he concluded, "the bottom line is, we need you to buy four hundred million dollars' worth of stock. It can't be debt, because debt hits our cash-flow covenants."

Mandl quickly agreed. The two kept walking for two hours, during which they negotiated every aspect of the deal. None of it was captured in writing. By the time they got back to the resort, AT&T had tied itself even more closely to the merger and to a future in cellular.

The money brought relief to McCaw's cash needs—as McCaw put it, the money added "freeboard" to the good ship McCaw Cellular. But it brought no real solution to the alliance-building problems Barksdale faced. The accounting alone would be a nightmare—just one of many. How, for example, would the companies divvy up the proceeds from calls traveling over the combined network? What if AT&T became unhappy and walked away? What new businesses could McCaw pursue on its own? Could McCaw use discounts granted by AT&T on long distance to undercut AT&T's own sales force? What sort of scenarios should be addressed in McCaw's ninety-nine-year lease on and use of the AT&T brand name, and how could McCaw deal with the many restrictions?

And finally, how would AT&T treat Craig McCaw as both ally and substantial shareholder? A legal analysis done for McCaw described this problem as similar to the one General Motors faced when it brought in Ross Perot and his EDS. AT&T would have to give McCaw special treatment to avoid fiduciary problems, a situation Ma Bell didn't appear to recognize.

Craig McCaw had concluded months earlier that the best approach was for AT&T to simply buy the company, but he worried that the telecom giant still didn't get it. Combining the two companies' services, marketing, and networks into one integrated system made sense. But the idea remained a tremendous leap for AT&T's ruling minds. "You can only lead them to water. You can't make them drink," McCaw had warned his negotiating team. "The culture of the company is bigger than the CEO, especially a regulated company."

Negotiations continued to drag. The deadline for the $400 million payment came. In February 1993 AT&T bought 14.5 million shares of newly issued McCaw stock at $27.62 a share. Meanwhile, the McCaw company began to work its way out of its liquidity crisis, buoyed in part by AT&T cash. There was even talk that McCaw might begin to show a profit in a year or so, the first black ink in its history as a cellular company. And now a new irony developed: As AT&T got deeper into its relationship with McCaw Cellular Communications, Craig McCaw began to see less of a need for AT&T.

Yet McCaw was influenced by a corporate culture as well. Despite his growing doubts about the merger, he realized that it remained the best deal for his company's shareholders. On a personal level, he saw that Wayne Perry wanted a long-term easing of his duties but didn't think anyone could take his place. A powerful desire to bring closure to the McCaw company was driving Perry, McCaw suspected. There was some truth in that. Yet Perry saw himself primarily as the "one guy who really believed in McCaw."

After still another negotiation session, this one at McCaw headquarters in Kirkland, Mandl and his staff finally began to talk of changing the alliance deal to an outright takeover. They presented the idea to Robert Allen, who gave the go-ahead. Since McCaw had already made his decision, once Mandl openly suggested the idea, the framework of a buyout emerged quickly.

As always, however, the details proved tricky. When Craig McCaw boarded an airplane for a flight to New York on a Friday in August 1993, he didn't know whether the deal of his life would go forward. He told Robert Ratliffe, his public relations aide, to prepare two press releases, one celebrating a deal and another praising the virtues of continued independence.

Meanwhile, Robert Allen was also flying into New York and hoping to rescue the deal. Allen had just spent a week in China, where he had been astounded by the opportunities to sell telecommunications services, especially cellular networks, which inexpensively leapfrogged the need to build traditional wired networks in an emerging marketplace. The trip strengthened his resolve to ally himself with the biggest cellular company in the United States.

The jet-lagged executives came to their meeting in New York assisted by platoons of lawyers, investment bankers, publicists, and others. But McCaw and Allen met alone that Saturday morning, August 14, for most of four hours, as the members of the McCaw board arrived in New York from Seattle, Boston, and elsewhere. The sixteen-person group included John and Bruce McCaw and John Giuggio, chief executive of Affiliated Communications. Keith McCaw, by then no longer a board member, also arrived.

Finally, at 7 P.M., McCaw and Allen shook hands in a hallway of the Waldorf-Astoria Hotel on a deal trading McCaw stock for AT&T shares. Based on the then current value of the two companies, AT&T would pay $12.6 billion for McCaw in what was technically a pooling of assets. McCaw addressed his board. "We have reached agreement," he said. "Obviously, they think this is a good business, and they're willing to pay for it." Alberg, a member of McCaw's deal team, also briefed the board. Other team members present included Wayne Perry, Roberta Katz, and Andrew Quartner.

There were questions from the board, none showing resistance to the deal but some probing for weak points. There was a bittersweet feeling at the meeting, especially for longtimers like Bruce and John McCaw, who had been with McCaw since the company's early days as a cable TV outfit in Centralia, Washington, the sole remaining asset from Elroy McCaw's estate. Letting go of the company would be hard. But the benefits of being backed by powerful AT&T were obvious.

Most of those present had heard Katz's line about marrying off a too-young daughter. But the suitor promised not to smother the bride's spirit. Ultimately, the McCaw team chose to believe Bob Allen's assurances. "I trust him," Barksdale said of Allen.

Someone pointed out one missing ingredient. Unlike the investment deal announced the previous November, which had offered the McCaws and other insiders $100 million plus another $600 million if AT&T decided to exercise their option to buy control later, this one gave no special consideration to the McCaw brothers, whose shares gave them voting control of the company. Craig McCaw had decided he wanted the deal with Allen to be simple, with no side deals for his family. "Jimminy Christmas," Hal Eastman, a director, exclaimed. "Can you believe he's doing this?"

Eastman admired McCaw. The deal with AT&T made sense for the company's future and for its shareholders, but not necessarily for Craig McCaw. McCaw was freely relinquishing something very central to his entire sense of himself. Eastman studied McCaw's tired face. Eastman felt he had been around him long enough to see the subtle signs. McCaw's decision hurt.

"I know this was painful, but I want to tell you how courageous it was," Eastman said.

"I can't really talk about it," McCaw replied.

* * *

Craig McCaw may have acted in part from a sense of personal sacrifice, but he and his family, as the McCaw company's largest group of shareholders, still benefited handsomely from the AT&T deal. Together they held 47.51 million shares of McCaw stock. Based on the closing prices of McCaw and AT&T shares before the deal was announced, the one-for-one swap of shares represented a gain of $528.2 million for the McCaw family, $185 million for Craig McCaw alone.

There was another benefit for shareholders: AT&T's annual dividend of roughly $1.20 per share. Based on previous years' dividends, the McCaws could expect an annual income of some $57 million.

The Saturday board meeting moved on to other topics. Investment bankers, lawyers, and others offered technical advice. John Giuggio, whom McCaw admired and enjoyed as a friend, was a feeble presence that day, drained by a three-year battle with cancer. He would be dead in three months. The son of immigrants, Giuggio had started with *The Boston Globe* as a messenger. He had seen incredible changes in the McCaw company, which he had served as a board member for twelve years. He considered Craig McCaw a genius. No wonder: Affiliated's investment in McCaw, dating back to 1981, had grown to $85 million. Now it was worth $2 billion.

"I can't believe the company we bought into ten years ago for twelve million is now selling for twelve billion," Giuggio said, struggling out of his chair to leave. Breaking off a conversation, Craig McCaw walked over to help Giuggio with his coat, open the door for him, and walk him to the elevator. It was the conclusion to a successful partnership.

Craig McCaw, his brothers, and the board talked past midnight, dining on take-out pizza and Chinese food. McCaw said nothing about his future plans except that he planned to serve on AT&T's board, to continue to follow his vision of the future and to be "a player"—whatever that meant. But nothing in the deal with Allen restricted McCaw from any role in the telecommunications business.

The following day, the AT&T and McCaw boards met separately and approved the deal, which was still subject to regulatory and court approvals. (At the final closing, months later, the transaction had dropped in value to $11.5 billion, reflecting a lower AT&T share price.)

On Monday at 9 A.M. London time, the board of British Telecom, which held 22 percent of McCaw, agreed to sell its shares to AT&T. Now all that remained was to tell the world. Craig McCaw and Allen were scheduled to speak at a news conference at AT&T headquarters with reporters from *The Wall Street Journal, The Washington Post,* CNN, and other organizations. The deal would make the network news and occupy the front page of newspapers across the country.

Money was not central to McCaw's life, as Steve Countryman had discovered back in Centralia many years earlier. But the deal boosted McCaw's stock holdings significantly from their current value of $868 million. Once the deal was signed, it would place him in the ranks of the world's billionaire elite. It would also make the McCaw family AT&T's largest single group of shareholders. Bruce McCaw's AT&T shares would be worth $680 million, John McCaw's $552 million, Keith McCaw's $637 million, and Craig McCaw's $1 billion.

In the next day's *New York Times,* a headline summed up the past ten years of Craig McCaw's life: BIG PAYOFF FOR HIGH-TECH GAMBLER.

One small detail delayed the king of cellular before announcing the sale of his kingdom. Leaving his hotel room at the Lowell that morning, Craig McCaw paused on the threshold. "I can't find my room key," he complained to Robert Ratliffe, patting his pockets.

It was an odd moment. At age forty-four, Craig McCaw was walking away from his life's work. Perhaps the missing key was an emblem for the coming disorientation in his life, a period that would end with some surprises and a painful personal transition.

Ratliffe just laughed. "I think we can mail it to them," he said. McCaw agreed, and they headed off together to the news conference.

20

"Master of the Obvious"

An Ambitious New Vision Takes Shape

When Craig McCaw got to that press conference, it wasn't long before someone asked him about his plans for the rest of his life. Would he retire? "If the truth be known, I haven't got a clue," he said. He didn't elaborate, but the remark said more about McCaw's personal interests than about his business prospects.

Soon afterward, he went fishing with Robert Ratliffe on a remote lake in British Columbia. Having just organized a PR campaign for one of the biggest friendly takeovers in history, Ratliffe, too, was pondering his future. Nothing, he concluded, could ever match what he'd already done. "My career's over," he told McCaw.

McCaw's response almost might have been directed at himself. "I think you've got a couple of careers left in you," he said. "You can do this again."

McCaw wasn't really clueless about his business future. He had many things going, including side bets in cable TV, radio, and small wireless distribution systems. He continued to watch promising new technologies. He had some ideas, but the man others saw as a visionary wasn't yet sure how events would unfold for him.

AT&T announced that Craig McCaw would join its board, representing the McCaw family's 3 percent ownership, the largest of any private shareholder group. McCaw said he would use that role to keep an eye on the old McCaw Cellular Communications, now renamed AT&T Wireless Services. James Barksdale would stay on as president, reporting directly to Bob Allen, a structure designed to maintain the wireless unit's independence and entrepreneurial spirit. (Barksdale, CFO Peter Currie, and General Counsel Roberta Katz later left AT&T Wireless to help launch Netscape Communications, which eventually waged a high-profile Internet browser war with Microsoft and was purchased by America Online.)

The other members of AT&T's board were all over sixty years old and came from politics, pharmaceuticals, banking, retailing—anything but telecommunications. McCaw would be the first outside director who was both young and knowledgeable about trends in the industry— making him either a potent ally of or a threat to Allen. Some at AT&T feared that McCaw, the maverick, could become an embarrassing gadfly, as Ross Perot had become for General Motors after it had absorbed the billionaire's Electronic Data Systems and Perot began publicly challenging Chairman Roger Moore's authority and policies.

Those who knew McCaw considered that scenario implausible. Author and futurist George Gilder imagined a different outcome—that McCaw would emerge as Allen's successor. That seemed unlikely to those who knew McCaw's distaste for large bureaucracies. Still, the son of Elroy McCaw may have felt a secret flicker of interest. Wayne Perry, for one, thought that McCaw didn't really want to be on the board but did want an open invitation, thus enjoying the status of board membership without the duties. After all, this was the man whose motto was "Flexibility is heaven."

There had been one odd twist in the sale negotiations that would later prove important. AT&T had suggested that McCaw agree not to compete with his former company. McCaw was willing, though he expected to be paid for giving up that right. "Craig would have retired out of telecommunications," claims Perry. Perry could not recall what figure was tossed out—perhaps $80 million, an amount that Perry regarded as relatively small, especially measured against McCaw's significant earning potential in the industry.

But AT&T had a problem with that plan. The $80 million would have put a damper on its earnings, so AT&T said no. "Okay" was all McCaw said. Perry says, "He was not disappointed. Craig easily takes reversals and can think about a new path."

But the door to a new McCaw communications company was open. From then on, McCaw would speak in only the haziest terms about his plans, pooh-poohing any question about his possibly competing against AT&T. After all, said McCaw, he wouldn't want to undermine his own sizable investment in Ma Bell.

As AT&T prepared to take control, McCaw quickly withdrew from involvement in the old McCaw company, but he left firm instructions with aides that the buyer should be fully briefed on what it had bought. Cellular still required huge amounts of cash and a push from management. "Tell them the facts," he said. "Don't fool around. Make sure they understand."

McCaw made some presentations to AT&T people and attended roughly twelve AT&T board meetings as a nonmember observer, speaking occasionally. At one meeting, the board was told that the company was canceling plans by the McCaw-AT&T division to join a cellular partnership serving Shanghai, China. The company wanted to sell switching equipment to the Shanghai partnership, but the Chinese were balking at giving AT&T too big a stake. Knowing how hard the McCaw people had worked for this deal, McCaw was deeply disappointed and said so at the board meeting. He considered this an example of AT&T's conflicting divisions: The division that made cellular switches now would be selling to companies that competed with AT&T's wireless group. (British Telecom had already refused to buy AT&T hardware.)

Since McCaw believed that cellular service offered greater long-term profits, the choice of which unit should be shed was easy. But he kept some of his thoughts private. He stopped short of saying AT&T should sell divisions, though that step seemed obvious to him. (And within two years, Allen would in fact spin off both the hardware division and Bell Labs.)

McCaw sensed that some of the board members couldn't understand what he was saying, while others apparently did but made no response. The silence made him uncomfortable. "I'm pushing the envelope here, and they're not saying 'Thank you for saying it,' " he later recalled. From that moment forward, he felt his views were unwelcome. Clearly, he was not destined for a long stay on the board. McCaw soon became at best a vaporous presence at AT&T.

The judicial and regulatory reviews of the merger took about a year, hitting some significant snags. BellSouth and Bell Atlantic fought a skillful rearguard action, asking for delays and restrictions. In February 1994 the Justice Department announced it would oppose the waiver needed for the merger to go forward. Then Judge Harold Greene declared that the proposed transaction would violate the 1984 AT&T breakup agreement because several McCaw licenses were jointly owned by regional Bell companies. The foundations of the deal appeared shaky.

But piece by piece, AT&T and McCaw won the needed approvals—with conditions. The Justice Department required AT&T to wait another year before putting its name on cellular service and before certain units could share plans and strategies with the McCaw division. Old McCaw customers must be allowed to pick any long-distance provider they chose.

The merger was formally completed on September 19, 1994. Every McCaw staffer was welcomed into the AT&T fold with a $2,400 bonus, various AT&T merchandise, and a T-shirt: WHO WILL LEAD THE FUTURE OF COMMUNICATIONS? WE WILL. *Fortune* magazine blessed the transaction with a cover photo of Allen holding a cell phone. "The McCaw acquisition is crucial to AT&T's strategy for the 21st Century," the magazine declared. "Now it must embrace its cellular baby without smothering it."

While McCaw Cellular Communications ceased to exist, McCaw himself remained interested in telecommunications. In fact, it became increasingly clear that McCaw wished he hadn't sold the company. He itched to get back into wireless. Once a cellular king, always a cellular king. Now he needed to find a new throne. But before embarking on such a search, he felt he had to distance himself from AT&T, whose vast holdings seemed to touch every facet of communications. Pressured by Allen to make a quick announcement, on October 21 McCaw publicly declined a place on AT&T's board, one of the most prestigious directorships in business.

"Much to its credit, AT&T is working exceedingly hard to develop a broad array of products and services that demystify and simplify the Information Superhighway for an increasingly broad group of customers," McCaw said in a press release. "Those very efforts make it difficult for me to make even minor contributions to the telecommunications industry and not be perceived to be technically in conflict with my duties as a director of AT&T."

In reply, Allen said he appreciated McCaw's "offer to be helpful. I look forward to maintaining a mutually beneficial relationship." In fact, however, from that moment on, AT&T never once consulted with Craig

McCaw. Having celebrated McCaw as the wireless genius, *Fortune* magazine tried to make a joke out of AT&T's loss: "If you lived in Seattle, would you want to sit on AT&T's board?"

McCaw never stated publicly what his potential conflict with AT&T would be, but most assumed it had to do with his interest in a newly available chunk of spectrum. The FCC planned to auction 30-megahertz licenses for a new generation of wireless technology, usually called PCS, for "personal communications services." The new wireless phones would use the 1850–1990 megahertz band, compared to 800 megahertz for cellular. Conventional cellular phones used a system in which messages were translated into wave patterns. PCS used a potentially more efficient digital system in which messages were converted into computer digits, or 0s and 1s. PCS offered the promise of lighter phones, longer battery life, a broad array of services that went beyond mere voice communication, and cheaper airtime. Bryant Hilton, manager of media relations for the Personal Communications Industry Association, a trade group, told the Baltimore *Sun* that PCS could attract 8.5 million subscribers by 1998 and might replace wired phone service for some consumers.

Based on this hope, many large companies were planning to bid on PCS licenses, including AT&T, Sprint, the regional Bell companies, and a joint venture involving cable giants Comcast Corporation, Cox Cable Communications, and Tele-Communications, Inc. (TCI). Notably absent was MCI, whose latest strategy positioned itself as a reseller by leasing capacity from license holders.

PCS, however, presented some technical difficulties. Because PCS used lower-power transmitters, more had to be built as compared to traditional cellular transmitters. And anyone launching a PCS service would have to compete with two cellular carriers that had already spent big money to build systems and win customers. These entrenched incumbents were already lowering prices, making it even more difficult for newcomers to generate revenue to pay off new-system costs.

For these reasons, many of the early entrepreneurs in cellular, including George Lindemann and John Kluge, saw PCS as a poor investment. They believed that the gold-mine days of grabbing licenses cheaply before others saw their value were over. Others agreed. "We've been looking for three years and we still can't find a business case for me-too cellular," Herschel Shosteck, a market economist tracking the cellular industry, told a reporter.

The FCC auctions for ninety-nine ten-year licenses in fifty-one markets started in December 1994. The FCC hoped to raise more than $10 billion for the U.S. Treasury. There was speculation on Wall Street that McCaw planned to use cash from the AT&T transaction to start assembling another collection of licenses. With all that spectrum up for grabs—to quote an old Craig McCaw insight—it had to be worth *something*. An AT&T spokesman, however, said that McCaw had no specific plans, only a desire to keep the field clear for whatever opportunities presented themselves. Meanwhile, McCaw kept his own counsel.

The wait ended quickly. Within weeks of severing his formal ties to AT&T, McCaw told the FCC that he had formed a company called ALAACR Communications to bid on PCS licenses in markets where AT&T already owned the maximum allowable frequency. McCaw wouldn't say what ALAACR stood for, but some wags interpreted it as "A Little Attempt At Craig's Return."

Some assumed that McCaw was bidding under some arrangement to benefit AT&T. But others thought that competition was the more likely motive, though McCaw's strategy targeted the cities AT&T could not get—for example, New York City, where AT&T already had a cellular license. McCaw figured he could operate those markets alone or perhaps in some future alliance with AT&T. To those following the PCS race, McCaw was the player to watch.

Characteristically, McCaw showed a large appetite for spectrum. Under auction rules requiring bidders to declare their overall goals, McCaw said he would pursue markets serving a combined 54 million POPs.

Since no one better understood the strengths and weaknesses of the cellular business, McCaw's interest in PCS gave it tremendous credibility. McCaw could create a whole new standard for wireless communication, declared Daniel Kranzler, a McCaw alumnus who had formed AccessLine, a Bellevue, Washington, telecommunications company. Because PCS allowed paging and other messaging, Kranzler speculated that McCaw could come up with a redefinition of the functions of a wireless communication device. "The key is, are there entrepreneurs out there who are wise enough and have enough vision so they could craft

PCS from the beginning so that cellular would have to catch up?" Kranzler told *The Seattle Times*. "That takes someone like Craig McCaw."

By December McCaw was bidding on licenses in New York, Minnesota, Salt Lake City, Alaska, Spokane, Portland, and other areas in an auction conducted from remote locations via computer modem. Working through four employees at a lakefront office near his old McCaw Cellular headquarters, McCaw submitted his bids electronically and waited to see where he stood.

As the bidding progressed, bidders could switch to different markets if they spotted a bargain. At one point, McCaw made the highest bid for New York City, $171 million. In another round, he bid $330 million. Then, in an effort to scare off Sprint from the Big Apple, he outbid himself in the next round with a new offer of $347 million. Noting that Pacific Telesis was getting little competition for the Los Angeles license, McCaw bid there, too. To top PacTel's $183 million, McCaw bid $300 million. Several rounds later, PacTel's offer hit $446 million. McCaw fired back with $470 million. PacTel's answer: $493.5 million.

The maneuvering drew attention and speculation from many quarters. "Craig O. McCaw confounds the giants with his wild and woolly PCS bidding," declared *The Wall Street Journal*. A PacTel spokesman said, "Our biggest concern isn't the other Bells—it's Craig McCaw."

Still, PacTel and others couldn't determine McCaw's goal. Was he bidding on certain markets in order to disguise a plan to bid later on other markets? At one point, McCaw was top bidder for eight markets. By the twenty-eighth round, McCaw's bidding totaled more than $800 million. The *Journal* quoted some who speculated that McCaw's real goals were New York and Los Angeles. "I'm a tiny player in a sea of giants" was all McCaw would say.

But all this excitement gave a false impression of McCaw's position. Rather than feeling victorious, he began to view the auctions as a diminishing opportunity. The bidding was going beyond what he thought were realistic amounts. Several bidders began dropping out, leaving McCaw as the only individual competing with the Bells and other giant companies.

Anyone who had watched McCaw carefully, however, might have known that he always had planned moves and countermoves. The master of the strategic "back door" had found another path to spec-

21

"The Michael Jordan of Telecommunications"

McCaw Strikes Gold in the Wreckage of Nextel

Morgan O'Brien's professional life had been hell till the message came from Craig McCaw.

In January 1995, as interest grew in McCaw's bidding on PCS licenses, O'Brien was trying to forget his troubles by taking a vacation on the Caribbean island of Saint Lucia. There he got the call that McCaw wanted to see him the next day in Washington, D.C.

Despite his pleasant surroundings, O'Brien was a man in trouble, an abrupt reversal from what had been a fabulous career, patterned in large part after that of Craig McCaw.

O'Brien had started out in the 1970s as a lawyer in an obscure section of the FCC, handling radio-dispatch licenses for Specialized Mobile Radio (SMR), the spectrum initially licensed for free by truckers, cabbies, and plumbers. He spent the 1980s at a Washington, D.C., law firm, representing mobile radio clients before the FCC. In 1987 O'Brien watched cellular soaring in value while SMR was largely ignored. Since cellular and dispatch spectrum were largely the same, both occupying the 800 megahertz airspace, the only difference between the two industries was artificial—an FCC decree limiting SMR's use. Yet the same amount of spectrum sold for just $100,000 with a dispatch license and $2 million with a cellular license.

O'Brien figured that if he could quietly buy up the dispatch licenses and get an FCC rule change, he could create a national radiotelephone system and make himself a fortune. Bringing in partners, O'Brien founded Fleet Call and did his first deal, buying two dispatch system in Fresno and Bakersfield, California, for $3 million. O'Brien didn't have the money, but knowing how long it took for the FCC to process a license change, he figured he had time to raise financing—the old "sign 'em quick, close 'em slow" approach McCaw had used.

Soon O'Brien was repeating in dispatch what independents had done in cellular, using methods inspired by his study of Craig McCaw. With borrowed money, O'Brien bought up small operators for what they considered ridiculously generous prices. He deliberately kept a low profile as he added to his collection of licenses.

Then O'Brien began converting the old analog dispatch systems to digital service using technology invented by Motorola. The Motorola Integrated Radio System (MIRS) used compression technology to enable the 14 megahertz of spectrum used by the old dispatch systems to provide as much service as the 25 megahertz given to cellular. The "communicator phones" combined several functions: two-way, group conversations, private calls, and digital messaging. A customer could dial someone directly and use the handset like a cellular phone for a private conversation or push one button and use it like an old-fashioned walkie-talkie to speak with several people at once. If MIRS worked as hoped, it would be far more powerful than conventional analog cellular phones.

In 1991 O'Brien obtained a waiver from the FCC that allowed him to use new digital technology to integrate his licenses. The following year he took Fleet Call public, soon renaming it Nextel. Then, in February 1994, he found a sugar daddy—MCI, looking to counter the McCaw-AT&T transaction. MCI anointed Nextel as its sole wireless play and agreed to invest $1.36 billion over a few years for an 18 percent stake. Ironically, MCI was using a Craig McCaw copycat to buy its way out of the mistake of selling Airsignal in 1985.

Much of the business press hailed the deal as presaging the next stage in wireless communications, launching a third competitor that would force the old cellular duopoly to improve service. O'Brien proceeded to announce an even bigger deal: $2.4 billion of Nextel's stock for ownership of Dial Page, one of Nextel's biggest rivals, and for Motorola's collection of 2,500 specialized mobile radio licenses. And in July he announced a third deal, merging with OneComm Corporation of Denver.

O'Brien couldn't resist publicly vaunting his triumph, the fruit of seven years of labor and more than 250 transactions. "We own North America. There's nothing left to buy," he crowed in the pages of *The Wall Street Journal*. Nextel could now promise eventual coverage of 95 percent of the U.S. population and all of the top fifty markets—210 million POPs, three and a half times the number reachable by the McCaw-AT&T cellular system. "Our national system is a replacement for the national telephone infrastructure," O'Brien declared, claiming that cellular companies were mired in old-age analog technology that would have to be junked. "I don't think they can cope with that. I don't think they understand it."

Certain details demanded attention, however. Nextel faced a loss that year of $500 million, and it would need $2 billion to build 4,000 cellular transmitters in order to bring digital service to its 1.5 million customers.

O'Brien had borrowed from Craig McCaw's playbook, but he had apparently missed some pages. In simple terms, O'Brien had run out of flexibility. Lenders and vendors now controlled his fate. McCaw had always been careful not to let his need for cash restrict his strategic choices. He never became too dependent on the maker of a switching system, especially if that compromised quality. O'Brien now saw his choices reduced to a few painful trade-offs.

Before the deal was finalized, MCI became uneasy with the erosion of its stake in Nextel, with how its name would be used by Nextel, and with concerns about the MIRS system. (In the early markets, many MIRS customers found voice quality poor.) Motorola, in turn, fretted over the shareholder rights given to MCI and threatened to exercise its right to veto any Nextel deals, including the MCI investment.

O'Brien worked hard to hold MCI and Motorola together, but in August he announced that MCI had broken off plans to invest in his company. Privately, he told friends that it pained him to see MCI walk away with its $1.3 billion in badly needed cash—but he wanted Motorola's dispatch licenses even more. Shares in Nextel, which had sold for $44 in February, skidded to $15 by mid-December.

And new problems loomed as Nextel's equity shrank, raising the specter of violation of debt agreements. Without waivers from bond-holders, Nextel could not complete its acquisitions of Dial Page and OneComm Corporation. As O'Brien approached his fiftieth birthday, his company was hitting its lowest point—sinking, some believed, into insolvency.

So O'Brien welcomed the call from Craig McCaw in January 1995.

The talk began casually. McCaw had been watching O'Brien's career for years. He knew about O'Brien's acquisitions, understood his goal, and knew that Nextel would inevitably emerge as the third wireless carrier. He, Wayne Perry, and others at McCaw Cellular Communications had discussed several options in regard to O'Brien: to leave him alone, to spend some money to buy key licenses he would want, to form an alliance with him, or to buy his company.

Both O'Brien and McCaw saw themselves as facing a common rival, the big regional telephone companies. But several previous meetings between them had been inconclusive. "I wanted to buy Nextel a couple of times, but Wayne slow-rolled me," McCaw said later. "He was dead wrong about that one." Perry thought that the FCC would block McCaw Cellular from buying Nextel and that McCaw had better uses for its money. So they simply watched Nextel grow, knowing it would eventually end the wireless duopoly.

Now O'Brien's troubles gave McCaw another opportunity. McCaw said he was interested in making an investment and offering strategic advice. This was great news for O'Brien. McCaw's involvement would restore Nextel's credibility, his money would ease its financing troubles, and his advice would vastly improve its strategic positioning. But what did McCaw want in return? Was this a bid for control or just a passive investment? Saying he wasn't sure, McCaw suggested that O'Brien put together a proposal and that they meet, just the two of them, without investment bankers.

Excited, O'Brien called several associates and told them to get working, gathering data and organizing their pitch. The next day, he faxed McCaw a proposal: In return for a seat on Nextel's board, McCaw could invest $120 million for 8 million shares ($5 a share higher than recent trading), plus an option to purchase another 8 million shares. Further, there would be no "standstill" provision to limit his additional purchases of Nextel stock.

McCaw turned negotiation details over to his aides from Eagle River, his personal investment company. They told O'Brien that the share price was too high, but perhaps McCaw could sweeten the deal by buying even more stock. The two sides met over the next four weeks, trading ideas and information. Later, O'Brien said he had done many such negotiations but had never met a group as efficient as Craig

McCaw's. "They immediately zeroed in on the most important issues," O'Brien said.

It quickly became clear that McCaw wanted to take control of Nextel for as little money as possible. He wanted approval of company policies, including executive hiring, strategic planning, marketing, and technology, which almost certainly meant dumping Motorola's troubled MIRS or looking for something else.

O'Brien now discovered what Affiliated Publications had learned a long time ago: McCaw likes control. For a brief time, McCaw's advisers had considered making a small investment in Nextel. But McCaw, typically, had bigger ideas. After deciding that Nextel's customer profile would not conflict with that of AT&T's wireless customers, McCaw quickly decided to raise the stakes with O'Brien: more of McCaw's money and a more expansive role for McCaw. It was a classic example of McCaw's leapfrogging the agenda. "Craig's thought was 'If we're going to do something, let's do it in a way that's significant,' " said his Eagle River aide Dennis Weibling.

Once O'Brien showed interest in McCaw's more expansive idea, talks went forward on two fronts, an enormous job for McCaw's small team. The McCaw people negotiated with both Nextel and Motorola while analyzing Nextel's problems. As they soon discovered, Nextel was in terrible shape: It had a weak management team, a dispirited sales force, and a product that didn't work. Nextel also had to work through complex mergers, move already dissatisfied customers to a new technology that was sure to have glitches, finesse bondholders upset with the company's feeble revenues, and end a costly feud with the sole supplier of their product.

McCaw's team decided that nothing could be done without new leadership. Motorola and Nextel were blaming each other for technical problems when both shared the blame. McCaw and Weibling flew to Chicago to meet with Robert Galvin, former chief executive of Motorola, and his son and corporate successor, Chris. After looking at the MIRS system, McCaw's team concluded that the necessary fix involved software, not transmission devices and other hardware. If Motorola could commit to fixing the system, then Nextel could be salvaged.

Motorola, which had been embarrassed by the glitches, saw in

McCaw's talents another incentive to make repairs: Nextel would become a bigger customer under him than it would under O'Brien. "McCaw would help create a world-class customer," Weibling said. McCaw liked the fact that both O'Brien and the Galvins wanted him.

During some of the most intense negotiations with Nextel and Motorola, McCaw wasn't even present. In March he spent three weeks near an airport in Georgia, where he was training on new jets: intense, demanding work that involved physically exhausting sessions by day and heavy reading of technical manuals by night. But at 1 A.M. McCaw would be on the phone with Weibling, reviewing how the negotiations were going, suggesting ideas, directing overall strategy. One weekend, Weibling flew to Georgia for face-to-face consultation.

McCaw kept pushing. Where O'Brien had failed, McCaw succeeded. Motorola agreed to increase the number of engineers assigned to the MIRS problems and find a way to make the system work with technology written by outsiders, which ultimately would lower costs to consumers. MIRS became IDEN, or Integrated Dispatch Enhanced Network. The reworked system used half as much signal compression as the previous approach, a technique that improved voice quality. O'Brien was impressed with McCaw's achievement. He "played the Motorola relationship beautifully," O'Brien says.

Conducted in secret, the three-way talks that had begun in January came to an end on April 4, 1995. Though the prices of wireless licenses had skyrocketed on the cellular and PCS sides, McCaw had found a bargain in Nextel. For a modest down payment and promises of further payments, he won effective control of a fledgling national wireless system that served the top fifty markets, 25 percent of Nextel's board seats, plus lucrative stock options.

The board of directors would still technically run Nextel, but key decisions would be made by an "operations committee" controlled by McCaw. The board could overrule this committee, but only by a two-thirds vote and after paying McCaw $25 million and other fees for not taking his advice. Furthermore, if Nextel's board rejected McCaw's advice, his stock would immediately begin accruing dividends of 12 percent, and his Eagle River investment company would gain the right to exercise the remaining options at $12.25 each. "It's an insurance policy that no one believes will be necessary," said Roger Nyhus, spokesman for Eagle River. It was also a powerful hammerlock on control of the company.

As part of the deal, McCaw agreed to put down $14.9 million, plus another $300 million at closing. If both sides met certain conditions, he and his brothers would invest up to $1.1 billion in Nextel stock at favorable prices over the next six years to ultimately own 23.5 percent of the company.

On the night before the deal was to be announced, McCaw and Morgan O'Brien met in New York for a gut check. McCaw always based his deals in part on a reading of the players, and he wanted to verify that he and O'Brien were comfortable with each other. McCaw wanted control. Was O'Brien at ease with that, and was he willing to let McCaw move Nextel in a new direction? They talked for four hours. Rather than resenting his loss of control, O'Brien felt relieved to be getting McCaw's talents. O'Brien had done all he could; now someone else would take over and bring Nextel to the next level.

"It didn't take me one second to think that through," O'Brien said later:

> I was enthusiastic from the outset because [McCaw] has a very special talent, insight, and ability to see the future. Plus he's bold. Look at his track record. It's like getting the world's most astute consultant. You can never buy McCaw's interest and talent. The only way you can get him is to have an arrangement where he benefits from his involvement.

On the morning of April 5, representatives of Nextel and Motorola were waiting for McCaw to say yes. When McCaw gave the signal, Nextel's investor relations director pushed a button, and the word went out on the wires. At the subsequent press conference, McCaw made it plain that Nextel was being repositioned as a supplier of unique services, especially wireless group conferencing, rather than as a competitor to traditional cellular. The "base-market opportunity," as McCaw called it, was not existing cellular users or the average house-wife, but the 17–18 million two-way radio users in mobile work groups, like truckers and newspaper photographers.

This made sense, because Nextel faced too many hurdles in offering competitive cellular-style service. As McCaw said:

> Nextel is logically concentrated on something that allows it to do something very well and something that others are not already doing. You do not ask a duck to fly really fast; you ask it to fly and land in water. Essentially, this product is amphibious—both instantaneous push-to-talk and also interconnect and data services.

McCaw called the Nextel technology unique but "perhaps less effective" than traditional cellular in direct-dial communication:

> If cellular is Chevrolets and Hondas, this is a Jeep. It's a more flexible product. You can have, for instance, five or six people working in stream-of-consciousness mode. They would pick up the receiver and reach the whole group or just one person. They could never accomplish that with a switch-based telephone.

Besides, McCaw said, he wasn't interested in trying to copy cellular. "I've already been there, done that, and it is not my intent to do what I've already done," he told reporters.

McCaw said his investment in Nextel closed the door on his interest in the PCS auctions. He joked that he had stayed in only to make sure New York and Los Angeles went for high prices: "It's a wonderful thing that I could help the government make more money."

McCaw turned aside the press's suggestions that he was a visionary, playing himself as someone who just got lucky. "I'm really just a simpleminded guy who likes to focus on one or two things at a time. . . . I'm not even sure what I've done," he said. Turning the tables on reporters, McCaw asked their opinion of his next purchase: "Is it the right move?"

It seemed so. Nextel's stock quickly rose 25 percent, making McCaw an immediate paper profit and burnishing his reputation for brilliance. "Like George Soros, Warren Buffett and a handful of others, McCaw has become one of those rare people whose investment decisions move markets," declared Bloomberg Business News. "A huge boost for Nextel," said the *Los Angeles Times*. "Yesterday, Craig

McCaw became the Michael Jordan of the communications industry," said *The Washington Post.*

McCaw swiftly made significant changes, including the departure of Wayland Hicks as Nextel's chief executive. According to McCaw's aides, McCaw had been stunned when Hicks, a former Xerox executive, seemed unaware of a new vibrator function on wireless phones. When McCaw picked up a phone and started talking, Hicks asked, "How did you know it was ringing?" (Hicks flatly denies the story, saying he knew all about vibrating phones.) McCaw wouldn't listen to Eagle River's arguments that Hicks's continued presence would help stabilize Nextel. McCaw felt so strongly about having an executive with technology smarts that he and Hicks agreed to part company even before a replacement had been found. Weibling, who had never run a large company, was named acting CEO.

McCaw made another curious personnel choice in naming Scot Jarvis, a former senior manager at the McCaw company with no technology background, to the job of fixing Nextel's broken systems. Jarvis was invigorated but a bit terrified by the assignment, feeling unqualified for the task of leading the Nextel and Motorola engineers. And it seemed a little crazy that a handful of people at Eagle River should be the de facto management team of Nextel. (No wonder Wayne Perry, still with AT&T, ridiculed Nextel as the *Titanic.*) Somehow the Eagle River staff had to get a new Motorola system designed, keep buying new licenses, complete the merger deals, and keep the Nextel bondholders happy. How would they do all this, exactly? "We had to make it up as we went," Jarvis admits.

McCaw reassured Jarvis that a small team like the one he had assembled was perfect for the job. Lockheed, he said, had designed and built a great airplane faster than anyone thought possible by giving a skunk works the job. "That's what we need," McCaw declared. So Jarvis kept at it, leaving McCaw to focus on other companies, other matters. McCaw skipped nearly all of the Motorola-Nextel meetings. "Craig has always been the man behind the curtain," says Jarvis. "You've seen *The Wizard of Oz.* Craig doesn't show up at these kinds of meetings."

Nonetheless, McCaw's influence could be seen in a thousand details—though this time the details affected people at an intimate level.

Nextel headquarters was supposed to leave New Jersey for Seattle to facilitate a reorganization, a culture change, and a dumping of unwanted personnel. Faced with uprooting their families, dozens of employees struggled to decide whether to stay or move; thirty or so bought houses in Seattle, while others announced plans to quit rather than move. Then McCaw abruptly canceled the move. Nextel would settle in the Washington, D.C., area, rather than in Seattle or New Jersey, to satisfy a demand by Dan Akerson, McCaw's choice for chief executive. No one knows how many house sales were halted as a result. If McCaw regretted the double disruption for employees, he never said so.

Akerson was an aggressive operations-management specialist who had served as president of MCI and chief executive of General Instrument, a cable TV technology company. He had a "kick-butt" style and the drive needed to make Nextel a serious competitor. Brian McAuley resigned as president to become a vice chairman.

By the following year, Nextel had been turned around. It had secured a $1.65 billion line of credit, executed the mergers with OneComm and DialPage, completed the purchase of the Motorola licenses, and built half of its planned transmitters. Service now extended to 200 cities, including New York, Los Angeles, St. Louis, Seattle, Washington, D.C., Raleigh/Durham, Charlotte, and San Diego.

Nextel's new communicator phone received good reviews during tests at the 1996 Summer Olympic Games in Atlanta. The new phones initially cost $400, about twice the cost analysts favored, and were still too big, but the service prices were attractive: just a dime a minute for dispatch calls and competitive rates for cellular calls. Pushed by its new chief operating officer, Tim Donahue, a former McCaw Cellular regional president, Nextel was aggressively selling itself to work groups such as doctors and nurses, real estate brokers, and others attracted to the push-to-talk feature linking a caller to one or more people instantly.

McCaw encouraged Nextel's management to emphasize what made its device unique. Don't sell it as another cellular phone, he urged. As McCaw told the *Journal*, the device needed a bold approach: "If you look at any of these things you say, 'Have the courage to be different and provide something that helps people, rather than the security of imitating what you know works.' If it works, someone else is already doing it." The simple sales tip seemed to sum up much of McCaw's philosophy: Be yourself, provide something that people need, find strength in your convictions.

By 1997 Nextel had completed its transformation from casualty to competitor. Akerson boasted that the company was now challenging Sprint, PCS Primeco (a regional Bells venture), and the old McCaw people now working for AT&T Wireless: "We're going to be all over those other guys like a bad case of measles," he bragged. None of those giants was yet losing sleep, but Nextel was being taken seriously. After Nextel dropped its roaming charges, AT&T was forced to follow suit.

Nextel was probably years away from profits, but McCaw was already raising the bar. Though O'Brien had predicted that Nextel management would focus on improving its U.S. network, McCaw drove to expand its international presence. A few years earlier, under its previous ownership, Nextel had specifically sworn off any interest in foreign markets. McCaw changed that. Nextel had already taken a 25 percent stake in Clearnet in Canada and a 17 percent stake in Mobilcom in Mexico. Now, moving on the tentative deal that AT&T had passed on, McCaw pushed Nextel to spend $23 million for a minority stake in a Shanghai, China, cellular system.

Working through an international subsidiary he had created specifically to explore wireless opportunities, McCaw also moved into the Philippines, Indonesia, and South America, winning a national license to serve Brazil and licenses to serve major markets in Argentina. Poorly served by the country's landline telephones, Brazilians had gone crazy over cellular phones. The number of subscribers in Brazil was growing by 46 percent a year, and average subscriber revenue was $119 a month—twice the U.S. figure.

McCaw was up to his old trick of buying cheap and early and letting others validate his foresight. He paid only about $1 a POP in Brazil; a year later, BellSouth essentially wrote a billboard saying CRAIG MCCAW IS A GENIUS by paying $144 a POP there. The contrast was even more extraordinary because BellSouth paid $1.5 billion for licenses to serve a *portion* of Brazil, while McCaw had paid $186 million to license *all* of Brazil.

Under McCaw's leadership, Nextel was capturing a share of the world's most explosive telecommunications markets even as McCaw largely disappeared from press coverage. More amazingly, McCaw largely disappeared from Nextel itself. Hardly anyone inside Nextel ever saw him. Tim Donahue, Nextel's number two, said, "I talk to him rarely." When they did talk, McCaw's advice was simple—the same message he had delivered at McCaw Cellular—move fast, but don't skimp on quality. Beyond that, he refused to talk about details. "Reporting to him is like reporting to the wall," Donahue said. "You tell him you want to do something and he says, 'Well, okay.'" A little weird? Yes—and it worked.

Within four years of that call from Craig McCaw to Morgan O'Brien, Nextel was an unqualified success. The value of its stock had increased sixfold; the company was challenging AT&T Wireless in ninety-two U.S. cities and offering service in ten of the world's twelve largest markets. Nextel served 3.6 million customers—more than McCaw Cellular's total the year it was purchased by AT&T.

McCaw could have cashed in his chips by selling the company to MCI WorldCom, the number-two U.S. long-distance company, once again in search of a wireless presence. MCI WorldCom saw its rivals forming huge wireless ventures (Bell Atlantic with Vodafone AirTouch and AT&T with British Telecom). As McCaw had predicted, wireless had become central to anyone's strategy in telecommunications. But the Nextel–MCI WorldCom deal collapsed in May 1999 over disagreements over price. (MCI WorldCom later bought Sprint, which had both long-distance and wireless businesses, for $129 billion, the costliest corporate buyout in U.S. history.)

McCaw, as always, had his back door. Nextel announced a $600 million investment from Microsoft and plans for a new product, Nextel Online, that would enable work groups to access the Internet and share information on intranets, internal company networks. It was a step toward the goal of transforming the handset from a mindless speaker with a bell into a smart device that could manage data or voices, assign priorities to calls, and connect to a smart system that would automatically hunt for and process data.

Nextel invited third parties to write software for this new platform, much as Microsoft encouraged other software firms to write applications for the Windows operating system on personal computers. In time, the little handset could become a powerful mobile device in what

McCaw and others called the ICE age—the era of convergence among Information, Communications, and Entertainment.

"The telephone doesn't know who it's calling, or if it's a right number, or if you want to talk, or if you want to talk about what the caller wants to talk about," McCaw once told *Red Herring* magazine:

> But all these issues can be handled with hierarchy software iterations between devices. . . . We believe that in the future, people will be willing to pay something to buy back their freedom. So we think that there's a great market for wireless, if only in the interest of achieving efficiency and forgetting the other human benefits. We're not many years from making wireless work well. If you're going to compete in a global environment, if you're going to work across time zones, deal with international issues, translate languages, you need this kind of device.

Nextel was flourishing, yet McCaw suddenly shifted Dan Akerson from chief executive to an unspecified role at Eagle River. In a very unusual public display of differences with a subordinate, McCaw let out word that he hadn't liked the way Akerson treated people. "Do Dan and Craig have the same management style? No, they don't," said McCaw's spokesman, Bob Ratliffe, evidently choosing his words with care. "Dan's tough and strong," he added, noting that McCaw is "softspoken, kind—not to say that Dan's not kind."

McCaw himself said nothing. The wizard stayed behind the curtain, quietly promoting Tim Donahue, a McCaw longtimer, into Akerson's job. Akerson remained chairman of Nextel's board.

One amazing aspect of this event was the lack of attention it received. At most large public companies, a chief executive's abrupt departure would be a source of continuing questions. Yet Akerson's departure was a one-day story, and Nextel's stock quietly rose some 4 percent. The market's calm reflected McCaw's prestige. People expected unusual moves from him. Instead of questioning his wisdom, as critics had early in his career, people now assumed his brilliance and took everything he did as part of a veiled strategy.

No one anticipated the breadth of ambition of McCaw's next

project. Having bought a remarkable collection of the world's wireless licenses, McCaw was ready to go beyond the world—literally. He was quietly preparing a bid for the space that surrounded the planet—a fantastic idea for a celestial monopoly of such potential risk and complexity that even his closest aides doubted it could be done.

22

"The Potential to Change the World"

Enter Bill Gates and Teledesic's "Internet in the Sky"

Bill Gates never traveled without something to read. Not even on this very special trip to Hawaii, where the Microsoft chief executive would marry employee Melinda French on New Year's Day 1994.

Gates was famous for his personal "bandwidth," computer slang for his ability to absorb information on a wide range of topics. He often focused his vacation reading on a single topic, like bioengineering, and would spend hours poring through books on that theme. Now, as he prepared to end his prolonged bachelorhood, Gates might have expected to focus purely on personal matters. But as he prepared to board a helicopter for the first leg of his trip, he paused to take a packet from an aide to Craig McCaw, a fellow Seattle billionaire whom he'd known casually for years.

The packet contained documents about a potential space-based communications system—an idea that attracted McCaw precisely because it seemed so crazy. Now Gates was interested. The king of software and the onetime king of cellular were about to join forces in the newest and wildest scheme of Craig McCaw's career.

* * *

The idea had begun with Ed Tuck, who, like McCaw's father, had gotten his start as a radio announcer. Tuck went into engineering in the 1950s and started a business making microwave communication links, the first of several technology companies he launched. Tuck made enough money to start a venture capital fund whose projects included a company that made handheld devices to receive signals from global positioning satellites, giving the user a highly accurate location. The military used such satellites for positioning ships at sea, and Tuck correctly figured that fishermen, hikers, and others would buy an affordable version to stay on course as they traveled. His Magellan device sold for less than $200 at Kmart.

But Tuck wanted to take the idea a step further. Why not use satellites not only to track one's own position anywhere on the globe but also to stay in touch from any location? Imagine being able to dial a phone and say, "Hi, Mom. I'm at the North Pole." Intrigued, Tuck decided to finance some preliminary research into how such a system could work.

By 1988 Tuck's idea had grown grand. The goal: an affordable telephone call from anywhere in the world. Stringing copper wire across Australia's outback or China's inner provinces would always be too expensive. But a satellite-based wireless system could bring service to all the people—more than half the world—who had never made a phone call.

Tuck shared the idea with business associate Gary Sutton, who told Tuck about a Washington State man he'd met at a Harvard Business School entrepreneurship seminar. Craig McCaw had said something that stuck in Sutton's mind.

"He'd always encouraged me when I saw something big, visionary, radical, to let him know," Sutton later told Thomas E. Haines of *The Seattle Times*. "And in six years, this was the first one [I told him about], the only one."

Sutton's call to McCaw led to a meeting in Los Angeles. Not many knew it, but McCaw had long been interested in space-based communications. Back in 1986 a little company called McCaw Space Technologies had tried to assemble a consortium to build a $380 million communications system using one satellite positioned over the Pacific Ocean and another over the Indian Ocean. One would serve Hong Kong and Asian cities; the other would serve Africa and parts of Asia and Europe. The company planned to offer teleconferencing, videotext, teletext, electronic mail, video feeds, high-speed data transfer, and point-to-point services. "We believe we are on the forefront of a revolution," Joe Walter, vice president of McCaw Space Technologies, said at the time.

Trouble erupted among the partners, and the idea fizzled. But Craig

McCaw remained fascinated by the communications potential of satellites. Meeting with Tuck in 1989, he asked how the system would work. The sheer ambition of the idea was appealing. "At first, it sounded grandiose and slightly crazy, so that of course intrigued me," McCaw says. "I said I'd like to know more."

For his part, Tuck was impressed at how quickly McCaw appreciated the idea. "After my experience with Magellan, I expected to spend years being ridiculed. McCaw is one of these guys who see the potential of things that other people can't see. He saw the whole gestalt and said, 'It's all here.' "

Not everyone around McCaw felt so confident. The board of McCaw Cellular Communications agreed to support some investment in the idea, but not much. Wayne Perry felt there were too many places where the project could collapse. McCaw was surrounded by skeptics. "They'd throw up their hands and say, 'This is completely naive. It'll never work,' " McCaw later recalled. Besides, as Perry said, McCaw Cellular was then facing huge demands for cash. Why pour valuable dollars into something so speculative? It was a sensible business attitude.

But McCaw wouldn't give up. In June 1990 he and Tuck put seed money into a company named Calling Communications. The company initially focused on satellite telephone calls as well as a much more ambitious idea: the space equivalent of fiber-optic service. (In terms of data throughput, fiber was a fire hose compared to the pinhole of traditional telephone lines.)

The company—later renamed Teledesic, a blend of "telephone" and "geodesic"—hired a small team of engineers. They were led by Dave Patterson, a former systems engineer for information technology at AT&T Bell Laboratories, ITT, TRW, and Sprint. He had been chief architect of Sprint's fiber-optic communications system. Now his goal was to find a way to supply high-end communication anywhere in the world while matching the cost and performance of land-based fiber-optic networks.

The idea of using satellites for this purpose raised tricky technical problems. To match the speed and capacity of fiber, a satellite system would need a huge breadth of spectrum; bands not normally used for satellites would be required. The system would need microwaves in the

"Ka" band, at the very high end of the radio spectrum. And because signals in that band were easily blocked by trees, buildings, and even rain, the system would need satellites almost directly overhead at any given time, so that signals would shoot up at no more than a forty-degree angle.

Next came the problem called "latency"—the delay between the time a signal is sent into space and the time it's bounced back to a point on the ground. A half-second delay was no problem for a simple video downlink from a satellite 22,320 miles in space; a viewer wouldn't know when the picture had originated. A similar delay would be annoying, perhaps, for a telephone call. But it would pose a serious problem for interactive computer communication, in which systems are constantly checking back and forth to detect and correct errors in transmission. So to minimize latency, a low earth orbit for the satellite system would be required.

All calculations pointed to one conclusion: To provide service across the entire globe, the system would need no fewer than 840 satellites, flying in twenty-one separate orbits some 435 miles above earth—plus another eighty spares in case any broke or were hit by space junk.

The number was staggering: *840 satellites?* No one had ever made that many. How would such a huge manufacturing task be accomplished? And what would it cost? A single hand-built satellite cost $100 million; multiply that by 840, and the numbers quickly get silly.

The engineers took some comfort in recent advances in computer manufacturing, which had cut the cost of making complex items such as microprocessors and hard drives. But the technical challenges facing the plan were still staggering.

And even if satellites could be made cheaply, launching them was another matter. At that point, all the companies and governments in the world launched a combined total of about seventy-five satellites a year. At that rate, even if Teledesic took over the entire world's launch capacity, it would take over a decade to deploy the Teledesic network. "We thought, 'This could be a killer,' " Patterson recalls. "But we sort of asked ourselves . . . just because no one had done it before, does that mean it can't be done?"

One hopeful sign was the fact that companies in France, Japan, and the U.S. were talking about creating new or expanded satellite launch systems, while the Russians wanted to use their huge nuclear missiles as satellite launchers. (Many were scheduled for destruction under arms-control treaties with the U.S.; why not send them into space instead?)

Then, of course, there was the space-based switching system—individual satellites receiving and forwarding huge volumes of data. To handle so much data traffic, each satellite would have to contain a sophisticated computer run by complex software no one had yet written.

Faced with these huge questions, Tuck and his team set to work. Tuck found that, in an almost spooky fashion, solutions to specific problems occasionally seemed to materialize out of nowhere. For example, the engineers were busy wrestling with the design of the satellite antenna when an entrepreneur happened to visit, asking Tuck to fund an adaptation of Reagan-era Star Wars antennas. Tuck was about to toss him out when he realized that the design had potential application to the Teledesic problem. Moments like this made Tuck feel that some angel was watching over the project.

Meanwhile, others announced big satellite projects, hoping to offer mainly global phone service and messaging. In June 1990 Motorola announced its $3.4 billion, sixty-six-satellite Iridium system for voice and one-way data transmission. San Jose–based Globalstar planned to launch a $2.2 billion, forty-eight-satellite system; Montreal-based Odyssey proposed a $3.2 billion, twelve-satellite system; and ORBCOMM, of Dulles, Virginia, planned a messaging system of thirty-six smaller satellites for $320 million. Finally, New York–based Loral and France's Alcatel, one of the world's largest telephone equipment makers, backed SkyBridge, a mix of sixty-four low-orbit and three high-orbit satellites. Against this backdrop, the Teledesic team kept working on their plan, by far the most ambitious of them all.

Then, in mid-1993, the board of McCaw Cellular cut off Teledesic's funding. "I didn't want it to die," McCaw told USA Today. "So I put my own money in it." After that, no one doubted who controlled Teledesic. The fledgling firm moved from California to offices adjoining McCaw's Eagle River Investments in Kirkland, Washington.

McCaw wanted to put someone in charge who shared his style of management. He had been dissatisfied with the candidates offered by a search firm—mainly people with satellite experience who lacked the personality he wanted. To McCaw, résumés meant nothing; he wanted attitude. As McCaw put it later, "I decided if I was going to put my money in[to Teledesic], I needed a cheap terrorist, a missionary who would live and breathe and die with this."

It happened that just that sort of person already knew people in the McCaw organization. Russell Daggatt was a lean, high-energy, intensely disciplined lawyer who had once worked at a Seattle law firm with Roberta Katz of McCaw Cellular. After Harvard Law School, he had worked for Flying Tiger, the air freight company. Daggatt had also worked in Japan representing IBM and American Express, and had coauthored a book on negotiating. Attracted to the energy and creativity at McCaw, Daggatt had told friends he wanted to work there.

The two men met for over four hours, during which McCaw subjected Daggatt to a series of soul-searching questions. One question probed Daggatt's grasp of strategic issues: What business was Federal Express in? Daggatt answered that FedEx sold not package delivery but peace of mind—the certainty of getting that crucial parcel delivered on time, "absolutely, positively," as FedEx's ads had it. That was the correct answer.

McCaw also offered various business scenarios and asked Daggatt to analyze the "value equation" in each. How does a business bring value to the customer? If Daggatt started talking about profit margins, McCaw stopped him. No, not profits, McCaw would insist—customer value. From such exchanges, Daggatt grasped an important point about McCaw's philosophy of business: "McCaw's approach to making money is indirect," he says. "It's how you create and build value. If you do that, there are lots of ways to make money. You're not going to make money very long if you're not creating value."

Daggatt got the job in October 1993, in part because McCaw liked his ideas for Teledesic's strategic direction. Daggatt had concluded that a pure telephone concept was a bad idea. Since others were rushing to provide that service, he argued for a more ambitious approach: broadband service that would be as powerful as that offered by land-based fiber-optic cables. In terms of capacity, broadband was to ordinary telephone service what a fire hose is to a soda straw—many times more powerful.

McCaw liked Daggatt's approach for several reasons. McCaw saw a future in which humans would return to a more nomadic lifestyle, working from remote locations rather than gathering in cities. Land-based fiber cables tied people to locations. He wanted a system that gave people the flexibility he craved in his own business and personal life. As he likes to put it, "Human beings from the time they discovered seeds have been enslaved towards places."

The industrial age hadn't involved much of an advance: "You move to a place, ruin it, and then move on." McCaw could see the results from his office window: A narrow four-lane highway crossed Lake Washington from Seattle, clogged with cars carrying people to central job sites. Many drivers took forty minutes or more to travel just a few miles. It was a colossal waste of time and energy.

Only in the coming information age would true freedom from place be achieved, and the technology offered by Teledesic could help, McCaw believed. Others might worry that disconnecting person from place had negative effects; for all their congestion and pollution, cities could be desirable as centers of culture, where people built communities and drew energy and ideas from one another. Some feared technology's dark side, but McCaw saw huge potential benefits in satellites.

"Now we're going back the other way, where machines are beginning to really serve us," says McCaw. "You can create the information communications structures that [support] a really different economy."

Daggatt's formulation also appealed to the sense of mission McCaw brought to telecommunications, the notion of empowering people to do their best. A global broadband system meant that anyone from Alaska to Zaire could access the same level of communications service, including teleconferencing, long-distance learning, and high-speed computer communications. An exporter in the Congo could use the same tools as a banker in New York City; a physics student in Tibet could be as well informed as a professor at Stanford. "It's inherently egalitarian technology," Daggatt says. Rather than view such a system as a threat, many nations, especially in the developing world, would welcome it as a great opportunity—if they could be made to understand its potential.

The system also had the potential to ride what some believed was the next big wave in communications, the worldwide network of computers known as the Internet. Years earlier, Apple cofounder Steve

Jobs had told McCaw about the Internet's potential. "It sounds great. How do we buy it?" McCaw had replied. It wasn't that easy, McCaw found. But he had come to regret not having invested in Internet-related companies. Teledesic presented another opportunity—almost an Internet in space.

Furthermore, because of its unique features and benefits, space-based broadband would not be threatened by advances in land-based wireless. Those advances would merely complement and feed demand for the space system. And finally, a more ambitious approach for Teledesic matched Craig McCaw's business style: It promised to be very high risk, hugely expensive, and controversial but, if successful, incredibly profitable.

Once Teledesic focused on broadband, "the company took on a whole different persona, a recognition that there was a whole different business to focus on," says McCaw. Now there was talk of changing the world. "I'm sort of into how things affect human beings," he says. A broadband Teledesic could affect billions.

Daggatt soon came to another crucial realization. The Teledesic team had focused entirely on technical issues, but the biggest problems facing the satellite system project would actually be political. No such system could operate without permission from the U.S. Federal Communications Commission, the U.N.'s International Telecommunications Union (a group that included the World Radio Conference), and scores of individual governments. Dealing with so many individual nations would be difficult enough, but not as difficult as winning approval from the FCC and the U.N. bodies, where rivalries, petty politics, and bureaucratic inertia could kill Teledesic's momentum. "We were naive," says David Patterson. "The real challenge was regulatory."

About this time, Bill Gates entered the picture.

At a Christmas party in 1993, McCaw had chatted with Gates about Teledesic, and Gates had agreed to read a briefing packet on his wedding trip to Hawaii. Later, at the AT&T Pebble Beach National Pro-Am golf tournament in February, the two talked some more. "I told Bill I wanted him to come with me, and I told him to close his eyes and jump," McCaw said later. "To his credit, he did jump."

Gates agreed to match McCaw's investment in Teledesic. Unlike McCaw, he remained largely a passive investor, getting information mainly from McCaw and Michael Larson, Gates's representative on Teledesic's board. Several times, McCaw and Gates put more money into Teledesic, a total that has never been disclosed. By early 1994 McCaw and Gates each owned slightly more than 30 percent of the company, while AT&T (through the old McCaw company) owned about 28 percent and Tuck's venture capital company owned about 10 percent.

Gates rarely talks about his involvement in Teledesic publicly, calling any discussion premature. But he once told *Fortune* that, as much as he liked the company's technology vision, the appeal of working with Craig McCaw drove the deal for him. "I wouldn't have invested in Teledesic unless Craig was involved," Gates said. "Craig is an amazing person. He thinks ahead of the pack and understands the communications business and where it's going better than anyone I know."

That remark was especially significant considering the fact that Microsoft was spending more and more of its time and money on communications-related interests. Microsoft wanted to spur the development of high-speed Internet access and related services to increase demand for its products. To that end, Microsoft would invest not only in McCaw's Nextel but also in cable systems around the world.

McCaw and Gates were reaching the same destination from different origins. Both were interested in various means of getting data to businesses and individuals. So it was friendship as well as strategic interests that brought the world's richest man to Teledesic.

But Gates's presence wasn't entirely positive. In some circles, Gates was considered a monopolist, a latter-day robber baron who wanted every scrap of market share in every business his company touched. Microsoft had been investigated by the Department of Justice and the Federal Trade Commission as well as the European Commission, and the company and its leader were the subject of an unending stream of criticism in the media and on a thousand hostile websites.

So Teledesic at first made no public announcement of Gates's investment. Publicity had helped Craig McCaw at times, especially when dealing with Wall Street or the banking community. But at this point, McCaw chose to keep a low profile, as he had in the early days of cellular. He knew the risk of powerful outside players taking an interest in his goal.

Teledesic remained little known outside of a small group of engineers and scientists until March 1994, when the company filed a request for spectrum with the FCC. Daggatt happened to be jogging along the Potomac River in Washington, D.C., when he saw the resulting headlines. Understandably, the media found it noteworthy that a twelve-employee company thought it could build and launch an enormous satellite system by 2001—a feat not even NASA would dare propose.

The press stressed the Gates-McCaw angle—the alliance of two technology superstars. But unlike previous stories about the business genius of these two men, the Teledesic stories carried a decidedly skeptical tone. "God save us. It's the stupidest thing I've ever heard of," John Pike, director of the Federation of American Scientists' Space Policy Project, told *The Wall Street Journal.*

McCaw wryly summarizes the news coverage: "They said these two spoiled rich kids have finally gone over the edge." Maybe so, but Teledesic found itself flooded with thousands of résumés, including many from engineers and manufacturing specialists who thought the project could work—and wanted in.

Daggatt felt bludgeoned by the initial public reaction and wouldn't give press interviews for a year afterward. But he had no time to recuperate. Instead, he was soon racing around the world, lobbying foreign officials to put Teledesic on the agenda for an International Telecommunications Union (ITU) meeting scheduled for October 1995.

The ITU was the only body that could grant worldwide use of radio spectrum. Typically, it began planning agendas for its meetings four years in advance, finalizing them at least two years in advance. Unless Daggatt could convince the ITU to bend that rule, Teledesic had no hope of getting regulatory approval in time to make its first launch in 2001 as scheduled.

But the ITU was a famously ponderous organization, run by consensus. Since each of the 186 member nations had equal voting power, any organized opposition could kill a proposal. And Europeans quickly denounced the Microsoft mogul's plan to "control" space communications. "Europeans tend to view this as a Bill Gates project, where we see it as a Craig McCaw project," Daggatt said later. "Bill has been extremely supportive of Teledesic, but he's trying to ensure there is no connection between Microsoft and Teledesic, mainly because Microsoft is his main focus and he doesn't want to do anything that would breach his duties to Microsoft."

Daggatt and several deputies hit the road, flying to Washington, D.C., Geneva, Rio de Janeiro, Djakarta, and other foreign capitals, trying to get placeholders for spectrum rights, just as an earlier group had gathered FCC spectrum licenses for McCaw Cellular. The Teledesic team hired consultants around the world to help them navigate local bureaucracies. The plan was to sell foreign officials on the benefits Teledesic would offer their local economy. Teledesic, the team claimed, would not supplant any local telephone systems but instead would serve them as a wholesaler. Nations could keep control of their systems; Teledesic would provide access only if a country wanted it. And because the satellites would offer equal service to every point on the globe, every country would enjoy equal benefit.

On one trip, Daggatt found himself in Rabat, Morocco's capital city, where he had a single afternoon to make his case. Over cups of Morocco's potent coffee, he met with half a dozen officials who, as leaders of an informal coalition of developing countries, could easily boost Teledesic—or torpedo it. Daggatt mustered all his persuasive skills to convince the Moroccans that Teledesic could satisfy their desire to expand their nation's telecommunications capacity without huge costs. The concept clicked. Morocco's minister of telecommunications stuck out his hand and a deal was reached, one of Teledesic's first significant international agreements. "We need services. We need capacity. We can cooperate with Teledesic," Ahmed Tumi, a Moroccan official, told *The Seattle Times*.

Earlier that summer, Teledesic had won the backing of the Clinton administration, which wanted to keep the United States a leader in telecommunications. The FCC would publicly lobby in its favor. That not only gave Teledesic a push going into the ITU meeting, where the company still hoped to win one of the coveted agenda spots, but also provided leverage for winning FCC licensing later.

McCaw and the top Teledesic leaders flew to Geneva for the ITU conference in late October 1995. McCaw made contacts while his staff launched a schmooze offensive. Lobbying was hardly a Craig McCaw strength or interest. "Craig is actually very shy and very unassuming in those kinds of situations. He's more inclined to stand back and not put himself forward," says Daggatt. Yet McCaw's low-key charm always proved helpful. "He tends to not seek out these big glamorous gatherings, but he does very well in them. When he does interact with people, he gets along well. [And] at the end of the day, he ends up having a good time."

The company's efforts included a luncheon for key ITU delegates and a giant $8,000 pizza party for hundreds of guests. When the conference opened, each of the 1,200 delegates found at his or her seat a free binder displaying Teledesic's logo. A motion was quickly made to add a proposal to set aside spectrum for any system passing data between moving satellites and stationary land antennas. Everyone knew which company that would help. The motion passed, but trouble lay ahead.

On the final night of the conference, European members who opposed Teledesic threatened to force a vote on the company. Confident he had the votes of the U.S. and developing countries, Daggatt negotiated with the Europeans up to the last minute, trying to convince them not to stand in the company's way. Finally, the Europeans bowed to pressure and permitted approval of the Teledesic plan, but some said they would try to force Teledesic to share the spectrum with competing firms.

"This is the concern," François Rancy, one European delegate, told *The Seattle Times*. "Not McCaw, but Gates, of course, is concentrating too much power. . . . There is a potential as a result of the '95 conference for a worldwide monopoly. And we gave it to Bill Gates." In any case, McCaw was thrilled with his victory. Without ITU approval, there would have been no choice but to shut down the company. "We were close to being annihilated," he says.

The next hurdle was the FCC application. As the company geared up for that challenge, McCaw was already preparing for Teledesic's next development phase. He brought in Hans-Werner Braun, who, as an engineer at the University of Michigan in the 1980s, had helped create the backbone of the Internet and had later worked at the San Diego Supercomputer Center. Charged with designing software that would link Teledesic to the Internet, Braun saw a chance to make history. "I think it will make a difference," he said of Teledesic. "I came here for that. I don't care about money. In fact, I don't think Teledesic pays that well."

McCaw also named David Twyver, former president of Northern

Telecom's global wireless operations, to a new position as chief executive. McCaw, who remained chairman, had talked Twyver out of taking a job as chief executive of Nortel, the Canadian phone giant. Twyver's biggest task would be lining up $9 billion in financing and building a network of manufacturers and suppliers. "This is definitely a high-risk project," Twyver told the *Los Angeles Times*. "But I'm working with two of the greatest entrepreneurs ever. And I think this has the potential to change the world as much as the first transcontinental railway."

* * *

Teledesic's streak of good luck ran out in August 1996, when a former ally became a rival for the same chunk of spectrum. Press accounts called it "a tug of war with billions at stake."

Alex Mandl, the man who had worked so closely with Wayne Perry to merge McCaw and AT&T, had quit his job as Robert Allen's heir apparent and signed on with little-known Associated Communications for $1 million a year and a $20 million signing bonus. Mandl's arrival gave sudden credibility to a small company that had been stealing moves from Craig McCaw—quietly gathering spectrum licenses that no one else thought had value.

Backed by communications engineer Rajendra Singh of Alexandria, Virginia, and the Berkman family of Pittsburgh, Associated had worked since 1993 to assemble free licenses for thirty-one cities that used the 18-gigahertz band. Associated wanted to use this band of spectrum to send data, video, and eventually voice to fixed receivers across a city, a system that would give businesses fast Internet access and other services without building infrastructure. Associated hoped to launch its service in 1997. The idea wasn't new. Xerox had proposed using this spectrum in 1978 for "digital electronic messaging" but, after winning FCC approval, had abandoned the idea, leaving the licenses available for anyone who wanted them.

Unfortunately, 18 gigahertz was precisely the piece of the spectrum that Teledesic wanted for sending and receiving data from its satellites. The FCC, which had helped Teledesic in Geneva, had goofed; two parties claimed the same piece of the spectrum. What to do?

Teledesic filed a petition with the FCC, asking the agency to block

Associated's plans because they would create interference with Teledesic's signals. Associated fought back. Both sides hoped for a speedily negotiated settlement of the problem, but skirmishes soon broke out in the news media. Daggatt suggested that Associated had pulled a fast one: "Raj Singh and the Berkmans were very clever in picking up these licenses with nobody noticing, but they seem to be cobbling these licenses together to create a new service that's never received policy review," he told *The Washington Post*. He added darkly, "There's also a question of the validity of some of these licenses."

An anonymous Associated official shot back: "We applied for these licenses over a number of years in a public process. For Teledesic, which is so involved in daily regulatory matters, to claim they didn't know what we were doing is a little disingenuous."

Associated had a point. Craig McCaw had known Singh since 1984 through Singh's engineering firm, LCC International, which designed grids for cellular systems. Singh had also designed the first systems for Nextel. The industry visionary could hardly claim he hadn't seen Associated coming.

McCaw's real advantage in the struggle with Associated was his long history of strong relations with the FCC. Since Elroy McCaw's first filing back in 1937, the McCaws had stayed friendly with regulators. Craig McCaw's top lobbyist was Richard Wiley, a former FCC chairman who also represented TCI's John Malone. McCaw's public statements coincided exactly with what the FCC wanted from license holders. He said the government had "entrusted" him with licenses to the public airwaves. Regulators loved to hear that.

"Having been regulated by the government and the FCC for many years, you sort of have a sense that the regulator is sacred," McCaw said later. "No matter how good your idea, you've got to have the regulator. Lots of good ideas have died through the failure to properly slalom the regulatory process." McCaw had no intention of letting that happen to Teledesic.

Fortunately, Teledesic had already converted the FCC into a teammate in Geneva; it had even donated $25,000 to a controversial nonprofit group that funded international travel by agency officials. (Michigan congressman John Dingell publicly criticized the arrangement, which had been approved by the FCC's general counsel.) To spearhead further lobbying with the agency, the company now hired the law firm of Gibson, Dunn & Crutcher, home to Scott Blake Harris, former chief of the FCC's International Bureau and a political ally of technology-savvy Vice President Al Gore. Harris had made frequent appearances at FCC meetings and won a plum appointment from agency chairman Reed Hundt to run the advisory committee preparing for the ITU conference.

Teledesic also found a surprise ally, the Pentagon, which quietly revealed that Associated's plans interfered with secret defense satellites linked to systems in Denver and Washington, D.C.

No one wanted this fight to continue. It made the FCC look bad and created delays for both Teledesic and Associated. To resolve the dispute, the two parties brought in a surprise choice for a mediator: Wayne Perry. Despite the fact that he worked for one Teledesic shareholder (AT&T) and was a close friend of another (McCaw), Associated agreed to let Perry broker a deal. A series of meetings were arranged in Perry's conference room, and most of the key parties gathered there—all except McCaw, who typically checked in by telephone while others handled the negotiations.

By February Associated and Teledesic had reached a deal. Associated agreed to move its services to a large swath of spectrum in the 24-gigahertz band in exchange for an undisclosed payment from Teledesic. The deal set aside a width of 400 megahertz—twice the amount used by all radio and TV channels combined—for Associated to share with other licensees offering similar services.

McCaw's old foe BellSouth and other companies protested, saying Teledesic and Associated had gotten too sweet a deal. They complained that the government was handing Mandl's company—soon to be renamed Teligent—the rights to spectrum that it otherwise would have auctioned. *The Washington Post* focused on McCaw's friendship with Reed Hundt and a donation of $50,000 McCaw had made to the Democratic National Committee just one month after the dispute began. For a time, a minicontroversy brewed.

Of course, both the FCC and McCaw spokespeople denied that politics had influenced the decision, and in time the rancor subsided. The following month, the FCC formally awarded Teledesic a license to operate in the United States.

Russell Daggatt felt great. He had won the FCC license in just three years, an amazing accomplishment. (Iridium, by contrast, had taken five years.)

The license approval made a publicity splash, but in truth the Teledesic satellite system remained more vision than reality. A large step toward realizing the dream occurred when the Boeing Company, the Seattle-based aerospace giant, announced that it would invest up to $100 million and become Teledesic's prime contractor. Boeing said it would assign up to 200 engineers to work on satellite plans for Teledesic.

In negotiating the deal, Boeing convinced Teledesic to alter its plans by using fewer but heavier satellites. Instead of 840 1,760-pound satellites flying 220 miles above earth, Teledesic would now use 288 2,860-pound satellites flying 435 miles above earth. The new approach called for satellites costing $20 million each, instead of $5 million.

The relationship had taken root three years earlier, when Daggatt and others called Boeing and asked to tour the 777 plant in Everett, north of Seattle, one of the most sophisticated manufacturing facilities in the world. The plant management put on an impressive show for the visitors, a minuet in which huge sheets of metal were rotated on cranes into precisely machined joints as workers fastened parts with titanium bolts. The performance illustrated Boeing's new approach to airplane building, born when company engineers had sat down with customers, engineers, and machinists to sketch ideas for an airplane that would be better for passengers, cheaper to operate, quicker to build, and easier to repair.

As they toured the plant, the visitors from Teledesic asked detailed questions of Alan Mulally, the vice president who ran the project. Mulally enjoyed the meeting. "They asked good questions. They were quick and smart. They were the sort of people I'd like on my team," he said in an interview. For their part, the Teledesic team was amazed. The intricately choreographed ballet in steel that Boeing presented was just the sort of miracle of design, engineering, and manufacturing that Teledesic needed.

Boeing, in turn, needed Teledesic. The aerospace giant was in the midst of a series of transformations. Phil Condit had recently become chief executive, bringing a management style that favored teamwork, delegation, and flexibility. Now his focus was the future: What would it take to keep Boeing in the phone book for the next hundred years? Looking for long-term strategic clout, he pushed Boeing into buying Rockwell International's aerospace and defense businesses and into merging with fellow aircraft behemoth McDonnell Douglas.

Clearly, Boeing wanted to dominate the world's commercial aviation industry and much of military aviation as well, but it also saw huge potential in several low-orbit private satellite projects in the offing. Even excluding Teledesic and the military, Boeing figured that the market to build and launch satellites would be $25 billion or more per year through 2005. "It looks like a good business opportunity," said Mulally, who later became president of Boeing Defense & Space Group, the division that would build Teledesic.

As one of the world's premier manufacturers, Boeing's presence gave Teledesic a huge boost. "In the past there has been a lot of skepticism," commented Marco Caceres, an analyst with the Teal Group, a Fairfax, Virginia, consulting firm. "But now with Boeing, they have a lot more credibility because Boeing is one of the world's biggest players in the commercial [satellite] launch business." John Hodulik, a satellite-industry analyst with Lazard Freres & Company, agreed. "The fact that Boeing is committing capital is important," he told *The Washington Post*.

Some predicted a culture clash between stodgy old Boeing and the embryonic Teledesic. But Mulally said that the two companies shared a vision of global communication. Boeing saw the 777 as "the forty-thousand-foot version of Teledesic," said Mulally; after all, each was an airborne system for connecting people and delivering information across the globe.

The analogy might be strained, but from its own operations Boeing appreciated the significance and potential of the Teledesic concept. They knew that world-class manufacturers needed fast methods of shipping data to far-flung partners from its own use of fiber cable to send engineering drawings and other data to facilities in Japan. They also knew that demand would grow for such data shipments, including high-capacity, interactive service. The only real question was, How much of that service would come from satellites? "Teledesic offers us an opportunity to figure out what the future of space-based telecommunications is going to look like," Mulally said.

No one expected an easy path ahead, but there were plenty of surprises in store. In June 1997 Motorola announced plans to launch its own broadband satellite system, $2.9 billion Celestri, to be operational by 2002. Motorola, still pushing its separate Iridium system for telephone calls, said it would ask the FCC for permission to use the same spectrum assigned to Teledesic.

Though Motorola's announcement lent further credibility to Teledesic's business plan, it also meant direct competition for financing and customers—to say nothing of spectrum. McCaw did not comment on the Motorola scheme, though Daggatt did. "It's an odd move. I don't know why they're doing it, other than to try to make life difficult for us," he said.

Reports surfaced concerning friction between McCaw's team and Boeing's over costs. *The Seattle Times* reported that the partners were up to $4 billion apart in their estimates of building costs. It was typical for a prime contractor to tussle with a client over costs, but this appeared to be a serious rift. Boeing was under growing financial pressure because of its difficulties in building the new-generation 737 airliners. Production problems got so bad that in 1997 Boeing reported its first annual loss in fifty years.

Boeing eventually reduced its role in Teledesic without withdrawing its investment. In its place, Motorola became a manufacturing contractor, and Lockheed Martin got the order to launch the first group of satellites, using three Atlas 5 rockets based in the United States and three Proton rockets in Russia.

Teledesic appeared to be surviving each challenge, while Iridium and the other satellite projects were running into serious financial problems. It was a big-money game, and nobody was better than McCaw at finding capital and maintaining credibility in such a fight.

It was too early to predict a winner in the satellite race, but Teledesic's odds were improving. Then McCaw, with no public explanation, replaced David Twyver as Teledesic's chief executive in a move that resembled the Akerson change at Nextel. McCaw named himself co–chief executive along with Steve Hooper, the former head of AT&T Wireless. Bob Ratliffe, McCaw's spokesman, would say only that McCaw and Twyver had differed over the best way to manage the company's growth. Hooper brought a skilled hand at financing, a looming challenge for Teledesic. To help with business development and government marketing, McCaw later brought in retired Admiral Bill Owens, former vice chairman of the Joint Chiefs of Staff.

In May 1998 McCaw announced a breakthrough: Motorola would drop the Celestri project altogether, join Teledesic as prime contractor, and buy a 26 percent stake in the company in exchange for $750 million in cash and design technology. The announcement solved two problems: Boeing remained a partner, but with a diminished role, easing those tensions; and Teledesic's chief competitor, the Celestri system, simply went away.

McCaw, who had always wanted Motorola in Teledesic, had been lobbying Motorola chief executive Chris Galvin as they worked together on Nextel. Even while Celestri sought the right to share Teledesic's spectrum, McCaw had stuck to his belief in not burning bridges to potential future allies. "When you're a competitor, you battle honestly, whether it's in the market or the regulatory environment or anything else," McCaw says. "You can fight like crazy . . . and shake hands afterward." (His ethical approach had practical benefits, because telecommunications companies' interests were so intertwined that it was often difficult not to deal with one another.)

Motorola joined two major foreign investors in Teledesic: Matra Marconi Space SA of France and Saudi Arabian Prince Alwaleed bin Talal bin Abdul Aziz Al-Saud. Increasingly, it looked as if Teledesic's first customers would be not the rural poor but large corporate-data consumers like banks and oil companies, perhaps in an alliance with a ground-based telecommunications company. "We view this as part of the global mix," McCaw says. "The challenge is to bring in integrated solutions."

McCaw was pleased. Though the inaugural date for operations had slipped to 2004, Teledesic was moving forward, defying the skeptics, achieving piece by piece what many had thought was impossible. Having seen the company survive a series of apparently fatal problems, McCaw joked that Teledesic had nine lives.

Building McCaw Cellular had been fun. It, too, had been an exercise in proving the skeptics wrong. But cellular had followed a path that, at least technically, was known. AT&T's research had predicted how cellular would work and win customers. It was clear that profits would eventually follow. But with Teledesic, McCaw was paving a wholly new path surrounded by a host of unknowns.

Those who watched him marveled at how he seemed to thrive in an environment of uncertainty. Ed Tuck saw McCaw as a master of chaos theory, a man who enjoyed finding clarity in the midst of confusion: "Craig manages to be involved in things that are closer to the optimum level of instability," says Tuck.

Constant change gave McCaw his cherished flexibility. In late 1999 he looked for ways to exploit the bankruptcies of London-based ICO Global Communications, which had failed to get financing to launch a satellite-based phone system, and Iridium, which couldn't make debt payments after consumers found its service expensive and unreliable.

Some saw the troubles for Iridium and ICO as reason to rethink the entire satellite-communications industry. With land-based wireless phones beginning to handle the Internet, critics said satellite services were costly, slow to deploy, difficult to adapt to changing technology, and too small a market. Yet once again, McCaw increased his betting and ignored the doomsayers. He considered starting Teledesic service sooner than 2004 or buying assets of both companies (seeing them as Nextel-like wreckages available at distressed prices). By December 1999 a group he led won control of ICO for payments of up to $1.2 billion. "What does Craig McCaw know—or think he knows—that no one else does?" asked *The Wall Street Journal*.

Some likened McCaw's interest in satellites to a *Star Trek* adventure, to boldly go where no man has gone before. But Craig McCaw, the amateur historian, prefers to draw inspiration not from Captain Kirk but from the great explorers of the past: "It's more like Columbus setting off from Spain and hoping there'd be things on the other side," says McCaw. "There's much more unknown here."

He loved it.

23

"Under the Radar"

*McCaw Makes Billions
in a Telecommunications Backwater*

In late 1994, shortly after closing the sale of McCaw Cellular to AT&T, Craig McCaw called Scot Jarvis, a trusted aide since 1985. Jarvis, who had remained with AT&T Wireless as a vice president based in California, was curious about the call from his longtime mentor. McCaw explained that he'd started an investment company, Eagle River, next door to the old McCaw Cellular headquarters in offices facing Lake Washington. McCaw said he needed Jarvis's services, and he promised fun. "Come on home," McCaw said. "We've got money to spend."

Jarvis didn't need much persuasion. He had enjoyed his time with McCaw immensely. But McCaw's current plans were vague. He wanted to make a few investments in communications, he said. Nothing too big—private stuff. He specifically said he wanted to "stay under the radar."

This represented a pivotal time for Craig McCaw both as a person and as a businessman. The sale of his company had triggered a profound self-reassessment. Without McCaw Cellular commanding his attention, he was now forced to see what remained in his life. The man who built back doors into every business deal had formed no strategy for life after McCaw Cellular.

So now, thinking it over, he decided to reinvent himself. A tycoon who already spent a considerable amount of time away from his businesses decided he wanted—more freedom.

McCaw decided to recast himself. He would shed some old habits—even his black-caterpillar mustache of many years would get the razor—and inject himself only where his presence was truly critical. He would skip board meetings of his own companies and monitor his deputies through global communications systems, checking in from Alaska or South Africa or wherever his interests happened to carry him. What did it matter whether the phone he used was in Seattle or Turkey? His spirit could be felt without his physical presence.

Like ancient humans, McCaw would be the nomad, a living illustration of his vision of work in the information age. Writing a new page for the Harvard Business School casebook, he would become what some termed the virtual executive.

McCaw uses a different term. "I'm much more of a highly interested consultant now than the guy involved in doing things," McCaw says. "I think that's probably a good role for me, in that I'm great at conceptualizing and I'm not as good at actually putting things in place." More than ever, he would delegate huge tasks and decisions to trusted lieutenants.

Scot Jarvis noticed the change soon after joining Eagle River. McCaw had been known for long absences at McCaw Cellular, but at least he had occasionally been visible to his headquarters staff. Now there was even less of him. "At Eagle River, he had made his billion. He had had the weight of the world on his shoulders, and I don't think he wanted that as much," Jarvis says. "He wanted to keep risk taking and building, but he didn't want to do it himself. As a result, he limited his communications so that really Dennis [Weibling] saw him most. Craig's a shy person by nature. He's even more shy now."

Some days, even McCaw's whereabouts were unknown. He might be down the hall in his office or in Jamaica, and Jarvis wouldn't know. McCaw was catching up on things he felt he had missed during his life as a chief executive of a public company. Exactly what that entailed was McCaw's concern. With the possible exception of Dennis Weibling and a few others, the boss's activities were a private matter. But as employees later discovered, McCaw at that time was working through a very difficult separation from his wife, Wendy.

McCaw had worked hard to keep his marriage off-limits to the news media, but his filing for divorce in 1995 opened an unavoidable window into his private world. Oddly, one of the most revealing sources was McCaw himself, who gave an interview about his personal story to *The Wall Street Journal*—perhaps trying to preempt the inevitable prying by reporters.

McCaw confessed that his professional success had damaged his personal life. "In many respects I had perhaps an unhealthy focus on the company and its needs, to my own detriment and to the detriment of my relationship with Wendy. My company was my children," McCaw said.

Now McCaw had realized he wanted more out of life. Nearly forty-seven, he wanted to have children and to forge closer ties with friends and family. Wendy, forty-six, had other priorities. She "wanted him to herself more," Steve Countryman, McCaw's friend from boyhood, said later. That apparently had been a central cause of their rupture. "I didn't attempt to extort her, and say if you don't do this, I'm going to do that," McCaw said. "I tried to convey the importance of those two things, friends and family. Maybe you can never have enough money, but it never really matters because money doesn't buy happiness. After a certain amount of reflection, I realized what was important to me and that wasn't important to Wendy."

In crass business terms, the partners no longer shared the same objectives.

He volunteered to the *Journal* that the split had not been caused by another woman. "I was 100 percent, completely faithful from day one of our marriage until after our separation," he declared.

Their shared life of extreme wealth—the yachts on two continents; the 780-acre island in Canada; the collection of luxury homes, each worth millions of dollars; the 4,500-acre ranch in Carmel; the jet aircraft—all that was over. But McCaw had a serious problem. His troubles with Wendy threatened his flexibility as an investor because she now claimed, under Washington State's community property law, an equal share of his fortune, then estimated at $1.3 billion.

What was worse, most legal experts tended to agree with her, though McCaw argued that his wealth had grown from a separately owned asset, the Centralia cable TV company he had inherited before their marriage. Since Wendy was claiming some $650 million of Craig's wealth, the divorce threatened his ability to use his assets for business transactions, including scheduled payments to Nextel. She wanted a sum from the estate equal to any investment he made over $5 million.

What became one of the largest divorce cases in U.S. history drew armies of lawyers, accountants, and divorce experts and generated thousands of boxes of paperwork. The basic argument was over how the

McCaw company had grown. McCaw's lawyers submitted charts that attempted to prove that the hundreds of transactions that had built McCaw Cellular Communications had arisen entirely from leverage against the brothers' cable company. In response, Wendy's lawyers argued that the distinctions between their personal and business assets had long been hopelessly blurred. To illustrate, she said she had consulted with Wayne Perry on personal tax questions.

The fight ensnared McCaw's mother and brothers, whose financial histories were probed by Wendy's lawyers. Platoons of lawyers, consultants, and advisers staked their positions. To outsiders it looked like hardball. Wendy's lawyers forced executives from AT&T and many of McCaw's associates, including Bill Gates, to give depositions. (Gates was questioned about the Teledesic partnership.) McCaw spent hours in meetings with his lawyers and with Wendy's. Legal experts speculated that a trial over her claims could take up to five grueling and expensive months.

For a man who cherishes his time and his focus, it must have been excruciating. This was one opponent who knew him as well as he knew her. "Craig McCaw may finally have met his match as a cunning, hard-nosed dealmaker: his wife Wendy," said the *Journal*. Wendy's lawyers say Craig had tried to dupe her by advising her "to feel under no pressure" from his divorce filing. Annoyed when she discovered that his lawyers had been scrambling to gather evidence for his case, she retaliated by trying to evict him from their waterfront home in suburban Seattle.

McCaw bristled at any suggestion that he was trying to take advantage of Wendy. "The amount of money she'd end up with irrespective is more than enough for anything she would want ever to do," he said. "I have a lot of goals and aspirations and if I were picking places to charitably expend my money, this would not be the first, understanding all the while that I wish only the best for her."

The only thing both sides agreed on was a desire to keep their personal affairs out of the public eye. Even so, some details emerged. In contrast to his mild-mannered public image, the *Journal* reported a bizarre Christmas Eve incident that involved McCaw's screaming at the couple's personal secretary after a job review, pacing for hours, and then breaking down in tears. The tale shocked McCaw's friends, who said it did not resemble the person they knew. "I've never seen him raise his voice to anybody," said Steve Countryman. But McCaw confirmed the report, saying the confrontation with the secretary had begun at Wendy's suggestion and that he had never intended to be hurtful or mean. "I don't think you will find a lot of people who will say I don't treat them with absolute respect," he protested.

Though most of the divorce court file was placed under seal by a judge, fragments of depositions were released. Wendy claimed the couple had had roughly $300,000 when they married in 1974. McCaw's mother set a value of $750,000, which suggested that the family had been better off after Elroy McCaw's death than even close friends believed. Much as McCaw would have wished otherwise, the court file hinted that this billionaire's lifestyle was more extravagant than that of the quiet kayaker seen in authorized photographs. As the divorce wore on, Wendy and McCaw continued to take turns using their boats, homes, planes, and a helicopter. Wendy preferred the Gulfstream IV, then considered the ultimate in personal aircraft. From her home in Santa Barbara, she faxed a note to McCaw's assistant requesting arrangements for the Gulfstream. "In a pinch the Citation [a jet valued at $5 million] would be OK. Just let me know," she wrote.

The divorce quietly ended after two years with Wendy's winning a huge settlement, including stock worth $460 million. Because the transaction affected so many shares of public companies, the settlement had to be disclosed to the Securities and Exchange Commission, but neither side gave public statements about the deal, whose exact terms were kept secret. But at last the lingering threat to McCaw's businesses was gone.

McCaw was free. Five months later, he married Susan Leigh Rasinski, a thirty-five-year-old investment banker with a Harvard MBA who worked in San Francisco. He bought them a $20 million estate in the Bay Area. By all accounts, the marriage to Susan made McCaw happier, more outgoing, and more committed to his personal life. "She has helped him pay more attention to what other people are thinking and doing and not be so self-focused in his own personal life," Countryman says. "She's been good for him." Susan took up flying lessons and, in due course, gave McCaw something he had long wanted: a son, named Chase.

McCaw was feeling more fulfilled than ever in his personal life, but he had not lost his restless business ambition nor changed his quirky style. At Eagle River, he would focus on a business opportunity, tell his staff to check it out, and sometimes lose interest even before they had completed the research. "Craig can get enamored with things," says Scot Jarvis. "[And then] the ardor can fade. It's hard to tell when he's [just] enamored and when he really wants you to move. You're supposed to predict, but there aren't many people who are good at predicting which ones he's really interested in and which ones are a passing fancy."

Wayne Perry knew better than anyone else how McCaw's thinking could take him down dead ends but also into opportunities no one else had seen. Despite his own obvious intelligence, Perry sometimes couldn't figure out the process by which McCaw got his ideas. "I used to try and go back and reverse engineer and see what it was—frankly, less to test him than to see if I could be a little ahead of it," says Perry. "[But] in spite of my work to stay abreast of a wide range of things, Craig McCaw is the first person in my life who used the words 'cellular' or 'Internet' to me—and he doesn't read as much as I do. I don't know where he gets it. I just hope he keeps a clear channel."

One of the most spectacular examples of both McCaw's intuition and his post–McCaw Cellular style of management had its origin in 1994. McCaw asked Jarvis and other top aides to study an obscure segment of telecommunications in which telephone traffic was carried by fiber-optic cables not owned by the regional Bell companies. Typically, the service involved connecting companies in major cities directly to long-distance carriers. It represented only about 0.2 percent of local calls—a minuscule backwater of telecommunications.

At first glance, this was not an attractive business: The tiny market was controlled by regional Bells, the regulatory environment was complex, capital costs were high, and competition from new entrants could easily depress margins. It wasn't like cellular in the early years, when competition had been limited to two players. The biggest player in fiber-optic service, Metropolitan Fiber Systems of Omaha, Nebraska, was losing money. This was two years before passage of the Telecommunications Act, which sought to open local telephone service to Competitive Local Exchange Carriers, or CLECs.

So as an opportunity for McCaw, this niche market didn't look good, or so his advisers thought. "There was no instant 'ah-hah!' to it," says Jarvis. "I understand," McCaw had replied. "Keep going."

So Jarvis and his team studied it again and gave McCaw the same message—and again McCaw rejected their advice. He wanted in. He believed that the growth of data, voice, and video would favor businesses that controlled "the pipes"—fiber cables. He also concluded that state and federal regulation of local exchanges would open. If fiber companies could be allowed to build their own switches and get reasonably priced access to the Bell switches, they could pick off customers.

As McCaw had learned from cellular, the sluggish Bells couldn't possibly hold 100 percent of the market. If both conditions were met, a niche business would explode in size. "McCaw could see that bandwidth would be more valuable," Jarvis says. "He could see the traffic was coming. He saw the CLEC industry before there was a CLEC industry."

McCaw formed a company called FiberLink, infused it with $55 million of his own money plus cash from loans, and told his tiny staff at Eagle River to get into the fiber business. He didn't tell them how—that was a detail for them to figure out. He suggested they consider buying some big players to catch up quickly, but he wasn't locked into that idea. He did want action—fast. As with cellular, he wanted his people to get established in as many markets as quickly as possible. Speed was so important that overpaying was forgivable, to a point. But unlike cellular, where McCaw had gained markets by buying small, established players, his team decided that it made more sense in this case to build markets from scratch.

Once the basic goal was set, McCaw spent very little time with Fiber-Link. He held the title of chairman and chief executive, but never came to a board meeting. Instead, he made himself felt in casual ways, including unannounced visits to Jarvis's office. "What did you buy today?" he would ask. Jarvis knew what that meant. McCaw didn't want to hear about a deal already done or one about to be done. He wanted an ever faster pace. That was his way of saying "Go," Jarvis says.

Like others who worked for McCaw, Jarvis sometimes marveled at how little his boss actually knew about his companies. Many privately grumbled about this aspect of McCaw's leadership. The positive side of his empowering approach to management was its ability to unleash people's creativity—the benefit that McCaw liked to celebrate. But there was a negative side, too. Some complained that McCaw just didn't work as hard as they did. He would be "off doing his thing" while they worked years of six- and seven-day workweeks, facing problems that he never knew existed.

Their criticism came from a deeply human need for praise from someone who really knew and appreciated what they had done. Many of McCaw's employees felt he didn't want to know about the difficulties of working in his world. At the same time, they felt a little guilty about their complaints. After all, McCaw had given them exciting careers and—no small thing—the opportunity to achieve great wealth.

Hard work was an unavoidable by-product of the extent of McCaw's ambitions. Once he chose a project, he wanted it to succeed at a spectacular level. Within six months of forming FiberLink, McCaw said he wanted it to eventually reach $1 billion a year in revenue, an astounding goal for what was still considered a niche business.

McCaw brought in Jim Voelker to be FiberLink's president, moving Jarvis to work on projects at Nextel and other McCaw investments. Voelker brought a deep background in telecommunications, especially with competitive-access companies. Voelker thought he had a bullish view of the CLEC business until he met McCaw, who saw FiberLink as growing into a big national player like MCI.

Like Jarvis, Voelker got very little direction from McCaw. "You know more about this business than we do. Go do what you think is right. Don't ask anybody around here for advice," McCaw told him, and he was half serious. Voelker would check in with people at Eagle River from time to time, but he seldom heard directly from McCaw. In fact, during one twelve-month period, he didn't speak to McCaw at all.

What seemed a long shot in 1994 started looking smarter by the month. FiberLink originally focused on small to midsize companies (typically with fewer than fifty access lines), offering them a package of local and long-distance services. In Spokane, Washington, FiberLink picked off US West customers. It didn't seem difficult. A FiberLink salesperson would visit a car dealer, for instance, and ask, "How's your phone service?" US West had never done that for a small company. In fact, US West's service was so widely criticized that the Washington State utilities commission ordered a rollback of its rates.

By 1996 FiberLink had changed its name to NEXTLINK, established itself in twenty-three markets in seven states, and was on a hiring binge. If all this sounded like the early days of McCaw Cellular, it seemed even more so when Wayne Perry and Steve Hooper left their jobs as vice chairman and chief executive, respectively, at AT&T Wireless to rejoin McCaw. Hooper became chairman of NEXTLINK and co–chief executive of Teledesic, while Perry became chief executive of NEXTLINK.

Their arrival coincided with the adoption of a more aggressive posture. Since the Telecommunications Act of 1996 had forced regional Bells to open their facilities to competitors, NEXTLINK could more easily enter bigger markets. McCaw wanted the company to adapt to this changed environment.

"You could march in the front door [of a regional Bell] and say, I've got my interconnection and colocation rights," says Perry. "You don't have to slip under the radar. You can go in the front door. This was classic McCaw. He's not a prisoner of any direction. His ability to turn on a dime and give nine cents change is unbelievable."

And rewarding. NEXTLINK went public in 1997. McCaw sold about 30 percent of the company, and the value of the shares rose 37 percent in the first day of trading. Analysts figured NEXTLINK would lose money for another two years, but the stock was well rated. Some argued that the company was well positioned to help long-distance providers, especially AT&T, expand into new markets without building their own networks. McCaw did well on the sale, making a paper profit of about $500 million on his original $55 million investment.

Each element of McCaw's empire was successful, but the management structure was extremely fluid. By mid-1998 Jim Voelker was out, replaced by George Tronsrue as president. (Voelker said the change was his own idea, keeping a promise to his family to spend more time with them.) NEXTLINK spokesman Todd Wolfenbarger said the move also involved bringing Perry into a more direct role as NEXTLINK readied itself for another series of strategic deals. "Craig probably felt more comfortable with people who had been close to him," says Wolfenbarger. But in a year, Hooper left, replaced as NEXTLINK's chief by Dan Akerson, who had moved from Nextel. Rather than move Akerson to Bellevue, Washington, McCaw moved headquarters to northern Virginia, where Akerson lived. Hooper remained co-CEO of Teledesic.

It all may have seemed chaotic, but it worked, and McCaw wanted even more for NEXTLINK. The company had grown to 3,000 employees and was able to borrow huge amounts of money for further expansion because lenders knew that McCaw met his commitments. In mid-1999 NEXTLINK paid nearly $700 million to acquire McCaw's favorite asset—spectrum—in a purchase of Local Multipoint Distribution Service (LMDS) licenses.

LMDS was a means of beaming data and voice over short distances to a switching office. Few in the press recognized what McCaw was doing—assembling his own nationwide telephone company, a smaller version of a Baby Bell. NEXTLINK could now provide fixed wireless coverage for 95 percent of the U.S. population. The fixed wireless system eliminated the toughest challenge of competing for customers, the "first mile" of service usually controlled by the regional Bell companies. McCaw was getting into position to offer bundled long-distance and local service, which the Bells and AT&T were taking years to do. Further deals with Level 3 Communications, Covad, and Speedus.com were struck with the goal of enhancing the service he offered to Bell customers.

Inside NEXTLINK, executives were talking about a goal of $10 billion a year in annual revenue, which they considered reasonable—just 5 percent of the $200 billion market for local and long-distance business. NEXTLINK could always get help from McCaw's other assets, including Nextel, Cable Plus, a private cable TV company that served apartment buildings in thirteen states, and eventually Teledesic. With cable playing an increasing role in the delivery of voice and Internet services, Cable Plus could become a stealth weapon for picking off even more Bell customers.

These certainly were interesting puzzle pieces, but how did they all fit together? Perhaps Craig McCaw was indeed assembling his own version of AT&T, becoming a latter-day version of Theodore Vail. But McCaw was hard to know and harder yet to predict. Maybe he did have a plan, or maybe he wasn't quite sure where he was headed. Yet each step along the way brought its own huge payoff. By late 1999 McCaw's share in NEXTLINK alone was worth $3 billion.

Not bad for the "interested consultant" who had never even set foot in a NEXTLINK office.

Epilogue

The Billionaire and the Whale

Clad in a diver's wet suit, Craig McCaw eased himself into the chilly salt water of a 2-million-gallon tank, gaining the notice of its occupant, a 7,720-pound whale. The powerful creature watched McCaw with its coal-black eyes, then swam closer to make contact. McCaw reached out with his arm . . . and experienced one of the greatest spiritual moments of his life.

Billionaires have their pick of toys, pleasures, and causes. This cause was Keiko, the killer whale with the droopy fin, star of the 1993 Warner Bros. movie *Free Willy*. McCaw had given millions to reading programs for public school kids in Seattle, to the creation of a park in central Seattle, to his alma mater the Lakeside School, and to other projects, but no philanthropy had so captured his attention and few had consumed as much of his money as returning Keiko to his home.

Keiko was some two years old in 1979 when he was captured off the coast of Iceland. He spent several years at aquariums in Canada and Iceland before being sold to the Reino Aventura amusement park in Mexico City, his home for the next ten years. In a small chlorinated tank, Keiko performed four shows daily, doing cheap tricks for dead fish accompanied by blaring rock music.

Warner Brothers paid the park $70,000 for Keiko's work in the film, a tearjerker about a whale that inspires a boy to reform. The hit movie attracted attention to the real-life whale whose health was deteriorating. One of about forty-eight whales in captivity, Keiko had lost 1,000 pounds and suffered from wartlike growths on his skin.

The whale's plight resonated deeply with McCaw. Why? No one really knew. Even his closest aides were baffled: It was one more Craig McCaw anecdote that supplied detail, but somehow only made his character more intriguing and more unknowable. Aides privately grumbled about the boss's excessive interest in the whale, a distraction from the billion-dollar deals. McCaw never seemed satisfied with Keiko's situation and kept shuffling his managers. Was all this a sign that McCaw had lost perspective? No one could ever separate the baffling from the brilliant in his personality.

Always sympathetic to animal rights causes, McCaw "decided [the whale's predicament] wasn't right, and someone ought to do something about it, and that I might make a difference," he says. Quietly and at first anonymously, he began pumping money into a foundation that bought the whale and moved him to a new $7.3 million facility at the Oregon Coast Aquarium in Newport. The goal was to improve Keiko's health, teach him how to survive in the wild, and eventually release him into his native waters as the first longtime captive whale ever set free.

After he moved to Newport in 1996, Keiko's health quickly improved, but his habits of domesticated life died hard. Friendly and playful with humans, he seemed more like a puppy than a wild animal. He couldn't hold his breath very long. Accustomed to eating dead fish, twenty-one-foot Keiko tried to hide when eight-inch live herring were dumped into his tank.

Keiko's presence transformed the town of 9,000, bringing an estimated economic benefit of $75 million a year through doubled attendance at the aquarium, salaries for veterinarians and other staff, and the sale of whale-related trinkets, including T-shirts and a root beer brand. The Free Willy Keiko Foundation spent $500,000 a year, and McCaw's own spending topped $3 million.

To McCaw's embarrassment, a feud erupted between the foundation and the aquarium when it became evident that Newport stood to lose its tourist draw. The aquarium claimed that Keiko was too weak to go free and accused the foundation of reckless haste. Insisting that Keiko was healthy, the foundation said the aquarium just wanted to keep its prize attraction. Each side presented marine biologists to back its claims.

The increasingly nasty dispute went to arbitration, and the aquarium ultimately discovered an old lesson about dealing with Craig McCaw: Always read the fine print. The contract between the aquarium and the foundation gave the latter sole power to decide when and where to move Keiko.

Some of the worldwide coverage played the battle as an amusing match between the eccentric billionaire and feisty Phyllis Bell, aquarium director, a characterization she ridiculed. "Yeah, right," Bell told *The Seattle Times* sarcastically. "We're in the same league. My car had a dead battery and wouldn't start this morning. Do you think that happens to Craig?"

To bring more credibility and prestige to the foundation, McCaw brought in Jean-Michel Cousteau, son of famed oceanographer Jacques Cousteau. Jean-Michel Cousteau said he might produce a documentary on Keiko for the Discovery Channel. McCaw seconded Cousteau's hope that the Free Willy Keiko Foundation might go beyond helping to free one whale and become an international leader in marine-mammal rehabilitation. "I would be sorely disappointed if we don't create more of a legacy," McCaw said.

McCaw surprised many by showing up at a news media luncheon honoring Cousteau. McCaw spoke of his fascination with Keiko. A celebrated practitioner of an executive's right to keep and bear squirt guns, McCaw noted that orcas, river otters, and humans are among the few animals that continue to play well past childhood. "I believe the child in all of us is the most enduring and frankly remarkable part of us, the ability to detach ourselves from the basic survival instincts," he said. He spoke of Keiko's obvious intelligence and the fact that the orca brain is bigger than the human brain, and discussed how whales communicate underwater with unique sounds.

Scientists even suspect that killer whale groups may have discernible dialects—an intriguing concept for McCaw, whose speculations about human communication once led him to suggest, in apparent seriousness, that the FCC should reserve spectrum for telepathic communications made possible by future brain implants.

It wasn't like McCaw to volunteer stories about himself, but he couldn't resist talking about his swim with Keiko. Keiko maneuvered as if to welcome the billionaire onto his back. When McCaw got on, Keiko wiggled to see how much effort it would take to bump his patron off. McCaw was charmed by what he called a "mystical" experience. He didn't say so, but it seemed McCaw and Keiko had gotten to know each other. The king of wireless communications—the quirky executive who shunned contact with strangers, even with some of his own employees—had evidently bonded with another life-form.

"The high point of my life spiritually is spending time with Keiko in the pool," McCaw told *The Oregonian*. "It's almost like dealing with an extraterrestrial, having a relationship with an intelligent being on a very personal level."

He would not give up on his blubbery friend. In September 1998 Keiko was rubbed with a white moisturizing balm, lowered into a giant tub of ice, and loaded onto an Air Force C-17 cargo plane. After a 5,340-mile flight, a first-of-its-kind deployment for the U.S. military, Keiko was lowered into his new home: a mesh pen in a bay near the fishing village of Heimaey, Iceland. "Is it a feel-good effort?" Craig asked. "If keeping your word to children is 'feel-good,' then certainly it is."

Sixty percent larger than his tank in Oregon, the pen made of graphite and Kevlar netting provided hope that Keiko could begin eating wild fish and get used to his native waters. But teaching a whale to stop acting like a pet was challenging. After a year, Keiko still required hand feedings. Some biologists doubted that Keiko would ever make the transition. Costs to maintain the whale had risen to $7 million and were escalating by $1 million each year. Keiko, with ten full-time handlers, probably had more personal attendants than his billionaire benefactor. As of late 1999 Keiko still lived in captivity, though his pen had been expanded fivefold.

The costs and the skeptics didn't bother McCaw. He had made contact with the whale species. He had sensed in them one of the most powerful motivators in his own life: a desire to be free. "Look into their eyes and you know they are intelligent and special," McCaw said. "Our moral imperative was to do our best to achieve as much freedom as he wanted, or was capable of, after all these years in captivity."

* * *

For any other billionaire, the effort to help a whale go free might seem a colorful sidebar to the larger story of his life. But for those who have followed Craig McCaw, the Keiko episode underscores essential aspects of his success.

His instinct for helping Keiko was, in a sense, the same humane motivation behind his career in communications: bringing freedom to others. McCaw wanted to sever Keiko's dependence on hand-fed salmon just as he wants to cut the leash that holds office workers to their desks. New wireless devices linked to powerful data systems would restore the nomad, allowing people to live where they wished and freeing them from the pollution and traffic jams of urban centers—or so he hoped.

The task of rescuing and airlifting the world's largest mammal was no more impossible than running a cable company from a Stanford frat house; sitting in a dinky office in Centralia, Washington, and dreaming of a cable TV empire; building a cellular company to rival the Baby Bells; or, as a part-time investor, assembling a space-based Internet that required a trifecta of money, technology, and unprecedented global manufacturing coordination.

Craig McCaw continues to ride waves caused by deregulation of telecommunications and the convergence of computing and communications. The changes in law and technology have produced exploding demand for voice communication, high-speed Internet access, video conferencing, and electronic commerce. The old telephone companies have enormous resources, direct links to customers, and brand names. The Baby Bells might seem well positioned to seize this opportunity, but they are weighted by enormous bureaucracies and antiquated systems. As their customers move quickly in new directions, they are like ocean liners trying to make sharp turns, buzzed by new-style powerboats.

McCaw's investments in NEXTLINK, Nextel, Cable Plus, and Teledesic are all pieces of the same puzzle. They add up to a share of what he thinks will be a $450 billion market for voice and broadband data services by 2010. They are claim stakes for the next frontier of communications.

The race is on to serve customers who want new services, such as data beamed to handheld devices or improved "pipelines" for high-speed Internet service at homes or offices. The many parts of McCaw's activities can be bewildering, so consider the ambition reflected by the single goal of just one company: NEXTLINK is building a fiber-optic system capable of transporting more than forty times the current U.S. long-distance traffic.

Picturing Craig McCaw on the back of a whale is not the obvious way to consider the future of telecommunications, but it highlights how the industry is less about the companies—because they seem to devour one another, change names, spin off, break up—and more about unique individuals who set the agenda and serve as models for a leadership style that works best in a quickened industry. More important, the new dynamic seems to require unconventional executives who can see "around corners," as colleagues have said about McCaw.

Craig McCaw does not occupy the chief executive's office at AT&T or MCI WorldCom, but his ideas are felt throughout the industry. He is one of a few gurus whose utterances are dissected for clues for the Next Big Thing. There are times when McCaw is so cryptic or clumsy in his expression that no one is clear on *what* he's saying. But his fundamental message hasn't changed: Think like an anthropologist about what people will soon want, and build for that future. When the people discover what they want, you'll be there to serve them.

Study his lifestyle. Strip away the toys of the billionaire, and you find the executive of a global company who needs to access information and coworkers at any time, from any place. The societal shift to data on demand everywhere, anytime is a logical evolution of his 1980s vision of the go-anywhere telephone. The cell phone got smart enough with microprocessors and software to screen calls, give alerts, and look for certain information. It's a short step to the handheld Internet browser that doubles as a telephone. These improvements delight gadget-loving Craig McCaw, but he's not surprised. He's been waiting for everyone to reach his vision.

What lies ahead for Craig McCaw? Expect the unexpected. He could spend years staying on course, expanding his companies, and enjoying the result. But just as his face begins to appear again on the covers of magazines that celebrate his triumphs, look for a change. He hates routine. He gets restless when a venture begins to succeed and his presence is less essential.

Having built and sold two national companies, McCaw could wake up one morning and decide to sell one or all of his present companies. One possible scenario would be a sale of Nextel to a bigger company that needs a wireless presence, or a sale of Teledesic to a huge global player such as AT&T. There could be important strategic reasons for such a sale, but he wouldn't sell his empire merely for strategy or money, but to move on to new challenges. Or he would find a way to make his routine more interesting. He could pull in new partners, raise his bets, and propose something even more exciting, built around something bigger than the parts of his disparate enterprises. But how could he possibly top Teledesic's celestial ambitions?

No one can yet say what McCaw's final legacy will be. It could be his known companies or some embryonic venture kept off the radar. Whichever, it will bear the influence of a great and wholly unique American entrepreneur. He has built large companies, brought liberating technology to millions of people, and made himself and others wealthy, but those are achievements matched by others. Putting the stamp of his unique personality on business, keeping private his secret places, resisting the powerful pull to be conventional, playing the wizard to a dumbfounded audience—Craig McCaw's greatest achievement may simply be staying true to himself.

Notes

1. "That Man Behind the Curtain"

4 lifestyle it housed: Details of the McCaw family lifestyle throughout this chapter come from interviews with Bruce McCaw, Craig McCaw, and Marion McCaw, and from the Elroy McCaw estate files with the King County Superior Court.

4 "played with the big boys": Flourence Glass interview.

4 "I do this all the time": Brigitte Rubner interview.

5 ". . . not an operations guy": Les Smith interview.

10 "Wizard of Oz": *The Seattle Times,* August 26, 1990.

12 "before Judge Greene got ahold of them": Andrew Kupfer, "Craig McCaw Sees an Internet in the Sky," *Fortune,* May 27, 1996, p. 62.

2. "A Bit of a Loose Skipper"

13 Elroy McCaw's career: Much of this chapter is compiled from interviews with Jim Adduci, Jane Chytl, Royce Hull, Bruce McCaw, Craig McCaw, Garland Norin, Elaine O'Toole, *Broadcasting Magazine,* August 1960, Elroy McCaw's estate file with the King County Superior Court, and various clippings on Elroy McCaw's career kept by *The Seattle Times* library.

18 "Hey, Jim": Jim Adduci interview.

18 losses for both stations: *Broadcasting Magazine,* August 1960.

19 become Manhattan Cable Television: Rick Sklar, *Rocking America: How the All-Hit Radio Stations Took Over* (New York: St. Martin's Press, 1984), p. 75.

19 "He locked out the studio orchestra": Ibid., p. 10.

20 "any goods or services in this world": Ibid., p. 11.

21 "masterstroke from a master broadcaster": Les Keiter with Dennis Christianson, *Fifty Years Behind the Microphone: The Les Keiter Story* (Honolulu: University of Hawaii Press, 1997), p. 52.

26 "my father in terms of sensitivity to opportunity": Interview with Craig McCaw by the American Academy of Achievement, May 22, 1997. Posted on Academy website: www.achievement.org.

3. "Money Was Not the Issue"

This chapter is based entirely on interviews with people named in the text.

4. "How Can We Build Our Dreams on This?"

41 "or climb higher": American Academy of Achievement interview.

5. "There's This Crazy Kid . . ."

48 "you can't fail": American Academy of Achievement interview.

55 "Your integrity is always challenged": American Academy of Achievement interview.

6. "Always Have a Back Door"

73 began to squawk and carry on: Brad Horwitz interview, *Comline,* McCaw Communications internal newsletter, June 1993.

7. "What Would Be in Their Best Interest?"

83 "being created and it was worthwhile": American Academy of Achievement interview.

84 10 kilohertz: John S. Bain and Winston E. Himsworth, "CMRS: Cellular Mobile Radio Telecommunications Service" (New York: Lehman Brothers Kuhn Loeb Research, October 7, 1981), pp. 10–11, 62.

84 an estimated 16 million using citizens band: W. B. Young, "Advanced Mobile Phone Service: Introduction, Background, and Objectives," *The Bell System Technical Journal,* January 1979, p. 2.

8. "We Were Dreaming of Dick Tracy"

90 "being subjugated needlessly to 1890s technology": American Academy of Achievement interview.

92 able to compete in price with pagers: Electronic Mail & Message Systems newsletter, October 15, 1980.

94 Erb threatened a court challenge: *The New York Times,* April 9, 1981.

94 operating cellular in seventy major cities: *The New York Times,* April 10, 1981.

96 1.5 million customers in the first full year: Bain and Himsworth, p. 23.

96 "easily achievable": Bain and Himsworth, p. 29.

96 among many applicants: Bain and Himsworth, p. 33.

101 "all this effort in order to file one application": *Broadcasting Magazine,* June 7, 1982.

102 "like to be in the long lines for the cellular radio": Ibid.

9. "I Can't Go to Bed Owing Somebody a Billion Dollars"

104 "get rich quick": Ibid.

107 "Most Attractive Cover Award": *Cellular Resources,* February 1983.

112 "driven by adversity": American Academy of Achievement interview.

10. "Like Negotiating with the Russians"

113 holding a new sort of telephone: *News Tribune* (Tacoma), October 14, 1984.

114 "if you ask for a lot": American Academy of Achievement interview.

121 "I see everybody buying cellular": *News Tribune* (Tacoma), October 14, 1984.

11. "What Do You Want for a Sacramento?"

122 another 567 for the third round: Tom Kerver and Arthur M. Hill, "Cellular Radio," *Cable Television Business,* January 1, 1984, p. 36.

123 "whose time will be very slow to come": Kevin McManus, "Wrong Numbers," *Forbes,* June 4, 1984.

133 had called off the cellular lotteries: *The Wall Street Journal,* October 4, 1984.

12. "You Went to Veterinarians When You Needed Brain Surgery"

134 "not trading chits in a game": Philip L. Cantelon, *The History of MCI: The Early Years* (Dallas: Heritage Press, 1993), p. 390.

134 "PROFITS YEARS AWAY": *The Wall Street Journal,* June 25, 1985.

135 at a cost of $9.6 million: *The Seattle Times,* August 13, 1985.

136 "Went to sleep on the job": Cantelon, p. 395.

13. "It's Getting Awful Lonely"

149 "risky, but it's a reasonable": *The Wall Street Journal,* July 2, 1986.

149 "enhance competition in the local telephone market": *The Washington Post,* August 11, 1986.

149 "compete for the long haul": *Financial World,* October 14, 1986.

150 "can't afford to buy Southwestern Bell": *The Washington Post,* August 11, 1986.

150 "it's getting awful lonely": *Forbes,* August 11, 1996.

150 have to sell eventually: *Communications Week,* July 21, 1986.

150 $63.3 billion of revenue in 1985: *Financial World,* October 14, 1986.

150 "doesn't pass the sanity test": Ibid.

151 $650 million a year: *The Washington Post,* August 11, 1986.

152 none of the forty or so providers: *Financial World*, October 14, 1986.

152 "we were spending": *Forbes*, August 11, 1996.

152 "have receded steadily and may now": *Financial World*, October 14, 1986.

14. "Where Do I Sell My License?"

155 "trusting the gods and calling psychics": *The Wall Street Journal*, July 21, 1986.

157 "an awful lot of wealth": *The Washington Post*, September 2, 1996.

157 "Monday-afternoon quarterbacking": Ibid.

158 equipped with a water cannon: Tim Donahue interview.

15. "The Mad Scientist"

165 "lucky to get 50 shares": *The New York Times*, August 4, 1987.

166 "dozens of small phone companies": *BusinessWeek*, December 5, 1988.

168 "have fun and enjoy": *Comline*, May 1988.

169 "something to behold!": *Comline*, November 1989.

16. "Take Tarawa"

179 chain of franchised art galleries: *Forbes*, January 8, 1990.

179 "not down the road": Ibid.

184 was a Bell obsession: *Newsday*, November 26, 1989.

190 "BellSouth has tried to make that": *The Wall Street Journal*, November 21, 1989.

190 "You can't build a national network": *BusinessWeek*, December 4, 1989.

190 "its taste for the fight": *The Wall Street Journal*, December 5, 1989.

191 "at what cost?" : *Forbes*, December 25, 1989.

191 generous but not excessive: *The Wall Street Journal*, December 15, 1989.

192 "may prove to be Pyrrhic": *BusinessWeek*, December 4, 1989.

17. "The Spirit Within Us Must Burn"

195 "issuing shares to a big U.S.": *The Wall Street Journal*, August 23, 1990.

195 in technical default on a big loan: *The New York Times*, September 29, 1991.

195 "The bad news isn't over": *Forbes*, November 26, 1990.

196 "Anything that jiggles": Ibid.

197 "distracted by all the hysteria": Ibid.

197 "expecting us to fail": *Comline*, March 1990.

18. "You're Marrying Off Your Daughter When She's Fourteen"

206 "deceptive in appearances": *The Washington Post*, September 24, 1995.

212 negotiating to buy one third: *The New York Times*, November 5, 1992.

213 "cellular and paging holdings": *The Wall Street Journal*, November 5, 1982.

214 "trying to mine platinum": *The Wall Street Journal*, November 6, 1992.

19. "Like Porcupines Making Love"

220 "dignified gathering of corporate": *Forbes*, March 1, 1993.

223 gave the go-ahead: *BusinessWeek*, August 30, 1993.

226 BIG PAYOFF FOR HIGH-TECH GAMBLER: *The New York Times*, August 17, 1993.

20. "Master of the Obvious"

230 "crucial to AT&T's strategy": *Fortune*, December 12, 1994.

231 "would you want to sit on AT&T's board?": Ibid.

231 replace wired phone service: *The Sun* (Baltimore), December 11, 1994.

233 "That takes someone": *The Seattle Times*, December 15, 1994.

233 "wild and woolly PCS": *The Wall Street Journal*, February 23, 1995.

234 "I pursue it": *The Washington Post*, April 6, 1995.

21. "The Michael Jordan of Telecommunications"

236 "nothing left to buy": *The Wall Street Journal*, August 31, 1994.

242 "with a switch-based telephone": *The Washington Post*, April 6, 1995.

242 "A huge boost": *Los Angeles Times*, April 6, 1995.

243 "Michael Jordan": *The Washington Post*, April 6, 1995.

244 "someone else is already": *The Wall Street Journal*, European Edition, September 11, 1997.

245 "bad case of measles": *USA Today*, January 14, 1997.

247 "this kind of device": *Red Herring* magazine, September 1993.

247 "not to say that Dan's not kind": *The Washington Post*, July 15, 1999.

22. "The Potential to Change the World"

250 "to let him know": *The Seattle Times*, September 29, 1996. Many comments in this chapter come from interviews by Thomas Haines of *The Seattle Times*.

250 "forefront of a revolution": *Satellite Communications*, November 1986.

251 "It'll never work": *USA Today*, December 23, 1996.

252 "it can't be done?": *The Seattle Times*, September 29, 1996.

256 "How do we buy it?": *Fortune*, May 27, 1996.

256 "business to focus on": *The Seattle Times*, September 29, 1996.

256 "The real challenge was regulatory": *USA Today*, December 23, 1996.

259 "We can cooperate with Teledesic": *The Seattle Times*, September 29, 1996.

261 "as the first transcontinental railway": *Los Angeles Times*, January 6, 1997.

261 "a tug of war": MSNBC, www.msnbc.com, October 1996.

262 "never received policy review": *The Washington Post*, September 15, 1996.

263 technology-savvy Vice President: *Los Angeles Times*, January 6, 1997.

265 "Boeing is one of the world's": *Los Angeles Times*, April 30, 1997.

265 "Boeing is committing capital": *The Washington Post*, April 30, 1997.

266 $4 billion apart in their: *The Seattle Times*, February 3, 1998.

268 "What does Craig McCaw know": *The Wall Street Journal*, November 18, 1999.

23. "Under the Radar"

270 "highly interested consultant": *The Seattle Times*, September 3, 1996.

271 "My company was my children": *The Wall Street Journal*, August 7, 1996.

Epilogue

281 "Yeah, right": *The Seattle Times*, November 20, 1997.

281 "fascination with Keiko": *The Oregonian*, February 10, 1998.

282 "Is it a feel-good effort?": *The Seattle Times*, September 10, 1998.

282 "Look into their eyes": Associated Press, carried by *The Seattle Times*, September 10, 1999.

Acknowledgments

Writing a book may not be as hard as living with a person writing a book. My love goes to my wife, Sally Tonkin, and our two children, Evan and Michaela. To them, I apologize for those many evenings away from them, for those vacations where I brought a laptop, and for those moments of grouchiness. And yes, I think the book is finally done.

Among friends and family, I owe Dan Butterworth for helping me understand the value of character in a story; Eugene Corr for showing me the value of character in real life; Susan and Joe Bennett, Cynthia Gannett, Evelyn Iritani, John McCoy, and Sally Tonkin for writing advice; Nancy Tonkin for providing a house in the sun; John and Cora Picken for providing a house near a lake; and Bill Prochnau and Laura Parker for the many years of good advice.

Kris Dahl at ICM helped get this book launched, counseled me during some difficult moments, and brought common sense to many problems.

I owe a debt at Times Books to former publisher Peter Osnos, who approved this project, to John Mahaney, who kept it going for so many years, and to Luke Mitchell, who got me to the finish line. A former Times Books editor, Karl Weber, brought good humor, patience, and insight to the manuscript. Beth Thomas did an excellent copyediting job. In the legal department, William Adams removed booby traps.

Those who helped me at *The Seattle Times* include: Paul Andrews, Frank Blethen, Mindy Cameron, Carole Carmichael, Steve Dunphy, Thomas Haines, Greg Heberlein (for those tricky math problems), Terry McDermott, and Carol Pucci. The staff of the *Seattle Times* library helped track down nuggets. Diane Albert, Dan Butterworth, and Beth Cooley hunted for errors in the galleys.

Craig McCaw agreed to help with the project, gave me a few interviews, and then became busy with matters of more importance to him. I shouldn't have been surprised. I knew that he disliked talking about his life and did not care to read anything about himself. He was always courteous and responsive to questions in our meetings. He allowed his employees, friends, and associates to talk to me and never made an effort to control what I wrote. I am grateful for the time he gave and especially grateful for his providing such interesting subject matter.

I owe special thanks to Bob Ratliffe, McCaw's longtime spokesman and friend. Bob took a risk by encouraging Craig to cooperate with me, and he helped enormously with my research.

In trying to understand Craig McCaw and the wireless industry, I relied heavily on reporting by *The Wall Street Journal* (especially by writers Mary Lu Carnevale, Leslie Cauley, Quentin Hardy, John Keller, Ralph King, Gautam Naik); *The New York Times* (Edmund Andrews, Geraldine Fabrikant, Mark Landler, Peter Lewis, Anthony Ramirez); *Los Angeles Times* (Jube Shiver Jr.); *The Washington Post* (Mike Mills); *BusinessWeek* (Peter Elstrom, John J. Keller, Jonathan B. Levine, Bart Ziegler); *Fortune* (Andrew Kupfer); *Forbes* (Fleming Meeks, Gary Slutsker); *The Seattle Times* (Paul Andrews, Michele Matassa Flores, Tom Haines, Tim Healy); and *USA Today* (Kevin Maney).

Some interviews for this book lasted an hour or less, but many lasted several hours. The author is grateful to those who wished to remain anonymous as well as the following individuals: Dawn Adduci, Jim Adduci, Barry Adelman, Dan Akerson, Tom Alberg, Robert Allen, Brian Almquist, Eldon Anderson, Bill Baldwin, Clyde Ballard, Jim Barksdale, Carl Behnke, Homer Bergren, Paul Blalock, Herman "Whitey" Bluestein, George Blumenthal, Vaughn Breaux, Jack Brennan, Carl Brophy, Roy Budde, Jim Byrnes, Richard Callahan, Cal Cannon, Patti Cannon, Jane Chytl, Joe Clark, Walt Conner, Steve Countryman, Peter Currie, Russ Daggatt, Bill Daniels, Tim David, Gardiner Davis, Mick Deal, John DeFeo, Charlie Desmond, Tim Donahue, Hal Eastman, David Endicott, Peter Erb, Peter Evans, Ace Feek, Flourence Glass, Bill Gough, Matt Griffin, Bob Hallowell, Mark Hamilton, Lou Hannum, Doug Hauff, Rick Hess, Steve Hooper, Ed Hopper, Royce Hull, Tom Hull, Scot Jarvis, Roberta Katz, Les Keiter, Gordon Kelley, Steve Lamont, Joe Liebsack, George Lindemann, Chuck Lyford, Larry Manthey, Joe Marino, Steve Markendorf, Brian McCauley, Bruce McCaw, Craig McCaw, John McCaw, Keith McCaw, Marion McCaw, Lawrence Minard, Fred Morck, Chuck Morris, Garland Norin, Morgan

O'Brien, Ellis Oliver, Steve Oliver, Dan Orr, Elaine Gwinn O'Toole, Sylvia Hoover Padgett, Lyn Pawley, Wayne Perry, Bob Ratliffe, Steve Rattner, Gordon Rock, Brigitte Rubner, Jeff Ruhe, Mike Senkowski, Bill Smallwood, Les Smith, Patricia Smullin, John Stanton, Stuart Subotnick, Gerald Taylor, Ed Tuck, Phil Verveer, James Voelker, Dan Waggoner, Dennis Weibling, and Richard Wiley.

Index